CW00872222

The

Better

Covenant

RON BAILEY

Dedication

To my wife Margaret

chief of very many
who have encouraged this project from its conception
and
prayed constantly for its safe delivery.

Acknowledgements

Firstly I want to acknowledge the very many in many parts of the world who have encouraged me for many years to 'get some of these things in print'. You see I *was* listening.

The things that we read and hear go much deeper than we can know. One of the features of several years spent reading and talking with fellow believers is that we can never really be sure quite what came from where. Much of what is written here is original, or so I think; it may be that it is not nearly so original as I thought it was. I have not followed any one school of theology so there will be thoughts expressed here which began in unlikely places. It would be unfair and unwise to identify any one above another but I want to acknowledge my indebtedness to the saints who have trod some of these paths before me and whose footprints have encouraged me to take less familiar routes.

I want, too, to acknowledge a little band of proofreaders who through the wonders of the Internet are located in the UK, Germany, Romania and the USA. Margaret, Mike, Gary and Robert... many thanks to you all!

And lastly my special thanks to Johan Companjen from Open Doors for his encouragement and kind foreword.

As is usual in these acknowledgements while expressing gratitude to many I acknowledge that all faults and errors are my own.

Let the words of my mouth and the meditation of my heart
be acceptable in Your sight, O LORD,
my strength and my Redeemer. Psa 19:14

Foreword: Johan Companjen

During more than 30-years of travel around the world, I have often noted that many Christians have little knowledge of the basic truths described in God's Word, the Bible. They know the stories from the Old and New Testaments, but fail to see the connection between them or God's overall, marvellous plan with mankind. So many Christians know so little about God's Covenant with His people.

That is why the book you hold in your hand is so important. Ron Bailey's clear description and explanation of God's age transcending covenants with his people paints the bigger picture. I have been blessed, challenged and encouraged to realize again, while reading Ron's book, that God has a wonderful 'master plan' – not only with creation but with all of mankind. I'm so blessed every time I read how the Lord 'went out of His way' to reveal His plans to mankind throughout the Bible, as Ron shares so clearly in this book.

"The Better Covenant" is solid spiritual food for all who are not satisfied with just emotions or good feelings, but have a desire to dig deeper into the truths of God's Word.

May this book be used to draw many into a covenant relationship with the Lord of the universe, the Saviour of mankind, our wonderful God and Father who longs for us to be part of His plan.

Johan Companjen

President Emeritus Open Doors International

The two covenants: Andrew Murray

"The New Covenant may become to us one of the windows of heaven through which we see into the face, into the very heart, of God."

"Blessed is the man who truly knows God as his Covenant God; who knows what the Covenant promises him; what unwavering confidence of expectation it secures, that all its terms will be fulfilled to him; what a claim and hold it gives him on the Covenant-keeping God Himself.

To many a man, who has never thought much of the Covenant, a true and living faith in it would mean the transformation of his whole life. The full knowledge of what God wants to do for him; the assurance that it will be done by an Almighty Power; the being drawn to God Himself in personal surrender, and dependence, and waiting to have it done; all this would make the Covenant the very gate of heaven. The Holy Spirit give us some vision of its glory."

Andrew Murray: "The Two Covenants" 1898

Preface:

Opinion is divided. Some say 'you must have a preface', others say 'no one ever reads a preface'. What is a man to do?

The New Covenant is one of my passions. It is the controlling model for my understanding of the Scriptures. From the time that I glimpsed the pattern of its covenants the book began to be a cohesive expression of God's plan for salvation. That discovery excited me; it still does. If any of what you are about to read is at all incoherent you can put that down to my excitement; in some states we see much more than we can say.

I long to express what I believe I have seen and this book is my attempt at that task. I pray you may catch something of the wonder of God's plans and expectations. What we now call the New Covenant was always God's plan and the death of His Son and the gift of His Spirit have now made this plan a living reality. May this book stir you to faith and prayer until it becomes your reality.

...for those who *never* read prefaces, the original preface is now placed where you can't avoid it... camouflaged under the title of Chapter 0:

Table of Contents

0: The artist's palette

The Bible is a strange book. It seems to pass quickly over really important historical events and then concentrates its attention on events that seem of hardly any consequence. Momentous events are dealt with very superficially and at other times it will take a couple of chapters to record family weddings or a funeral. Some people think the Bible has no sense of proportion.

There is a method however in its 'strangeness'. The Bible is not trying to be an encyclopedia or a world history, it is a special 'God's eye view' of events that are recorded for the truths that they contain; it is a "salvation history". It is God's way of introducing us to some amazing ideas which he then uses to speak living truth into the hearts of men and women who trust him. The apostle Paul once wrote that the events of some parts of the Old Testament *happened to them as examples, and they were written for our admonition, upon whom the ends of the ages have come.* 1 Cor 10:11 NKJV.

There is some 'heavy' teaching in this sentence; it seems to suggest that some of the things that happened thousands of years ago actually happened with Christians in mind and that apparently minor events were recorded because of their lasting significance.

When children begin to learn language they don't usually begin with a dictionary but they simply notice how 'Mother' uses the word and then build up a personal definition in their minds. Part of the reason for the Old Testament, according to Paul, was just this; it was creating a series of ideas, which could be used later to build more complex truths.

Here's a different illustration; a painter may choose to create a colour that cannot be bought in a tube. He makes a quantity of it on his artist's palette and when he wants to use it he has it immediately to hand. God has been doing something similar with the Bible. He has created a palette of ideas and truths that he can then use whenever he wishes. Bible words and ideas don't really have 'definitions'; they have 'histories'. The best way to understand a Bible idea is not to start off with the dictionary, not even a Bible dictionary. The best way is just to read the Bible slowly and repeatedly and see how that word or idea is used. In the way that the artist can return to his palette of ready-made colours so the Bible often does the same thing, taking a word or an idea that has a significant history and using it to trigger memories and emotions. This is why personal names and even place names can be very significant in the Bible's "salvation history".

There is a word that we don't often use in modern language; it is the word 'covenant'. Here is the entry in my Oxford online dictionary...

Covenant: noun

an agreement.

• Law - a contract drawn up by deed.

• Law - a clause in a contract.

• Theology an agreement that brings about a relationship of commitment between God and his people. The Jewish

faith is based on the biblical covenants made with Abraham, Moses, and David. See also Ark of the Covenant,

...But that is only a small part of what it means. Our English word 'covenant' comes from a French word which means 'to agree', in the sense of 'coming together in agreement'. We shall see that this is a key part of what a 'covenant' really is. It is a special kind of legal agreement that has benefits and responsibilities for those parties who 'agree' to it.

There is another key part of what a 'covenant' is; a covenant creates a relationship. In this sense it is more than a promise. Most often it is a promise with a built-in condition. Sometimes the conditions aren't obvious but they are nearly always there. This should give us our clue as to why God is so interested in 'covenants'. He is not interested in just blessing people as they pass by but has always intended to enter into relationship with them. If most of our explanation of what it means to be a Christian is expressed in terms of an 'experience' or an 'encounter' with God, it is easy to miss the fact that those encounters were designed to prepare the way for a lasting relationship.

I notice that my dictionary wanted us to know that 'the Jewish faith is based on... covenants'. This is true but it is also true, but often forgotten, that the Christian faith is also based on a covenant. As Jesus shared his final meal with his disciples he took the traditional cup of wine, that practicing Jews still use in their Passover celebration, and added another dimension to it; *... He also took the cup after supper, saying, "This cup is the New Covenant in My blood, which is shed for you. Luke 22:20. NKJV.* We may presume that he expected the disciples to have some idea of what he was talking about, but for many who read these words today they are in an unbroken code. His physical blood was still in his veins when he made this statement, so just what did he mean? And what did he mean by 'the *New* Covenant'?

This takes us back to the beginning of the trail in understanding the New Covenant. Almost 600 years before Christ the prophet Jeremiah declared that God had a plan to create a covenant, a New Covenant; *"Behold, the days are coming, says the LORD, when I will make a New Covenant with the house of Israel and with the house of Judah—* Jer 31:31. NKJV. Why would God create a New Covenant? After all the Jews already had quite a few covenants, why another one?

The dictionary also drew our attention to a particular 'legal agreement' that God had made when it spoke of the 'ark of the covenant'; this was ancient Israel's most sacred religious object. The relationship between God and his ancient people was based upon the legal terms of a covenant, an extraordinary agreement that changed the whole nature of who these people were and set them on the way to their breathtaking destiny. That legal agreement was kept safe in the centre of their camp in a special repository called "the ark of the covenant." In fact the agreement was in duplicate; one copy was in Moses' handwriting on parchment, the other copy was in God's handwriting and was written in stone. We shall see the significance of this later in Chapter 2.

So why would there be any need for another covenant? The answer is simple; the earlier one failed. It was not the fault of the terms of the agreement that caused it to fail, or the reluctance of God; it failed because the people failed to keep their side of the covenant. The New Testament letter to the Hebrews makes this point very carefully; *Because finding fault with them, He says: "Behold, the days are coming, says the LORD, when I will make a New Covenant with the house of Israel and with the house of Judah—* Heb 8:8. NKJV. God did not 'find fault' with 'it' i.e. the covenant, but with 'them' i.e. the people.

So let's see if we can see what God is teaching us when he uses the language of 'covenant'. We will dip into a few passages of Scripture to slowly create our colours on our own artist's palette. We shall need to add several different colours or ideas to get the shades just right, but if we can succeed in that effort we will begin to see the significance of Christ's words that the New Covenant was in his blood and why, as Andrew Murray once wrote, "The New Covenant may become to us one of the windows of heaven through which we see into the face, into the very heart, of God."

1: The trail begins

Although we may seldom hear the language of 'covenant' in our modern contexts, in ancient times it was one of the ordinary facts of life. When I bought my house I discovered there was a 'covenant' that I had to agree to. It is a very simple one; it says I must agree not to keep chickens or pigs in my garden. In some countries this would seem a strange condition but, living in a town in England, it was designed to make sure that all the houses that are so close together would not become like small farms. I had to agree to that covenant before I could buy the house. Even though I had the money to buy it and could fulfill all the other conditions I still had to agree to this one, no chickens or pigs!

In ancient times there were many agreements or covenants that controlled the lives of ordinary people. In fact, the word for 'covenant' is used over 300 times in the Bible. In our different Bible versions we may find the word translated as 'covenant' or 'alliance' or 'treaty' but the underlying word is 'covenant'. The word is the constant backdrop to the salvation history that is the storyline of the Bible. If we dig down beneath the surface, just a little, we hit 'covenant' every time. In fact, it all started with a 'covenant'. In the prophecy of Hosea, in the New International Version, we have this statement; *Like Adam, they have broken the covenant-- they were unfaithful to me there.* Hosea 6:7 NIV. Older translations usually have the words 'men' instead of 'Adam' here but most modern translations have noticed that the original Hebrew word was 'singular' and that, in Hebrew, it is the name 'Adam'. It seems that Adam was in an agreement or covenant with God and that he broke that agreement by an act of treachery.

A Covenant with Adam

We can see something of the terms of that agreement or covenant in the account of Adam's creation. If we read the account carefully we discover that Adam was not created 'in Eden' itself; he was first created and then placed in Eden. His placing in Eden was accompanied by words that gave him full access to every tree in the garden with a single exception; by implication his stay in Eden was conditional. One single tree, the tree of the knowledge of good and evil, was strictly prohibited on pain of immediate death. (Gen 2:15-17) We know the story only too well; Adam broke the covenant by committing an act of treason and lost his right to Eden... and more, so much more.

So we can already identify one of the colours to add to our artist's palette in this story. If we follow the story carefully we discover that this covenant/condition was originally made between two people, God and Adam. Eve shared in the covenant because of her relationship with Adam but the original covenant was made with 'one man'. Adam was the representative, or federal head for the coming race. He was that 'one man' who betrayed God and everyone related to him and represented by him has suffered some of the consequences. This next sentence will take us almost to the end of the trail, but this is why God ultimately had to start again with another 'one man' as Paul explains in his letter to the Romans; *For as by one man's disobedience many were made sinners, so also by one Man's obedience many will be made righteous.* Rom 5:19. NKJV. The phrase 'one man' is repeated; firstly speaking of Adam and secondly of Christ. Paul tells us that Adam was a 'figure' or template for Christ. Here is another colour to add to that palette; often a covenant has a 'representative' who 'agrees' the covenant on behalf of others. That kind of representative might be called a legal middleman or an agent or to use the bible word 'a mediator'. It is just one of many concepts which will need to be added to the palette if we are to understand why the Bible works in covenants.

Adam himself created another covenant, and of a kind that we are still familiar with today, the covenant of marriage. When God presented Adam with his partner Adam responded in a particular way; *And Adam said: "This is now bone of my bones And flesh of my flesh; She shall be called Woman, Because she was taken out of Man."* Gen 2:23 NKJV. Now what does this mean? So far as the Bible record tells us Eve's flesh didn't come from Adam, only the bone came from Adam. So why does Adam use this kind of language? Flesh and bone used in this way is a Hebrew idiom; just the way the language works in Hebrew. It is the legal language used to create a family. Many years later we have the record of the tribes of Israel coming under king David's rule. For a few years David had been ruling over his own family tribe of Judah but the time came when the whole nation united together under his rule. The spokesman for the non-family tribes used this kind of language when he proclaimed *"Indeed we are your bone and your flesh."* The story goes on to tell us that *King David made a covenant with them at Hebron before the LORD. And they anointed David king over Israel.* 2 Sam 5:1-3 NKJV. "We are your bone and your flesh" means we are one family; a new entity, a family had been created. Adam's covenant became the basic building block of all marriage formulas; from this time on Adam and Eve were 'one family' and no longer just two individuals. We are still adding to that colour palette, a covenant often creates a new legal entity.

What is perhaps even more amazing is that centuries later God used this marriage covenant imagery to show his new relationship to the people of Israel; *"When I passed by you again and looked upon you, indeed your time was the time of love; so I spread My wing over you and covered your nakedness. Yes, I swore an oath to you and entered into a covenant with you, and you became Mine," says the Lord GOD.* Ezek 16:8 NKJV. Ezekiel is describing what happened to the people of Israel at Sinai during the time of Moses; they became 'the bride of Jehovah'. They became God's people and God became 'the God of Israel'; a phrase that is used almost 90 times in the Bible. Again we shall need to return to this idea later to appreciate it fully.

A Covenant for the earth, with Noah

There are 300 references to covenant in the Bible and we will not be tracing each one. We will, however, take a brief look at another covenant in the book of Genesis before we move on. If we tried to understand the word covenant by reading through the Bible from cover to cover, the first time we actually meet the word 'covenant' would be in the record of Noah and the flood. We are introduced to the terrible wickedness of those days and hear of God's intention to bring the judgment of a flood upon the earth. But even in the proclamation of the coming judgment there is some good news; *And, behold, I, even I, do bring a flood of waters upon the earth, to destroy all flesh, wherein is the breath of life, from under heaven; and every thing that is in the earth shall die. But with thee will I establish my covenant; and thou shalt come into the ark, thou, and thy sons, and thy wife, and thy sons' wives with thee.* Gen 6:17-18 KJV

I have switched back to my old English version of the Bible here to make an important point. In modern English we have lost the use of the second person singular personal pronoun i.e. Thee, thine, thy. The plural personal pronoun 'you' now has to serve two functions; it may mean 'you personally, 'just you' or it may mean 'all of you together'. Sometimes we can tell the difference from the context and sometimes we can't. Gen 6:17 is one place where we could easily miss the fact that this is a personal covenant that God is making with Noah. We could paraphrase it by saying "I will establish my covenant with you personally, just you, and you personally and those who are personally related to you will share in its benefits." I am trying to bring out the idea of 'relationship' again. The people who were saved in the ark had a personal relationship with Noah, as the old version says, *"thou shalt come into the ark, thou, and thy sons, and thy wife, and thy sons' wives with thee."*

This is another example of a representative or mediator; Noah was going to be the 'representative' or 'mediator' and the only means of safety would be to be 'with Noah'; no one else would survive. The way that 'salvation history' records this story is fascinating. It describes a whole world of corruption and then states that in this sea of evil and violence there was a solitary 'righteous man', Noah. The rest of the people have corrupted their way but one man is left standing, Noah. Those who are rightly related to this 'last man' will also survive as a result of the covenant that God has made with him. Does this remind you of anything? A thoroughly corrupt world and one man left standing? A man in a unique relationship with God who makes a way of salvation for all those who will come to him? Can we see a shadow of Christ here?

As we follow the story through the next chapters of Genesis we discover that this promise is repeated but in a different way; *And I, behold, I establish my covenant with you, and with your seed after you;* Gen 9:9. KJV. Again I have used my old English version to show the contrast; this time the covenant is not to the individual 'thee' but is now extended to 'you' - in the plural. It is now extended to every-one and every-thing that has shared Noah's experience in his ark. The covenant that God made with Noah is now benefiting all those who shared his experience.

There is an unexpected reference to Noah and his flood in the writing of Peter where he describes Noah's flood as a kind of baptism. *...once the Divine longsuffering waited in the days of Noah, while the ark was being prepared, in which a few, that is, eight souls, were saved through water. There is also an antitype which now saves us—baptism (not the removal of the filth of the flesh, but the answer of a good conscience toward God), through the resurrection of Jesus Christ,* 1 Pet 3:20–21 NKJV. That may not be easy to grasp but Peter is declaring that what happened to Noah was a kind of pattern, or template (the Bible word is 'type'). It was, says Peter, a template or prefiguring of baptism. Let's see if we can interpret this. Those who shared 'Noah's baptism' shared his survival. Those who came to Noah and were with him shared God's judgment on sin and... survived; it is a pattern for the future. Those who share Christ's baptism will also share his survival. We shall need to set this aside for further examination later, but the evidence is building. And in the story of Noah there is yet another colour to add to our palette. The account, in its apparently pedantic way, declares that "only Noah and those who were with him in the ark remained..." Some versions add the word 'alive' but technically it is not there. We are being introduced to another vibrant colour; this is the Bible's first use of the verb linked to the noun 'remnant'. We shall add this colour to our palette later in Chapter 11 but, for the time being, we will just take note at this point that Noah and those who shared his baptism became 'the remnant'. (Gen 7:23) God was going to begin all over again with a remnant. All the promises made to the race were now carried by the remnant. God's whole plan for the human race is contracted to a tiny group of people who are now the sole bearers of human destiny.

A Covenant with Abraham

And then, finally for this chapter, there is another colour, so subtle as to be easily missed but which will be necessary to make God's living definition of the word covenant. It is an unexpected use of the word 'covenant' that you may not have noticed at all in Genesis. Abraham, or Abram as he was at that time, pitched his family tent in a place called Mamre. The account makes it clear that the land itself actually belonged to Mamre who was one of three Amorite brothers; *...Abram the Hebrew, for he dwelt by the terebinth trees of Mamre the Amorite, brother of Eshcol and brother of Aner; and they were allies with Abram.* Gen 14:13 NKJV. Most Bible translations translate this as 'allies' or 'confederates' but the original Hebrew is fascinating, it says that Mamre, Eschol and Aner were 'masters of a covenant' with Abraham. As the story unfolds it looks as though the condition for Abraham pitching his tent on Mamre's land was some kind of simple military alliance. Abraham and his people would be expected to join the Amorite brothers if they were attacked. The three Amorite brothers were the 'senior' partners and Abraham was the 'junior' partner in this alliance. This is a telling instance of a covenant in action; a legal agreement made between Abraham and his Amorite landlords. It was designed to provide both Abraham and the brothers with mutual defense in time of attack. As we read through the story we find that not only Abraham's 318 personal servants but the servants of Mamre, Aner and Eschol too were part of the raiding party that rescued Lot.

We are being introduced to yet another ingredient of 'covenant', a defensive shield against outsiders. Many of the less noticed Bible covenants are of this kind; they are military alliances. Later it seems that Abraham raised his hand and committed himself to God alone and, for his part, God undertook to be Abraham's 'shield' and his 'reward.' (Gen 15:1) It is time well spent in tracing these covenants through the Bible to see what the word really meant in those ancient times. Bible words, remember, don't have definitions, they have histories. Let me illustrate at this point. In Northern France there is a pleasant seaside resort where English children sometimes spend a day's holiday/vacation. Hundreds of children associate the name of that seaside experience with a happy day at the beach, but for a whole older generation of British people the name of the town brings back other memories; the town is called Dunkirk. It was the scene of a time of great danger and an amazing escape to safety for the British Expeditionary Force during the early part of the Second World War. Similarly Bible words have their own history and we can only understand the truths of the Bible as we learn the history of some of its great words.

In this chapter we have seen the care and precision with which the Artist began to create just the colours he required on his artist's palette for the final picture. We have seen the colours of representation and mediator-ship. We have added the colour of the creation of new entities with new destinies and responsibilities. We have added the colour of 'the remnant', a human life raft in which the hopes of a whole race are carried on the shoulders of those who survive the judgments. We have seen how covenants provide a legal framework in which its members find a shield for protection. There are many more hues on God's palette but these will suffice for the present. We shall need to try to keep these ideas in mind, ready on our artist's palette, as we move forward into the Bible's concept of 'covenant' and the place of 'covenant' in salvation history.

2: The Sinai Covenant

Let's establish an important point right at the beginning of this journey. The topic of this book is the New or Better Covenant but when the Bible speaks of the 'New' or 'Better' Covenant it is using the language of contrast. In the prophecy of Jeremiah and in the book of Hebrews the New Covenant is described by means of contrast with an Old Covenant. We need to identify this earlier 'old' covenant and then ask how it differed from the better covenant, and what happened to make it 'old'.

A Covenant with Abraham and with Isaac and with Jacob

Through carefully recorded details we can trace the covenant that God established with Abraham and then with Isaac and then with Jacob, but this Abrahamic covenant was not the 'old' covenant referred to in the letter to the Hebrews.

Let's identify that 'Old Covenant' first and then, in Chapter 4, backtrack to examine the earlier covenant with Abraham.

As we move from Genesis to Exodus the scene moves from the land of Canaan to the land of Egypt and the record of God's dealings moves from individuals to that of a larger people-group. The move of Abraham's grandson to Egypt came as a result of a personal invitation from the Pharaoh to Abraham's grandson Jacob or as he is often called, Israel. It was God who renamed Jacob and the new name was the result of a personal encounter that took place in Genesis 32. In the earlier part of Genesis Abraham, Isaac and Jacob all have personal encounters with God. With each one He establishes his 'covenant' individually and for that reason is called the God of Abraham, the God of Isaac and the God of Jacob: *Moreover God said to Moses, "Thus you shall say to the children of Israel: 'The LORD God of your fathers, the God of Abraham, the God of Isaac, and the God of Jacob, has sent me to you. This is My name forever, and this is My memorial to all generations.'* Ex 3:15 NKJV. As the story unfolded in Genesis it related mainly to these men and their families but in Exodus it begins to broaden.

The blood descendants of Abraham, Isaac and Jacob were numbered at 70. The older English version says 'these came from the loins of Jacob'; the 70 were Jacob's bloodline. (Genesis 46:26,27) This number does not include the wives of Jacob's/Israel's children; this is just the number of blood descendants. There were many more than this who actually migrated to Egypt. Pharaoh's invitation was not just to the immediate family of Israel, but specifically to their 'households' i.e. their servants, retainers and others who were part of their community at that time; *And Pharaoh said to Joseph, "Say to your brothers, 'Do this: Load your animals and depart; go to the land of Canaan. Bring your father and your households and come to me; I will give you the best of the land of Egypt, and you will eat the fat of the land.* Gen 45:17-18 NKJV. Some of these 'households' were probably quite large. In an earlier story we discover that from his 'household' Abraham was able to raise a trained militia of 318 men. If we grant each of those warriors a wife and a couple of children we begin to get an idea of the size of Abraham's 'household; that would give us a moderate estimate of 1500 souls. Abraham was a clan leader.

From family to nation

During their time in Egypt that family community grew enormously. The bloodline and non-bloodline 'households' became thoroughly integrated into 12 'tribes' or clans which were given the names of the original family's 12 sons; Reuben, Simeon, Levi, Judah etc. By the time they came to leave Egypt under Moses there were something in the region of 3 million of them. They were no longer a 'family' they were a large and distinctive 'people group'. Even though they had become bond-servants to the throne of Egypt they now had their own community leaders called 'elders'; the group had developed structure and a cohesive identity. As we move from Genesis to Exodus the size of what is happening changes dramatically; we move from stories of individuals to the story of a nation and we are reading the account of the way in which that nation becomes 'God's Nation'.

The descendants of Abraham and their households had become the bond-slaves of Pharaoh and their conditions just got worse and worse as Egyptian rule became increasingly oppressive. The Bible refers to this period as 'being in an iron furnace'; the heat was turned up and the 'nation' was under crippling persecution. In their distress they called out to God and God responded to their prayer: *Then the children of Israel groaned because of the bondage, and they cried out; and their cry came up to God because of the bondage. So God heard their groaning, and God remembered His covenant with Abraham, with Isaac, and with Jacob. And God looked upon the children of Israel, and God acknowledged them.* Ex 2:23-25 NKJV. God had not forgotten his covenant relationship with Abraham, with Isaac and with Jacob and he 'recognised' those who prayed as the families of these three patriarchs. Then begins the story of the Exodus and the forming of this great multitude into a nation with a specific purpose. It is worth taking a little time to follow the story.

We can break the account up into two fairly obvious parts; first, their escape from Egypt and secondly, their arrival at Mount Sinai. Part of their escape was the event we call the Passover. Judgment came on all the eldest sons of the Egyptians and would have come on the eldest sons of the people of Israel too except for their obedience. Moses received a command to institute a special memorial feast which many Jews keep to this day, the Passover. Although the people were in such vast numbers God was still dealing with them in terms of 'families and households'; *Speak to all the congregation of Israel, saying: "On the tenth of this month every man shall take for himself a lamb, according to the house of his father, a lamb for a household."* Ex 12:3 NKJV. They splashed the blood of the sacrifice on the doorframes of their homes and ate the shared meal of roast lamb. In every home where there was blood on the doorposts and roast lamb on the table the eldest sons were safe, but in every other home, even if they were blood descendants of Abraham, the eldest sons were under sentence of death. They were instructed to make an anniversary of this event throughout their generations.

It was this memorial Passover meal that Jesus shared with his disciples in the upper room some 1400 years later. It was at the end of this Jewish annual celebration of redemption that we read; *the Lord Jesus on the same night in which He was betrayed took bread; and when He had given thanks, He broke it and said, "Take, eat; this is My body which is broken for you; do this in remembrance of Me." In the same manner He also took the cup after supper, saying, "This cup is the New Covenant in My blood. This do, as often as you drink it, in remembrance of Me."* 1Cor 11:23-25 NKJV. In the Exodus story it was some days after the Passover that this redeemed people finally entered into a covenant agreement with the God who had delivered them. In strict time order, the redemption came before the covenant but it was the shed blood and the meal of roast lamb that prepared the way for the covenant. The people of Israel were under the power of an evil king and that power had to be broken before the covenant could be established; no man can serve two masters. That Passover night, they began their journey to freedom and to Sinai and to a promised land.

At one point the fleeing escapees became hedged in between the Red Sea and the avenging Egyptian army and this became the scene of the famous event in which Moses stretched out his hand over the sea... the people of Israel entered a corridor of water and passed through safe and absolutely dry. (Ex 14:21-22). When the Egyptian army tried to follow the walls of water caved in and the entire Egyptian army was drowned. It is interesting to notice how the Bible ends this account; *Thus Israel saw the great work which the LORD had done in Egypt; so the people feared the LORD, and believed the LORD and His servant Moses.* Ex 14:31 NKJV. Moses is one of the most important people in the Bible and certainly the most important person in the Old Covenant; Moses was the intermediary between God and man in the coming covenant. In that covenant there was one mediator and his name was Moses.

Baptized into Moses?

Many years later when Paul refers to this crossing of the Red Sea he describes it in a particular way; *all our fathers were under the cloud, all passed through the sea, all were baptized into Moses in the cloud and in the sea,* 1Cor 10:1-2 NKJV. Does that strike you as being a curious way to describe the events of Exodus 14? Why would Paul describe this event as a baptism? We already noted that Peter called the events of Noah's flood a baptism too. Although we are getting ahead of ourselves, we need to use these New Testament statements to help us as we try to understand the underlying truth for which these events have been recorded.

We may be helped by another statement of Paul's; *Or do you not know that as many of us as were baptized into Christ Jesus were baptized into His death? Therefore we were buried with Him through baptism into death, that just as Christ was raised from the dead by the glory of the Father, even so we also should walk in newness of life. For if we have been united together in the likeness of His death, certainly we also shall be in the likeness of His resurrection,* Rom 6:3–5 NKJV. There's that same phrase we read earlier, 'baptism into...' In 1 Corinthians Paul says the people of Israel were 'baptized into Moses' and now here in Romans he says those who are baptized into Christ are 'baptized into His death'. In ancient times the word 'baptize' was sometimes used in recipes for pickling onions! So now we have moved from painting to cooking! One recipe is very specific. You begin by blanching the onions in boiling water and then you marinate the onions in the pickling spices, but the words used for blanching and marinating are very instructive. The word for blanching is baptO which means to dip and the word for marinate is baptizO which means to submerge and saturate. The effect of baptizing onions in this way was that it united the blanched onion with all the flavours that were in the pickling spices, and the key word there is 'united'; this is also the sense of Paul's reference to 'baptism into Christ', it unites. A baptism sometimes had the effect of uniting the item being baptized with the element in which the baptism took place. There is some very important truth here but for the time being we will just concentrate on this simple aspect of it. The events at the Red Sea united the people with Moses, they became 'one with him'. They would share his destiny.

Moses was the human author of the first five books of the Old Testament and for the nation of Israel he was one of the most important persons in their history. He became their living link with God; the mediator of the Sinai Covenant and the Jewish people never forgot it. Many years later a recently healed man mischievously asked some religious leaders if they wanted to become disciples of Jesus, their answer was unmistakable; *Then they reviled him and said, "You are His disciple, but we are Moses' disciples."* John 9:28 NKJV. 1400 years after Moses' death they were still Moses' disciples. The record of Moses' life and work is thrilling. His relationship to God was 'face to face', that is, it was 'without a mediator'; there was no one in between Moses and God, but there was someone between God and the nation of Israel and his name was Moses! The story of Moses is factual but it is not recorded just because it is true but because it has lasting relevance. As well as being a real flesh and blood individual Moses was a prefiguring or foreshadowing of Christ himself. At his birth an evil ruler tried to kill him; the same was true of Christ. There are many other parallels between Moses and Christ but perhaps the most amazing one is that Moses offered to give up his own eternal relationship with God to make a propitiation for the sins of his sinful people; *"Yet now, if You will forgive their sin—but if not, I pray, blot me out of Your book which You have written."* Ex 32:32-33 NKJV. There are both parallels and contrasts. Moses' offer was rejected; Christ's was accepted. We could spend much time following the story of Moses and his covenant and the time would not be wasted but we must press on...

Arrival at Sinai and Covenant

Having escaped from Egypt Moses brought the people to the foot of Mount Sinai and then ascended the mountain to speak with God; God gave him a message for the people. If we follow this account carefully we will see several ascents and descents of this mountain as Moses fulfills his role as intermediary or mediator. The message was stunning. The people were no doubt excited at having a promise of their own land (Ex 6:4, 8) but this message went much further; *"You have seen what I did to the Egyptians, and how I bore you on eagles' wings and brought you to Myself. Now therefore, if you will indeed obey My voice and keep My covenant, then you shall be a special treasure to Me above all people; for all the earth is Mine. And you shall be to Me a kingdom of priests and a holy nation.' These are the words which you shall speak to the children of Israel."* Ex 19:4-6 NKJV. This was not only the promise of promised land, but a promise that God would enter into a solemn and binding covenant by which these descendants of Abraham and their households would become God's own nation. Moses faithfully conveyed the message to the waiting crowds and their response was immediate; *Then all the people answered together and said, "All that the LORD has spoken we will do." So Moses brought back the words of the people to the LORD.* Ex 19:8 NKJV. In other words a resounding 'yes'!

It is easy to identify the conditional clauses in this agreement. 'If' you fulfill these obligations 'then' you will be...

The implications are very clear. If you do this then this will follow, if you don't do this then this will not follow. This is a classic covenant and that is what God calls it. What God promises is truly amazing. If they agreed to the terms of the covenant God would give them an exclusive destiny even though the whole world and all its nations already belonged to him. This vast gathering would become God's special treasure, God's unique possession. They would be 'His' in a way that no other nation was 'His'. They would become a 'kingdom' under a king's rule but not like the other kingdoms of the world, they would become a kingdom, not of warriors or scholars or financiers, but a kingdom of priests; they would become God's personal servants. And they would become 'a holy nation'. There's the word at last; they would become a *nation*, and a nation separated to God for God's own purpose. What a destiny! Little wonder that they all said 'yes'.

But this covenant has terms and conditions and Moses returns to God to get the details of the covenant agreement. This is the part we call the 10 commandments and the judgments. Exodus 20-23 gives us the details of the legal agreement that the people were about to sign up for. In Exodus 24 Moses returns to the people and repeats and then records, in his own handwriting, the terms of the covenant and again the people unanimously give their assent; *So Moses came and told the people all the words of the LORD and all the judgments. And all the people answered with one voice and said, "All the words which the LORD has said we will do." And Moses wrote all the words of the LORD. And he rose early in the morning, and built an altar at the foot of the mountain, and twelve pillars according to the twelve tribes of Israel.* Ex 24:3-4 NKJV. From this moment this document is called 'the Book of the Covenant' and may have been the first part of our Bible to be written down. Moses now reads this document to the people, so that there can be no doubt as to what they are signing up for, and again their response is unanimous; *"Then he took the Book of the Covenant and read in the hearing of the people. And they said, All that the LORD has said we will do, and be obedient."* Ex 24:7 NKJV.

The Blood of the Covenant

In between these two resounding affirmations of the covenant lies another event. Moses instructs the people to build a simple altar and to offer two kinds of sacrifices to God; whole burnt offerings and peace offerings. He collects the blood from the sacrificed animals in a basin and sprinkles half of it on the simple altar with its burning sacrifices, and the remainder of the blood he keeps in the basin. Then, for the third time, the people give their full-hearted consent to the terms of the covenant and Moses sprinkles the rest of the blood on the people (Exodus 24:8) and on the book (Heb 9:19). The people of God owed their existence and their destiny to a Book-based covenant and shed blood; this covenant was to be thoroughly 'bible-based'. By this act he 'united' the altar, the book of the covenant and the people with the same 'blood of the covenant' and uses words which were surely in the mind of Christ in that upper room;

> *And Moses took the blood, sprinkled it on the people, and said, "This is the blood of the covenant which the LORD has made with you according to all these words." Ex 24:8 NKJV.*

> *Likewise He also took the cup after supper, saying, "This cup is the new covenant in My blood, which is shed for you." Luke 22:20 NKJV.*

When Christ used these words in the upper room he added the word 'new' to make a clear contrast between the covenant that he would make and the covenant that Moses had made. The two covenants and their two mediators must always be carefully distinguished. We will miss much of what God is revealing if we do not distinguish these two separate covenants.

Under God's direction Moses then added another ingredient of the Sinai Covenant, the Priesthood and its Sacrifices. The Priesthood and the sacrifices are a little like a 'maintenance clause' of a legal agreement. A single sin would have shattered the Sinai Covenant, as it would have broken the people's side of the agreement. To prevent this disaster God instituted the priesthood under Moses' brother Aaron. As a result of the priests' activities in conducting sacrifices for sin the peoples' sin would not be held against them. Later we shall see that the New Covenant has a High Priest too and a new pattern of law; *For the priesthood being changed, of necessity there is also a change of the law.* Heb 7:12 NKJV. The Law and its Priesthood were integral parts of the Sinai Covenant, neither could function without the other. Both the Old and the New covenants come with a built-in priesthood, and neither can function without its officially appointed High Priest, but they are different kinds of priesthood. The Sinai Covenant making was interrupted by a tragedy which overtook the 'new nation' even in its earliest moments and threatened the termination of the covenant and the people, but when we reach the end of the book of Exodus we find the Tabernacle with its priests is up and running and God has taken up residence among his people.

These events took place about 1400 years before Christ and for the rest of the Old Testament we have the Sinai Covenant as a background against which all its history is acted out. It is good to remember this key fact that from Sinai to Calvary the backdrop of the Bible is the 'Old Covenant'. It was kept very imperfectly by the new nation and at times not kept at all. During the times of Samuel, Saul and David the Ark, where the Covenant agreement was kept, became separated from the Tabernacle and consequently some of the requirements could never have been fulfilled. The blood of atoning sacrifice, which was shed at the altar, could not be sprinkled on the missing ark and so technically the Day of Atonement did not take place for over a hundred years. There were other breaks too later in their history. Nevertheless that Covenant agreement between God and his new nation was in force during all those 1400 years. God added other covenants but they never took the place of the Sinai Covenant; that covenant was the one fixed point of all the passing years.

In this chapter we followed the history of Abraham's descendants and their households and the way in which they became integrated into a new entity, a kingdom of priests and God's own nation. We noted the original Passover meal that marked their deliverance and paved the way for the Covenant to be ratified. We saw the unbreakable bond between the Law and the Priesthood and the statement in Hebrews that teaches us that the New Covenant is a change both of Law and Priesthood and we reminded ourselves that the Sinai Covenant is the permanent backdrop to the whole of the Old Testament from Exodus to Malachi. Finally we saw again the way that Christ distinguished 'the New Covenant' from the Sinai Covenant.

3: An Old Covenant

I am tempted to say that when the Sinai Covenant was first instituted it was really a 'new covenant' but I think that might lead to some confusion! There was a time when it was 'new' and we need to see what took place that made it 'old'. In Paul's letter to the churches in Galatia, he tells us that the Sinai Covenant was added and was only temporary; we will return to that statement later in Chapter 4. Certainly it was a new experience in the lives of the nation of Israel and from its inception the pattern of their lives would be radically changed. In particular, 'God had moved into the neighbourhood'! If we are familiar with the Bible story this may now not seem very remarkable but it will be good to remind ourselves that the Tabernacle that Moses was instructed to build was not a meeting hall like those that we are familiar with. It was really a mobile palace where God sat on a throne and reigned in the midst of his people. Like a desert chieftain God had his tent right at the centre of the camp and the rest of the people pitched their tents around him. As with any oriental king, not everyone was permitted into his presence only his most trusted servants. This would be true of God's palace too, the rest of the people were allowed into the outer courtyard but only his chief ministers, the priests, were allowed into the palace itself and even then one part was set apart exclusively for God; not even the chief minister/priest was allowed there except for the ceremony of Atonement, just once a year.

A summary of Israel's history

When God finally moved in there was no doubt about it. Not even his ministers could stand the impact of his presence. The consciousness of the presence of God was so overwhelming that the priests were unable to function. Presumably, they could only bow in awe at the scene of God coming into his throne-room. (Ex 40:33-35) Alas, in spite of such wonderful beginnings, the story of the nation of Israel was a story of national failure. Many individuals knew God for themselves and were faithful servants but the nation as a whole was a terrible failure. The last book in the Old Testament seems to summarize a thousand years of failure; *"I have loved you," says the LORD. "Yet you say, 'In what way have You loved us?'* Mal 1:2 NKJV. It is a great but tragic summary of the Old Testament story; *I have loved you, but you...* God's faithful love is contrasted with the nation's obstinate failure.

The individual family clan-tribes of Israel retained their own identities and at times fought each other but ultimately they all united under a king, David. In some ways, this was the high point of Israel's nationhood. When they recognised David as king they were in their own land with all enemies subdued and unanimous consent that David should be their only ruler. We referred to this event earlier when they declared that they were David's 'bone and flesh'. A covenant was enacted at that time between the nation and its king. (2Sam 5:1-3) Things were looking good... briefly. In less than a hundred years it had all unraveled again. David's grandson Rehoboam decided he would show 'who was in charge' and the nation split along its traditional fault lines; ten and a half family tribes broke away and left David's grandson with just the rump of a nation.

Although we can see the folly of men in these events the split was actually God's punishment on David's dynasty. The breakaway kingdom known as 'Israel' really was 'Israel' to all intents and purposes and only the tribe of Judah was left to the dynasty of David. (The family tribe of Judah, some Levites and a trickle of other families stayed loyal to 'the house of David'.) 'Israel', the nation-state in the north, rapidly went downhill; its rulers were just one disaster after another. They turned away from the true God and became passionate followers of other gods. As a result God told them he would punish them with banishment; the whole 'nation of Israel' was ultimately exiled into the territories of the super-power of Assyria. Other captive peoples were then brought in to the empty land and the nation-state of 'Israel' was no more. The nation-state of 'Judah' in the south survived somewhat longer but its leaders were a patchy group of the good and bad.

You are not my people... you are my people.

Just as 'Israel' in the north was about to come to an end God sent the prophet Hosea to warn them that the coming events were his sentence upon their betrayal of the covenant. Hosea's prophecy is specifically addressed to that northern kingdom known at this time as 'Israel'. This part of Bible history is often difficult to follow due to the fact that the books are not in chronological order and it becomes difficult to follow the story line and to insert the books of the prophets into the right part of the historical timeline. Take a look at the book of Hosea just to get the flavour even if you don't understand all the details. It begins with a tragedy that results in a divorce. God uses the formal language of divorce as he speaks to 'Israel'; *Then God said: "Call his name Lo-ammi, For you are not My people, And I will not be your God."* Hos 1:9 NKJV. The phrase 'You are not my wife and I am not your husband' which we find echoed in Hosea 2:2 was patterned on the formal way in which a divorce was enacted. Well that's that then. It is all over for 'Israel', but wait... what is this next message from God to 'Israel'? *"Yet the number of the children of Israel Shall be as the sand of the sea, Which cannot be measured or numbered. And it shall come to pass in the place where it was said to them, "You are not My people,' There it shall be said to them, 'You are sons of the living God.'* Hos 1:10 NKJV. Notice too the switch from 'people' to 'sons'. Apparently it is not the absolute end, there is to be another chapter to their extraordinary story.

This may already seem confusing but there is an added complication to the story. Under the Sinai Covenant's special laws a man could not take back a wife that he had divorced if that wife had become the wife of another man. (Deuteronomy 24:40) So how is God going to take the northern nation-state of 'Israel' back as his 'bride'?

There is a feature in prophecy that frequently makes prophecy difficult to understand. Sometimes a Bible prophet begins by speaking about things close at hand but then in the next sentences may begin to speak of events hundreds of years in the future. There is an old illustration that is often used to try to explain this phenomenon. If you look towards a range of mountains you will see the high points and sometimes they seem very close together but if you actually make the journey on the ground you may find that there are deep valleys between those high peaks. They were not visible from your first vantage point and you may not have been prepared for them. Your first view was not a lie or a mistake but all the details were not available in the earlier view. Times alter perspectives; this is an important principle of Bible interpretation. We can see this in the prophecy of Hosea. In one breath he says 'you are not my people' and in the next breath he says 'you are my people'. Are these two statements in contradiction to each other? No, it's just that there was going to be a very deep valley between these two peaks.

As a separate nation-state the northern 'kingdom' of 'Israel' had received its divorce papers; it was over. However God's purposes for the people of that nation-state were not finished. The nation-state was finished but not God's plan for its people. The next verses begin to show us the plan. *Then the children of Judah and the children of Israel Shall be gathered together, And appoint for themselves one head; And they shall come up out of the land, For great will be the day of Jezreel!* Hos 1:11 NKJV. When we find references to 'Israel' and 'Judah' like this we need to give some thought to whom we are referring. We have two nation-states in view, the northern nation-state of 'Israel' and the southern nation-state of 'Judah'. The way that God was going to fulfill his plan would be to reintegrate the two nations into one nation under one head. He would 'gather them together' and there would be 'one head' over the reconstituted nation. The shame of the past would be lost in the new entity that God would bring into existence. There would no longer be two nations and two kings but one nation and one king. This promise is going to be a vital link to the words of later prophets who will take up this theme and declare it in their own unique ways.

It was in 722 BC that the tragedy finally struck. The northern nation-state of 'Israel' was conquered by the super-power of Assyria and its family tribes were expatriated and absorbed into other parts of the Assyrian empire. 'Israel' was finished or as the Bible expresses it so dramatically; *The virgin of Israel has fallen; She will rise no more. She lies forsaken on her land; There is no one to raise her up.* Amos 5:2 NKJV. The southern nation-state of Judah limped on for another 130 years but finally God's judgment came on her covenant betrayal too. Jerusalem and Solomon's Temple were engulfed in flames and the people of Judah were exiled into the empire of Babylon. This time another prophet had predicted it; *The land shall be entirely emptied and utterly plundered, For the LORD has spoken this word* Is 24:3 NKJV. What a tragedy. It seemed as though "Israel's" wonderful destiny was in utter ruin. Surely this must be the end?

A new exodus, a new thing and a new covenant

Even before these two different exiles took place God had begun to speak about a return and had used the language of their history; *Therefore, behold, I will allure her, Will bring her into the wilderness, And speak comfort to her. I will give her her vineyards from there, And the Valley of Achor as a door of hope; She shall sing there, As in the days of her youth, As in the day when she came up from the land of Egypt.* Hos 2:14-15 NKJV. Notice the phrase 'as in the days when she came up from the land of Egypt'. This will become a familiar theme for other prophets. God is describing his intention to restore the people to their land and is using the language of the 'exodus'; he is promising a second 'exodus' and using the language of their history to prepare them for the future. The details will be very different; this time they will escape not from Egypt but from Babylon and all the other places of their exile. It will not be a repeat of the Egyptian event but a 'new exodus'. This is how Isaiah described it in a long passage that is well worth quoting here; *Thus says the LORD, your Redeemer, The Holy One of Israel: "For your sake I will send to Babylon, And bring them all down as fugitives— The Chaldeans, who rejoice in their ships. I am the LORD, your Holy One, The Creator of Israel, your King." Thus says the LORD, who makes a way in the sea And a path through the mighty waters, Who brings forth the chariot and horse, The army and the power (They shall lie down together, they shall not rise; They are extinguished, they are quenched like a wick): "Do not remember the former things, Nor consider the things of old. Behold, I will do a new thing, Now it shall spring forth; Shall you not know it? I will even make a road in the wilderness And rivers in the desert. The beast of the field will honour Me, The jackals and the ostriches, Because I give waters in the wilderness And rivers in the desert, To give drink to My people, My chosen. This people I have formed for Myself; They shall declare My praise."* Is 43:14-21 NKJV. This passage contains the famous promise that God is proposing to do a 'new thing'. That will be another part of the repeating refrain, 'a new thing'.

As the judgments struck and during Jerusalem's last days the prophet Jeremiah began to declare God's plan but this time not in the language of a 'new exodus' or a 'new thing' but of a 'New Covenant'; *"Behold, the days are coming, says the LORD, when I will make a New Covenant with the house of Israel and with the house of Judah— not according to the covenant that I made with their fathers in the day that I took them by the hand to lead them out of the land of Egypt, My covenant which they broke, though I was a husband to them, says the LORD. But this is the covenant that I will make with the house of Israel after those days, says the LORD: I will put My law in their minds, and write it on their hearts; and I will be their God, and they shall be My people.* Jer 31:31-33 NKJV.

We can see lots of familiar themes here. The 'New Covenant' will be made with the 'house of Israel' and with 'the house of Judah' although later this reconstituted nation is simply called 'the house of Israel'. There are reminders of Egypt here too and the 'Sinai Covenant' and the strong statement that the 'New Covenant' is going to be different. This is going to be important later. This is not a repaired Sinai Covenant or a Sinai Covenant with some new additions; this is going to be a 'New Covenant'. Isaiah had said don't even think about the 'old things', God is going to do a 'new thing'. Now Jeremiah takes up the same truth; this will not be the Sinai Covenant Mark II, this is will be a 'New Covenant'.

It is this statement of Jeremiah's that re-labels the Sinai Covenant; *In that he saith, A New Covenant he hath made the first old. But that which is becoming old and waxeth aged is nigh unto vanishing away.* Heb 8:13 ASV. Many modern versions opt for the word 'obsolete' here but I have quoted from the American Standard Version to keep the link with the word 'old'. You will notice we have jumped from the Old Testament to the New Testament here because the writer to the Hebrews is telling us that the 'New Covenant' that Jeremiah promised has arrived and the Sinai Covenant is now 'old'. From the moment that Jeremiah gave his prophecy the Sinai Covenant was potentially the 'Old Covenant'. Later we shall see what it was that actually made this Sinai Covenant 'old'.

The promise of a remnant

There is yet another thread that we must examine and this will link us to our final comments about Noah in Chapter 1. The prophet Isaiah uses the word 'remnant' to describe those who will return. I can still recall shopping from the 'remnants stall' in the open market with my mother. It is interesting how 'words have histories'. A remnant is what is left when everything else has gone. Isaiah uses the word to say that although God's judgments have justly come on the house of Israel and the house of Judah, the destruction has not been total; a remnant will survive and that remnant will return. *And it shall come to pass in that day That the remnant of Israel,*

And such as have escaped of the house of Jacob, Will never again depend on him who defeated them, But will depend on the LORD, the Holy One of Israel, in truth. The remnant will return, the remnant of Jacob, To the Mighty God. For though your people, O Israel, be as the sand of the sea, A remnant of them will return; The destruction decreed shall overflow with righteousness. Is 10:20-22 NKJV. Some time ago I tried to calculate just what percentage this 'remnant' might represent. If we think of the 'remnant' initially as those who returned from the exile during the times of Zerubbabel and Ezra and Nehemiah we are talking about less than 50,000 people. I have calculated that the population of the nation during David's day was closer to seven million. The 'remnant' was a tiny proportion of the original united nation.

Later the prophet Ezekiel takes up the theme and speaks of the 'remnant' but he also adds his own ingredients to the promises. He speaks of the returning exiles and repeats the idea of Hosea that they will be one nation under one king. God even gives him a miraculous illustration to make the point. (Ezek 37:15-17) But Ezekiel adds some details that make it more complex too. He says that the 'one king' who will reign over the reconstituted nation will be David; *I will establish one shepherd over them, and he shall feed them—My servant David. He shall feed them and be their shepherd.* Ezek 34:23 NKJV. As Ezekiel is prophesying over 400 years after David's death this is going to need an explanation. Ezekiel is really promising the return of the Davidic dynasty and more. This will give us a pointer to the future because the descendant of David that Ezekiel promised is Jesus of Nazareth, the son of David, and Jesus himself would later use words which were a clear echo of Ezekiel's prophecy; *And other sheep I have which are not of this fold; them also I must bring, and they will hear My voice; and there will be one flock and one shepherd.* John 10:16 NKJV.

As we promised, we shall need to retrace our steps for a while because there is yet another covenant that we need to examine and this is even 'older' than the Sinai Covenant. In fact it will stretch back all the way to Abraham and then, moving forwards, will find its fulfillment in the person who is the real subject of both of these covenants, Jesus Christ himself; the Son of David and the Son of Abraham. These two key Old Testament characters appear side by side as the New Testament begins its own story: *The book of the genealogy of Jesus Christ, the Son of David, the Son of Abraham:* Matt 1:1

In this chapter we traced the history of the nation-states of Israel and Judah and saw how comprehensively God brought his judgment upon them. We traced the separated states and saw that we need to distinguish the different ways that the word 'Israel' is used. Sometimes it refers to the separate northern nation-state of 'Israel' but when that nation becomes 'no longer a people' the name of Israel becomes the label for God's reintegration of remnants from both 'the house of Israel' and the 'house of Judah' into a reconstituted 'Israel'. We also saw that it was promised to this reconstituted 'Israel' that David would reign over them and that Christ clearly saw himself as the fulfillment of this prophecy.

4: A day in the life of Abraham

Here is the back-track that we promised back in Chapter 2. It was a very long day. It began in starlight and ended in starlight. The first part of it was full of bustle and things to do and the second part was mysterious and silent.

There are very large gaps in the Bible storyline. They are not really omissions; it's just that what we have has been carefully selected to keep us on the track of salvation history. As mentioned before, one aspect that often takes new readers of the Bible by surprise is the unevenness of the way it records time. Abraham's story is a case in point. It takes 4 chapters to cover 25 years; (Gen 12-15), then it takes 5 chapters to cover one year; (Gen 17-21). In the story of Abraham it is mostly gaps; there is a 13-year gap between the end of Genesis Chapter 16 and the beginning of Genesis Chapter 17. The narrative is not a full biography but a recording of 'the steps of the faith of our father Abraham' and sometimes, between one step and the next there can be a lengthy pause. If we remember the unevenness of time's passage in the Bible the fact that a whole chapter, Genesis 15, records one single day suggests that this day is of some particular significance.

Abraham obeyed by faith

Abraham, or Abram as he was called at that time, left Ur in Mesopotamia and stayed for some time in Haran. He was 75 years old when he began the journey from Haran and arrived in the land of Canaan. (Gen 12:4,5) In the area of Shechem he had an experience of God; this seems to have been his second such experience. Back in Ur God had appeared to him with an abrupt instruction; *The God of glory appeared to our father Abraham when he was in Mesopotamia, before he dwelt in Haran, and said to him, "Get out of your country and from your relatives, and come to a land that I will show you."* Acts 7:2-3 NKJV. The land is not specifically promised at this stage; it is just a simple instruction to leave Ur. In fact, there is no promise of anything at this stage, just a simple command. The promises will come later. The letter to the Hebrews describes the moment of this first encounter with God as the obedience of faith; *By faith Abraham obeyed when he was called to go out to the place which he would receive as an inheritance. And he went out, not knowing where he was going.* Heb 11:8 NKJV.

We shall see that the full promise of an inheritance comes later in this same chapter; *Now the LORD had said to Abram: "Get out of your country, From your family And from your father's house, To a land that I will show you. I will make you a great nation; I will bless you And make your name great; And you shall be a blessing. I will bless those who bless you, And I will curse him who curses you; And in you all the families of the earth shall be blessed."* Gen 12:1-3 NKJV. We often conclude that this was the original promise to Abraham and his descendants of the land, but as the record stands at this early stage it was a destination rather than an inheritance. The command breaks neatly into three sections; God's instruction to Abraham, God's personal promise to Abraham of a huge family and, lastly, of the worldwide implications of the first two sections. The promise of a country as his personal inheritance was implied but not specifically stated at this early point. The main thrust of this encounter with God is that Abraham would be blessed as he obeyed God.

It was when Abraham actually arrived at his destination in the land of Canaan that God promised that he would give the land that he was standing on to Abraham's posterity. The Hebrew way of saying that is... *Unto thy seed will I give this land: and there builded he an altar unto the LORD, who appeared unto him.* Gen 12:7 KJV In this reference the 'land' is promised to Abraham's 'seed'. Modern versions usually switch to the word 'descendant' which is an accurate translation but it breaks the link with many Old Testament 'seed promises'. These are a sequence of promises scattered from Genesis onwards that trace the line of descent from Adam to Mary. This first explicit promise, regarding the land, was actually a promise to Abraham's 'seed'. At the risk of being archaic I will stick to the word 'seed' now so that we don't lose the connection.

The Seed is Christ

Let's take a huge jump through about 2000 years to the letter of Paul to the churches of Galatia; *Now to Abraham and his Seed were the promises made. He does not say, "And to seeds," as of many, but as of one, "And to your Seed," who is Christ.* Gal 3:16 NKJV. We have jumped almost to the end of the story but sometimes that is necessary to see the journey's aim. There is a happy coincidence in the way our English language works and the way that the Hebrew language works here. If, in English, I were describing a grain of wheat I would describe it as 'a seed', using the singular form. If I were describing 10 grains of wheat I would describe them as 'seeds', using the plural form. If I were describing a barn full of wheat I would describe it as 'full of seed', reverting to the singular use of the word 'seed'. Something similar happens in Hebrew which means that most of the times that the Hebrew word 'seed' is used in the Bible it is used in the singular form, although not always. Now Paul does not believe in coincidences; he believes that the Holy Spirit has inspired the way the language works at this point. Let's see if we can follow his reasoning.

Paul has noticed that in these promises that are scattered through the book of Genesis the Hebrew word for 'seed' is always in the singular. He would be aware that in the commonly used Greek translation of the Old Testament of these passages the word for 'seed' was always in the singular too. He draws our attention, in Gal 3:16, to the fact that these promises were not made to 'seeds' as though it were hundreds of thousands of individuals in focus, but these promises are made to 'one individual seed'. Taught by the Holy Spirit he then makes his amazing link. The promises of the 'seed' had a double focus; they had immediate relevance for Abraham and his descendants but were also focused on a single person in the future, and that person was Christ himself; the Seed of Abraham. *Now to Abraham and his Seed were the promises made. He does not say, "And to seeds," as of many, but as of one, "And to your Seed," who is Christ.* Gal 3:16 NKJV.

As we noticed earlier sometimes in Scripture we can begin with something which is close at hand and then 'suddenly' jump to something much more distant. So as God has made his promises to Abraham he has always had a further peak in view and not just the nearer peak of Abraham and Isaac. Of course, the promise as Abraham received it was fulfilled initially in the birth of his son Isaac, but the greater fulfillment of the promise is found in Christ himself; the Seed of Abraham. I said, 'let's see if we can follow his reasoning', but this is not so much reason as revelation; Paul has seen something that was always there but was only revealed at the appropriate time. To understand this deep Bible truth we need to re-read the story of Abraham with Paul's revelation in mind.

God always intended to bring 'blessing' not only to the physical descendants, or seed, of Abraham but also to all nations. Abraham was to be not just the recipient of a personal blessing, but the channel through which God's blessing would reach every nation. Again we see Paul makes this connection a little earlier in the same letter to the Galatian churches; *so that in Christ Jesus the blessing of Abraham might come to the*

Gentiles, so that we might receive the promised Spirit through faith. Gal 3:14 ESV

A witness to the making of a covenant

Let's try to put Abraham's long day into the context of his life and this 'promised Seed' and see if we can see its significance. It followed close on the heels of a time of conflict when Abraham had led a mission to rescue his nephew Lot. Lot had become caught up in a combined attack of four city-state kings against the territory where Lot lived. Lot had moved into the city of Sodom and was taken captive in the attack. Abraham's rescue mission was successful and he and his allies were able to bring Lot and his fellow captives home. On his return journey Abraham met a mysterious character named Melchizedek, the king of Salem, who pronounced a blessing on Abraham. In consequence Abraham made an oath that he would, from that time, be dependent upon "the LORD, God Most High, the Possessor of Heaven and Earth". His dependence on God rather than on political alliances left him vulnerable but God more than filled the gap by promising to be both his shield and reward.

This additional promise seems to have provoked Abraham to remember God's earlier promise and he points out that God has not yet delivered on that promise. "What is the point of more blessings if it all dies with me?" is the force of Abraham's prayer. God points him to the starlit skies and asks him if he is able to number them and adds; *So shall thy seed be.* Gen 15:5 KJV. The word 'seed' is in the singular but it is a clear promise of vast numbers of physical descendants. (Apparently, we can see about 5000 individual stars with the naked eye!) This is a key moment in Bible history as its sequel tells us that... *And he believed in the LORD, and He accounted it to him for righteousness.* Gen 15:6 NKJV. This total trust in God alone and no other becomes the pattern for 'justifying faith' but we must leave that theme for another time, although it is a vital Bible truth. God then makes the promise even more specific; Then He said to him, *"I am the LORD, who brought you out of Ur of the Chaldeans, to give you this land to inherit it."* Gen 15:7 NKJV. Abraham now has a clear geographical inheritance in view, but he seeks reassurance; And he said, *"Lord GOD, how shall I know that I will inherit it?"* Gen 15:8 NKJV. It is in answer to this question that we have the record of a very mysterious event.

God instructs Abraham to prepare the scene for the making of a covenant. This is the way in which covenants were often made; a corridor of sacrificed animals would be prepared and those who were to agree and confirm the covenant would step into this corridor of death and make their mutual oaths and promises, 'on pain of death'. Abraham would have been very familiar with this way of sealing an alliance. There is actually another example of this kind of covenant making much later in the Bible story; *...the men who have transgressed My covenant, who have not performed the words of the covenant which they made before Me, when they cut the calf in two and passed between the parts of it—* Jer 34:18f NKJV. So Abraham did as he was instructed and waited for God to turn up. And he waited... and he waited, through the heat of the day when the vultures swooped in to eat the bodies of the covenant sacrifice victims. Abraham drove them off and waited... and waited.

The deep sleep

At dusk, just as the sun was setting, Abraham fell into a deep sleep. It was not just the natural sleep of exhaustion but a trance-like sleep. Sometimes the Bible uses the repetition of words and ideas to create emotional links with other passages of Scripture. This is not the first 'deep sleep' that we find in the Bible. Adam had experienced such a 'deep sleep' many years before. This kind of 'deep sleep' is something that God uses from time to time. It was in this kind of 'deep sleep' that later some men received visions from God and this is what happened to Abraham at this time. When Adam slept like this God took hold of a rib and from the rib he made woman. While Abraham sleeps God will take hold of something of Abraham's and he will not release his grip until his purpose has been completed. There is a verse in Hebrews which may have this in mind; *For he does not indeed take hold of angels [by the hand], but he takes hold of the seed of Abraham.* Heb

2:16 DARBY. We need to keep in mind, as we read these passages, that other dimension of truth that says 'the Seed was Christ'.

The 'deep sleep' for Abraham is a time of horror and great darkness. With regard to the physical descendants of Abraham God gives a brief future history; they will experience alienation, captivity and affliction but there will be an 'exodus' in which they will be brought back to this very land on which Abraham is currently sleeping.

Finally the sun sets and in his deep sleep trance Abraham witnesses a remarkable sight. Two parties do enter the corridor of death as makers of covenants did of old, but Abraham is not one of them. The symbols used are a smoking furnace and a flaming torch. The Bible adds no comment and we will do so with caution. One of the aspects of God's character revealed in the Scripture is that he is a 'consuming fire'. This is a fire that is not just a dramatic sight but has a telling impact on something or someone. The fire consumes and the evidence of that will be the smoke. Does this speak of the righteous justice of God that must execute judgment upon the sinner and his sin? There is another symbol, a flaming torch. Do we see here a representation of God as revealed in Christ, the faithful and true witness? Of this we can be quite sure that Abraham, in his deep sleep, would have seen this as the making of a covenant in which he was not a party but a witness.

The oldest promise

Let's go further back than Abraham. When Paul wrote to Titus he spoke about God's truth and the hope of eternal life but it is the way in which Paul describes that eternal life which takes our breath away; ...*the truth which accords with godliness, in hope of eternal life which God, who cannot lie, promised before time began, but has in due time manifested His word through preaching, which was committed to me according to the commandment of God our Saviour;* Titus 1:1-3 NKJV. This is a typically long sentence from Paul and we need to break it down a little. The last part of the sentence speaks about the preaching of the gospel and its hope of eternal life but it is the earlier part that is hard to grasp. Paul speaks of *'eternal life which God, who cannot lie, promised before time began'*. That raises an obvious question. If God promised 'eternal life'...'before time began'... to whom did he promise it? This is God accommodating his language to finite minds and it is telling us that the plan of 'eternal life' for mankind is older than mankind itself. Before anything existed God's plans were laid and the plans included the 'hope of eternal life'. If this 'conversation' took place before 'time began' it can only have been a conversation within the Godhead. In fact, it is a conversation between Father and Son before time began.

It is a theme that 'blows the mind' but the plan of salvation for a sinful race was not put together hurriedly when 'things went wrong'. It was in place before anything was made; God is never taken by surprise. Later in the story of Abraham and Isaac there is a foreshadowing of Calvary itself as the Father and the 'only' Son agree to fulfill the will of God. As father and son make their way to the place of sacrifice there is a little phrase in the older versions of the story of Genesis 22 which is pregnant with powerful truth; it provides a repeated progress report of the events of that day with words that almost sound like the chorus to a song; "the two of them went together" (Gen 22:6,8.) It seems that what we have in Genesis 15, witnessed in his deep dream vision by Abraham, was an enactment, on earth, of an agreement, in which 'two of them went together', and in which the Son would reach through generations of history and 'take hold of the Seed of Abraham' in order to fulfill a promise made 'before time began'.

This certainly fits the pattern of Paul's thinking. When he speaks of the temporary season of the Law Covenant he asks a rhetorical question and then answers it; *What purpose then does the law serve? It was added because of transgressions, till the Seed should come to whom the promise was made; and it was appointed through angels by the hand of a mediator.* Gal 3:19 NKJV. Stretching back behind the Law Covenant there was a promise that had been made to Christ himself; 'the Seed to whom the promise was made'. This is a very clear statement in Galatians that the covenant that Abraham witnessed was one in which a promise was made to the Seed.

This 'taking hold of the seed of Abraham' becomes a hidden thread in the Old Testament story. Some years ago I conducted a series of studies as an overview of the whole of the Old Testament for a small church in North London; we called the series "Following the Seed". At times it truly seemed that everything hung on a thread but with all the heights and lows of the Old Testament we can trace 'the Seed'. God's purposes would not be frustrated by the failure of men. He had taken hold of the Seed of Abraham and held on to it tenaciously until its glorious culmination in Jesus Christ; the Seed to whom the promise was made.

In this chapter we examined the amazing account of a day in the life of Abraham, a day whose events pictured the stretch from eternity past to eternity future. We saw that God had set his purpose before the creation to make his Son the means of bringing salvation to a whole world. We walked on tiptoe through one of the most mysterious passages of the Bible and saw the shadows of an eternal covenant between the Father and the Son.

5: The Making of a Covenant

Now that we have done our back-track to Abraham and his covenant let's move forward in time again to the Sinai Covenant. So if the Sinai Covenant was 'added' to the Abraham Covenant we see that on occasion we may have more that one covenant operating at the same time. The Sinai Covenant was a temporary addition to the covenant made with Abraham. In fact, quite often there are many covenants operating at the same time but they are working at different levels and it is not easy to keep track of them as we read the Scriptures. The narrative of the Old Testament is like an old tapestry. As we view the tapestry our focus may be fixed on an event or a particular colour of thread. Some themes and threads may seem to disappear from the tapestry only to reappear much later. Sometimes the tapestry has a background colour that becomes so familiar that we hardly notice it. Of course if we viewed the tapestry from the rear we would see the unbroken threads that are not visible from those who only view the front of the tapestry.

The 'Seed of Abraham' is one of those coloured threads, which is easily missed. Often it vanishes from view but it is continuing unbroken through triumph and disaster. That thread finds its culmination in the person of Jesus Christ. As we have seen, at times it seems forgotten for year upon year only to reappear without warning. And then there is the background colour of the Sinai Covenant. This is always present but we become so used to it that we can fail to notice it. As we have said, from its beginning at Sinai to its end at Calvary that Sinai Covenant was the backdrop to the whole of the Old Testament. It is this covenant that the New Testament describes as the Old or First Covenant. Paul tells us that it was 'added' to the 'Seed of Abraham' covenant; *What purpose then does the law serve? It was added because of transgressions, till the Seed should come to whom the promise was made; and it was appointed through angels by the hand of a mediator.* Gal 3:19 NKJV. That single verse is vital to our understanding of the Old Covenant. It was to be in force only 'until the Seed should come'. The Sinai/Old Covenant was added and it was temporary.

The Purpose of the Sinai Covenant

That Sinai Covenant, given through Moses, served many purposes. It served as a restraint on outward sin. It served as a means of measuring how great personal failure was; it showed how bad sin was by quantifying it. In many ways it showed how hopeless our condition was if acceptance with God depended on our performance. And it served as a kind of tenancy agreement for the land of Israel.

The central part of the Sinai Covenant is usually known as the Ten Commandments or, as the Hebrew language called it, 'The Ten Words'. It will help to understand just what these Ten Words were about if we view them in a wider context. In his letter to the Romans Paul tells us that the 'work of the law' is written on the hearts of all nations; *for when Gentiles, who do not have the law, by nature do the things in the law, these, although not having the law, are a law to themselves, who show the work of the law written in their hearts, their conscience also bearing witness, and between themselves their thoughts accusing or else excusing them)* Rom 2:14-15 NKJV. The other nations may not have the 'words of the law' but they have the impact of the law, the 'work of the law' within them. Later Paul declares that of all the blessings ancient Israel enjoyed, the written 'word' was the greatest; *What advantage then has the Jew, or what is the profit of circumcision? Much in every way! Chiefly because to them were committed the oracles of God.* Rom 3:1-2 NKJV.

The nation of Israel had the explicit 'words of the law' and consequently no excuse for any ignorance of God's will. *The secret things belong to the LORD our God, but those things which are revealed belong to us and to our children forever, that we may do all the words of this law.* Deut 29:29 NKJV. This is a statement given at the 'second giving of the Law' or Deuteronomy. There will always be truths of which we are ignorant but we are not held accountable for these. The people who became God's nation at Sinai would certainly be held accountable for what God had clearly revealed to them. Later God made it very clear that extra privilege brings extra responsibility too; *Hear this word that the LORD has spoken against you, O children of Israel, against the whole family which I brought up from the land of Egypt, saying: "You only have I known of all the families of the earth; Therefore I will punish you for all your iniquities."* Amos 3:1-2 NKJV. For those who had clearer knowledge, the consequence of their failure would be increased. The covenant people would be held accountable for *all* their failure. The clear knowledge of God's will was to be an enormous blessing and a great burden.

All peoples have an instinct or a moral sense. It may be almost buried under centuries of darkness but men and women have a sense of what is 'fair' and, unless their consciences have become completely desensitized, they know how people ought to behave towards them and consequently how they ought to behave towards others. Individuals may make brave (or foolish) claims that they are without law and therefore free but at heart we all know this is untrue. 'Lie detector' tests are based on the science that although we may be very proficient at telling lies whenever we do so we trigger a kind of spiritual smoke alarm which alters the rhythms of our bodies. This universal sense of right and wrong was brought into sharp focus in the Ten Words given to Israel and it had a God-wards factor too in making God the centre of our affections and allegiances.

A unique covenant in a unique setting

The original version of the Ten Words gives its context very clearly. They were given to a specific group of people and were not scattered generally into the public domain. This is how the Ten Words are introduced; *And God spoke all these words, saying: "I am the LORD your God, who brought you out of the land of Egypt, out of the house of bondage. "You shall have no other gods before Me. "You shall not make for yourself a carved image—any likeness of anything that is in heaven above, or that is in the earth beneath, or that is in the water under the earth; you shall not bow down to them nor serve them. For I, the LORD your God, am a jealous God, visiting the iniquity of the fathers upon the children to the third and fourth generations of those who hate Me, but showing mercy to thousands, to those who love Me and keep My commandments. "You shall not take the name of the LORD your God in vain, for the LORD will not hold him guiltless who takes His name in vain."* Ex 20:1-7 NKJV. That is a long quotation but I wanted to show that these words were addressed to men and women who had had a vivid experience of God and a group of men and women who were about to become God's special people. The Ten Words were not broadcast into the whole world; they were addressed to a very exclusive group of people, God's people, God's own nation.

That group of people had Egypt behind them and the Promised Land in front of them. We can see this in the way the 5th Word is tailored; *honour your father and your mother, that your days may be long upon the land which the LORD your God is giving you.* Ex 20:12 NKJV. In its precise application it can only apply to the people of Israel. Does that mean non-Israelites do not need to honour their parents? Not at all, although it is instructive to see how Paul changes this 'commandment' when he is writing to non-Israelites; *Children, obey your parents in the Lord, for this is right. "honour your father and mother," which is the first commandment with promise: "that it may be well with you and you may live long on the earth."* Eph 6:1-3 NKJV. The particular application and promise of a long life in the Promised Land has gone and in its place we have 'on the earth'. This should help us to understand the nature of the Ten Commandments; they were Israel's personally tailored version of universal law. They were the unique conditions of an exclusive covenant that God was making with ancient Israel.

This becomes even clearer when we come to the book of Deuteronomy. The time is Sinai plus 40 years and the people are poised to enter the Promised Land under the leadership of Joshua. The Covenant is renewed and the people are reminded that their conquest and keeping of the promised land will depend upon them keeping the Covenant; *"Now this is the commandment, and these are the statutes and judgments which the LORD your God has commanded to teach you, that you may observe them in the land which you are crossing over to possess, that you may fear the LORD your God, to keep all His statutes and His commandments which I command you, you and your son and your grandson, all the days of your life, and that your days may be prolonged. Therefore hear, O Israel, and be careful to observe it, that it may be well with you, and that you may multiply greatly as the LORD God of your fathers has promised you— "a land flowing with milk and honey.'* Deut 6:1-3 NKJV. We could pursue this conquest-based-on-covenant into the book of Joshua and see it outworking there but we need to pause to examine some of the details of the Sinai Covenant.

Moses led the 'nation' to the foot of Sinai and God summoned him into his presence. We have seen that Moses will now function not just as a leader but also as the mediator of a covenant between God and the nation that has been redeemed from bondage in Egypt. The scene is set for the making of a covenant; *And Moses went up to God, and the LORD called to him from the mountain, saying, "Thus you shall say to the house of Jacob, and tell the children of Israel: "You have seen what I did to the Egyptians, and how I bore you on eagles' wings and brought you to Myself. Now therefore, if you will indeed obey My voice and keep My covenant, then you shall be a special treasure to Me above all people; for all the earth is Mine. And you shall be to Me a kingdom of priests and a holy nation.' These are the words which you shall speak to the children of Israel."* Ex 19:3-6 NKJV. We need to notice, as we have said, that it is addressed to people who have already experienced redemption. Egypt and its patterns have gone and are no longer a threat. For the first time in living memory the people are genuinely free to make their own choices. Up until this time they have been Pharaoh's slaves, bound to do his will, now they are free to choose their own master.

A 'classical' conditional covenant

We have already seen that this is a classic conditional covenant; if you do this, these consequences will follow; a classical 'if-then-else' statement. The implications are very plain; if 'a' happens then 'b' will follow. The opposite implication is equally plain; if 'a' doesn't happen then 'b' will not follow. Their destiny hangs on their choice. God is willing and able, but what of the nation? They give their enthusiastic assent; *So Moses came and called for the elders of the people, and laid before them all these words which the LORD commanded him. Then all the people answered together and said, "All that the LORD has spoken we will do." So Moses brought back the words of the people to the LORD.* Ex 19:7-8 NKJV. So Moses returns their decision to God and the process of Covenant has begun. At this initial stage Moses is establishing the general principles of this agreement. At the initial stage the finer details are not spelled out; they will follow.

We will not trace all the details of this amazing process but we can note that the 'details' of the agreement were divided into the 'Ten Words' and the 'judgments'. Before this process is completed a tragedy will intervene which will require a new start but we will just follow the process itself. Moses returns to the people with the full details of the covenant, all the 'Words' and all the 'judgments' and again the people are enthusiastic in their response; *So Moses came and told the people all the* words of the LORD and all the judgments. And all the people answered with one voice and said, "All the words which the LORD has said we will do." Ex 24:3 NKJV. At this response Moses creates a hand-written copy of the covenant and its demands. It will be one of two copies of the Law. One, the people's copy will be in Moses' own handwriting; the second, God's copy, will be written on stone in God's own handwriting. The human copy will become known as 'the Book of the Covenant'.

People, book and altar joined by blood

There is now a curious interlude. Moses himself creates a simple altar and erects 12 stone pillars to represent the 12 family tribes. Then he instructs some young men to conduct a whole-burnt offering and a peace sacrifice. These are ancient forms of worship that are much older than the Sinai Covenant itself. The blood from the sacrifices is caught in a basin and Moses sprinkles half of it on the altar and its burning sacrifices. Next Moses takes up his own copy of the Covenant, the Book of the Covenant, and reads it to the assembled crowds. For the third time the enthusiasm of the people is expressed in a unanimous assent to the terms of the covenant. Moses now sprinkles the remainder of the sacrificial blood onto the people themselves... and according to the letter to the Hebrews, on the Book of the Covenant. (Heb 9:18) He then announces that the Covenant is in force; And Moses took the blood, sprinkled it on the people, and said, "This is the blood of the covenant which the LORD has made with you according to all these words." Ex 24:8 NKJV.

It is a sobering reflection, that if we had visited this spot a year later the only evidence of the extraordinary happenings there would have been this altar with its 12 sentinel stone pillars; a silent testimony to the fact that at this moment in history this people became inseparably linked with the worship and service of God.

According to the terms of the agreement that God had instituted this motley group of refugees had now become a nation, God's nation; ...if you will indeed obey My voice and keep My covenant, then you shall be a special treasure to Me above all people; for all the earth is Mine. And you shall be to Me a kingdom of priests and a holy nation...' Ex 19:5-6 NKJV. The word 'holy' originally, in the Hebrew language, meant something separated for a particular purpose. I recall a meal in Ireland many years ago when the wife cut the first slice of a large pie and told the children to put it into the oven for 'your father's dinner when he comes home from work'. I remember saying 'that is exactly what sanctification means'. Although all the nations of the earth owe allegiance to God this nation had become 'God's Kingdom' in a unique and exclusive sense; a single slice out of the whole world. It would be in this nation that God's kingly rule would be worked out. From this moment on, and as long as this covenant might last, God and this people would 'belong' to each other, exclusively.

Israel's marriage covenant

Ezekiel later expressed it in the terms of a marriage contract; *"When I passed by you again and looked upon you, indeed your time was the time of love; so I spread My wing over you and covered your nakedness. Yes, I swore an oath to you and entered into a covenant with you, and you became Mine,"* says the Lord GOD. Ezek 16:8 NKJV. In this beautiful poetic language Ezekiel declared that this was the moment when the nation became the bride of Jehovah. God never forgot this moment even though the marriage was a stormy one; *Thus says the LORD: "I remember you, The kindness of your youth, The love of your betrothal, When you went after Me in the wilderness, In a land not sown. Israel was holiness to the LORD..."* Jer 2:2-3 NKJV.

It was this same prophet who saw that first covenant as a betrothal and marriage who first expressed the promised hope of another covenant against the backdrop of terrible failure; *Behold, the days are coming, says the LORD, when I will make a New Covenant with the house of Israel and with the house of Judah— not according to the covenant that I made with their fathers in the day that I took them by the hand to lead them out of the land of Egypt, My covenant which they broke, though I was a husband to them, says the LORD.* Jer 31:31-32 NKJV. From the time of this Sinai marriage covenant

Israel's spiritual promiscuity is called 'adultery' and it becomes one of the great parables by which God declared his love and his people's faithlessness.

So the marriage is agreed and sealed but it is a conditional covenant. What is going to happen if one of the partners defaults in keeping its side of the covenant? The first transgression of the covenant will make it null and void. How can this covenant be maintained in such an unequal alliance? The answer to that must be our next consideration and will open up yet another gallery of wonderful pictures to communicate God's truth to our hearts.

In this chapter we saw that the Sinai Covenant or Ten Commandments were a local application of universal moral law. Only the nation of Israel signed up to this particular expression of unchanging morality but every man knows the truths of these laws. We may not know the Ten Commandments but the 'work of the law' is written in the hearts of all men, everywhere. We saw that by the terms of this covenant God and Israel were joined as in a marriage and Israel's later breaking of the covenant was spiritual adultery.

6: The Covenant of Levi

The priesthood and a complicated system of sacrifices provided the maintenance aspect of the Sinai Covenant. In the last book of the Old Testament the prophet Malachi refers to this as a 'covenant with Levi'. (Mal 2:4,8) The introduction of this idea comes very abruptly in Exodus 25. The details are given only after the Covenant has begun and the instructions start with a list of materials that Moses is to gather together. The list includes precious metals and stones, fabrics, oils, spices; it is quite a list. The purpose of this collection is stated very plainly; *And let them make Me a sanctuary, that I may dwell among them.* Ex 25:8 NKJV. A sanctuary is a place set apart from ordinary use for a particular purpose. We use the word in this way when we speak of a Bird Sanctuary. The Bible use however always has the sense of being set apart for God's particular use; it is a holy place.

It was God's presence among the people that gave them their unique identity (Ex 33:15–16) and God's presence could only be ensured if the place were holy.

A home for God

We have grown used to the idea now but it might be helpful if we could try to imagine just what kind of impact this statement must have had on the people who had just 'signed' the covenant. It is one thing to have a ruler in another country watching from afar but how do we react to the thought of him moving into our neighbourhood? Small children are sometimes admonished with the warning 'God is watching'; for Israel he would not be a distant watcher but 'God with us', a very different prospect.

This would have been the pattern for a desert chieftain; his personal residence would be at the heart of the camp. The residence in this case will be a tent, not unlike the tents of his people but much grander. It was called The Tabernacle, just a name for a tent. I was once the pastor of a local church that was called 'The Full Gospel Tabernacle' and it was always fun to explain to outsiders that it just meant a tent where God could be 'at home'. We should not miss this simple introduction to the idea of the Tabernacle. Lots of ceremonies would take place here but at its heart its simple purpose was to be a place where God could 'dwell', and that idea is built into one of the Hebrew words which is used to describe this structure; the Mishkan, a place to lodge. The Tabernacle, from the outside was not impressive. It was a rectangular box covered with hides with dimensions of approx. 45 x 15 x 15 feet. (13.7 x 4.5 x 4.5 metres) In turn, that 'box' was surrounded by a courtyard 50 x 100 feet (15.25 x 30.5 metres). Not very large for three million people! But that was the whole point; this was not a 'dwelling place' for three million people but for one person. The Tabernacle had no pews, or pulpit or worship band; it was just "God's place."

Inside the box was a different story. All the furniture was gold or overlaid with gold and the only light came from a seven-branched lampstand with seven small lamps and from the ruddy glow of a charcoal altar for incense. The 'wall hangings' were woven with strands of gold thread and silver and pictured celestial creatures called Cherubim. It must have been breathtaking to see. We have commented earlier how The Clan Leader's chief servants were allowed to stand in this antechamber to the throne room, but the ordinary people of the Covenant were only allowed as far as the courtyard. The chief servants stood here poised to obey their Chieftain; that was the original idea of being a priest.

The throne room itself was separated from the antechamber by a thick embroidered curtain with those same images of Cherubim. Behind that curtain was a gold plated chest known as The Ark of the Covenant. Inside the chest was one copy of the Covenant written in stone in God's own handwriting and by the side of the chest lay the second copy of the Covenant written on parchment in Moses' handwriting; *So it was, when Moses had completed writing the words of this law in a book, when they were finished, that Moses commanded the Levites, who bore the ark of the covenant of the LORD, saying: "Take this Book of the Law, and put it beside the ark of the covenant of the LORD your God, that it may be there as a witness against you;"* Deut 31:24-26 NKJV. The two copies of the Covenant showed the continuing sense that God's presence with his people was based on an agreed Covenant. The chest had a detachable lid of solid gold and images of those same Cherubim in gold stretching over it. Christians have come to know this as the 'Mercy Seat' but in effect it was God's throne from which he reigned over his Covenant people; *The LORD reigns; Let the peoples tremble! He dwells between the cherubim; Let the earth be moved!* Psa 99:1 NKJV. And he reigned over his 'holy nation' in accordance with the Covenant agreed at Sinai.

A home fit for God

These chief servants are the people we usually call priests and their unique work was to be fully available to serve the king. In this they were acting as representatives of the whole nation who, according to the terms of the Sinai Covenant, were a kingdom of priests. The priests however were not permitted to stand in the throne room; they were not even allowed to enter it on pain of death. The only exception to this law was on a single day every year when the Chief Priest performed a ceremony known as Yom Kippur or the Day of Atonement. To understand the significance of Yom Kippur we need to remind ourselves of the purpose of the Tabernacle; it was created so that God could live in the midst of his people. God is a Holy God and he can only reside in a Holy place in the midst of a Holy People. This again was part of the original covenant agreement; the covenant people were to be a 'kingdom of priests', a 'holy nation'. Clearly this is going to pose problems if the people are not a 'holy people'. How are we going to stop the covenant coming to an abrupt end when the people of the covenant breach it?

The ceremony of Yom Kippur is described in the book of Leviticus; the priests' service book. It is an exercise in patience to pick our way through Leviticus 16 to identify all the intricate details of this special day. Every year the ceremony would mark the facts that God was a holy God and his people were an unholy people. The Chief priests and his assistants who were actually his sons first needed to be fit to perform the ceremony so a sacrificial bull was slaughtered as a Sin Offering for the priestly family; *And Aaron shall bring the bull of the sin offering, which is for himself, and make atonement for himself and for his house, and shall kill the bull as the sin offering which is for himself.* Lev 16:11 NKJV. To modern ears this all sounds barbaric but one of the main themes in the symbolism of these sacrificed animals was to illustrate just how costly it is to deal with sin and its consequences. A price must be paid to make a way into the presence of God and the price would be a life; in the Old Covenant the symbols only show the 'shadow' and 'pattern' of the reality that one day would have to take place.

The chief priest then took a censer of smoking incense and some of the blood of the sacrificed animal and having entered the throne room through the heavy curtain sprinkled the blood on the golden lid that covered the Ark of the Covenant. As he did so he took his own life into his hands. If the sacrifice was accepted then the chief priest would be accepted, if the sacrifice was rejected the chief priest would die. By this ceremony the priest's own personal sin and the sin of his own priestly family was 'atoned' or covered over. In Egypt God had recognised the blood-splashed doorposts and his judgment 'passed over' those who sheltered under the sign of the blood. Now the chief priest's own sin would be 'passed over' and the priest himself would be spared. The Bible word for this act that makes it possible for God to 'pass over' sin is 'propitiation'. A price was paid and instead of judgment reconciliation became possible. If we move briefly from the shadow to the reality we find that Paul described the death of Christ at Calvary as the place where a price was paid and reconciliation was effected; *being justified freely by His grace through the redemption that is in Christ Jesus, whom God set forth as a propitiation by His blood, through faith, to demonstrate His righteousness, because in His forbearance God had passed over the sins that were previously committed,* Rom 3:24-25 NKJV. There we have it plainly, because of shed blood God accepts the offender and 'passes over' or 'looks beyond' the sins.

When the chief priest was ceremonially 'right with God' he began the second part of the ceremony. This time a sacrificial animal would represent not just the priestly family but the whole covenant people; *Then he shall kill the goat of the sin offering, which is for the people, bring its blood inside the veil, do with that blood as he did with the blood of the bull, and sprinkle it on the mercy seat and before the mercy seat.* Lev 16:15 NKJV. This time the animal was a goat and it was actually one of a pair of goats. In the destinies of these two goats more deep spiritual truths would be illustrated in 'shadows' and 'patterns'. In effect the destinies of these two goats would express two aspects of one truth. One of the goats must be sacrificed and blood, the symbol of life poured out in death, again sprinkled on the golden lid that covered the Ark of the Covenant; the place that our English Bibles usually translate as 'Mercy Seat' but is actually referred to as 'the place where propitiation takes place'.

Now, the truth of the cost of covering sin having been illustrated, the chief priest turned his attention to the second goat that is usually called the 'e-scape goat'. Another truth must now be illustrated. Sin must not only be paid for, it must be removed from God's presence. The chief priest laid both his hands on the head of the scape goat and named all the offences of the nation against God; *Aaron shall lay both his hands on the head of the live goat, confess over it all the iniquities of the children of Israel, and all their transgressions, concerning all their sins, putting them on the head of the goat, and shall send it away into the wilderness by the hand of a suitable man. The goat shall bear on itself all their iniquities to an uninhabited land; and he shall release the goat in the wilderness.* Lev 16:21-22 NKJV. The 'e-scape' goat is released into the wilderness carrying away the people's sin. In its symbolism the two goats represented a single 'goat' that died for sin and consequently removed sin from God's presence.

Again to modern ears this all sounds very strange but in its powerful pictures God was teaching vital lessons to his people. In this Sinai Covenant pattern there was to be an annual resetting of the 'dials'. All the accumulated sin of the covenant community would be recognised, acknowledged, confessed, paid for and put away. Only as a result of the continual 'maintenance' of the Covenant through a priesthood would it be possible for God to continue to be resident among the people of the Covenant. Only through this system of symbolic truth would God's full purposes be possible; *And they shall know that I am the LORD their God, who brought them up out of the land of Egypt, that I may dwell among them. I am the LORD their God.* Ex 29:46 NKJV.

The inseparable link between covenant and law

It is important to understand the link between the Sinai Covenant and the Covenant priesthood. In fact, they are inseparable. The priests become the guardians of the Covenant and their work of 'reconciliation' is a vital element of the Sinai Covenant. The two are inseparable; they must stand or fall together. The chief priest that we have been talking about was Aaron, part of the family of Levi and for this reason the Sinai priesthood is usually called the Aaronic or Levitical priesthood. It was trusted exclusively to Aaron and his male descendants. When the role of Moses as the initiator of the covenant is completed it will be the role of the priests to keep things on track. They become the 'teachers' of the nation.

Only the priestly family could function in this way and when even a member of the royal family trespassed into this area of authority God's summary judgment was visited upon him. (2 Chron 26:16-21).

This authority of the Levitical family to be the nation's priests is also called a covenant; *"Then you shall know that I have sent this commandment to you, That My covenant with Levi may continue," Says the LORD of hosts. "My covenant was with him, one of life and peace, And I gave them to him that he might fear Me; So he feared Me And was reverent before My name."* Mal 2:4-5 NKJV. Comparatively, for its size, the book of Malachi has more to say than any other book in the Bible about covenant and it is Malachi who uses a wonderful picture of the coming Christ who he describes as 'the messenger of the Covenant'. (Mal 3:1) I wonder how many Christians think about Christ as the 'messenger of the covenant'? We can't spend much time with Malachi but there is a powerful repetition of an idea that can be identified. The name 'Malachi' means 'my messenger'. His prophecy rebukes the priests because they have failed as 'messengers of the covenant'. (Mal 2:7,8) He prophesies the appearance of John the Baptist who he calls a 'messenger' and says that John will prepare the way for the 'messenger of the covenant'. The book of Malachi stands at the end of the Biblical history of the Old Covenant/Testament and, in its message, it reveals the final failure of the Old Covenant, and a thrilling promise of what is to come.

Let's repeat the statement; the Sinai Covenant cannot work without the Levitical Priesthood; they are inseparable. The Levitical Covenant was really a covenant within a covenant, or a particular aspect of the Sinai Covenant; they are one. The writer to the Hebrews draws our attention to this as he explains the significance of who Christ is and his present role; *Therefore, if perfection were through the Levitical priesthood (for under it the people received the law), what further need was there that another priest should rise according to the order of Melchizedek, and not be called according to the order of Aaron? For the priesthood being changed, of necessity there is also a change of the law.* Heb 7:11-12 NKJV. That last sentence is key; the Levitical priesthood and the Sinai

Covenant must stand or fall together. If one is changed the other must be changed.

The Sinai Covenant background to the Old Testament

Let us repeat a statement. The backdrop to our Old Testament is the Sinai Covenant and the Levitical Priesthood. At times the priesthood functioned very imperfectly but every new beginning brought the nation back to its origins. Even when the nation changed to a monarchy the priesthood is the continuing backdrop. Kings of the nation were required to be 'bible-based' i.e. they had to base their reign on the fundamentals of the Sinai Covenant. When a king came to the throne one of his first duties, was to create his own personal Bible and to meditate on its truth daily; *"Also it shall be, when he sits on the throne of his kingdom, that he shall write for himself a copy of this law in a book, from the one before the priests, the Levites. And it shall be with him, and he shall read it all the days of his life, that he may learn to fear the LORD his God and be careful to observe all the words of this law and these statutes, that his heart may not be lifted above his brethren, that he may not turn aside from the commandment to the right hand or to the left, and that he may prolong his days in his kingdom, he and his children in the midst of Israel.* Deut 17:18-20 NKJV. The significance of this is that even though the pattern of government might change the underlying facts of life had not changed. The coming of monarchy did not change the foundations of the nation that was that they were God's nation by specific covenant, and the kings were required to remind themselves daily that this was so.

The monarchy and the Davidic covenant are really part of the Sinai Covenant. In historical terms the monarchy was 'added' many years later but it was foreseen and provided for right here in the book of Deuteronomy. The monarch was required to live in accordance with the Sinai Covenant and, necessarily, if the Sinai Covenant ever ceased this aspect of the covenant would cease too.

The scenes of priesthood changed greatly through the 1400 years that the Sinai Covenant was in force. Priesthood moves from Tabernacle, to Temple to ruin, to restored Temple and in the days of Christ to a Temple built by someone who technically wasn't even a member of the covenant nation. There were many stops and starts to the sacrificial ceremonies of the Temple but on 17 July AD 70, as the Roman armies prepared for an all-out attack on the Temple, the priests were forced to suspend the holy rite of Tamid, the daily sacrifice of a lamb, the supply of fresh victims having finally given out. The last sacrificial lamb had been sacrificed and the Levitical priesthood has now been obsolete for almost 2000 years. Christ's death brought the Sinai Covenant and its Priesthood to an end and the physical ceasing of its ceremonies was inevitable. Those who lived in the years leading up to AD 70 saw it coming very clearly. The writer to the Hebrews is speaking to people who were in danger of being drawn back into a covenant that had now passed its 'sell by date' and he speaks of Jeremiah's promise of a New Covenant, adding as a final comment; *In that he says New, he has made the first old; but that which grows old and aged [is] near disappearing.* Heb 8:13 DARBY.

In this chapter we saw the significance of the Levitical priesthood and its scheme of offerings and sacrifices for sin. The Sinai Covenant was only able to be kept functioning because of sacrificial systems that God had built into it. We saw that the annual Day of Atonement served to 'reset the clocks' and to start every year afresh. We saw the inseparable connection between the Sinai Covenant and the Levitical priesthood and that a promise of a New Covenant must, of necessity, bring in a new kind of priesthood and a new pattern of law.

7: A Day in the life of Moses

Haven't we been here before? That's usually the reaction to reading the book of Deuteronomy for the first time and the reaction is understandable that's why it's called Deutero - second and nomos - law. It is the second giving of the law and the whole book is the account of a single day. It is another illustration of the variable passage of time that we find in a chapter-by-chapter reading of the Scriptures. In fact it was Moses' last day.

Starting all over again

Forty years have passed since the original establishing of the covenant and the giving of the covenant law. All those bright expectations are in the dust now. The sequence of the first five books of the Bible is significant. Genesis is the book of beginnings that ends with the family of Jacob/Israel in Egypt. Exodus tells the story of how their migration resulted in their slavery and the way in which they were released from their service of Pharaoh and brought into the service of God by redemption and covenant. Leviticus gives the instructions for the 'maintenance element' of the contract, the priesthood and the nations sacrificial patterns. Numbers begins well and quickly becomes a disaster.

After a year building the Tabernacle, and with the Covenant up and running, the nation is ready to make the short journey to the Promised Land. The armies are mustered and the chains of command are in place. The journey is scheduled to take 11 days but their refusal to believe and to obey God resulted in a 40-year detour during which an entire generation died, having left Egypt but never arriving in the Promised Land. The book of Deuteronomy begins at this exact point in their history; *It is eleven days' journey from Horeb by way of Mount Seir to Kadesh Barnea. Now it came to pass in the fortieth year, in the eleventh month, on the first day of the month, that Moses spoke to the children of Israel according to all that the LORD had given him as commandments to them,* Deut 1:1-3 NKJV. Don't miss the point of those verses. The 11 days journey had taken 40 years. Now they were poised to enter the land from the East, rather than from the South, and Moses gathers the nation for his final sermon.

What follows in the book of Deuteronomy is not just a repetition of Exodus and Numbers but is the setting of the scene for a brand new beginning. Spiritually, however, they will be brought back to the original starting point, which is that Covenant. In fact Deuteronomy has more actual references to the Sinai Covenant than any other book in the Bible. When Moses has reminded them of their history up to this point he begins his message; *And Moses called all Israel, and said to them: "Hear, O Israel, the statutes and judgments which I speak in your hearing today, that you may learn them and be careful to observe them. The LORD our God made a covenant with us in Horeb."* Deut 5:1-2 NKJV. That will be the foundation of all that he has to say. If we were to continue the metaphor of a sermon we might say that was his 'text'; *The LORD our God made a covenant with us in Horeb.*

He then makes a clear contrast between the kinds of covenant that Abraham, Isaac and Jacob had known by saying; *The LORD did not make this covenant with our fathers, but with us, those who are here today, all of us who are alive.* Deut 5:3 NKJV. The Sinai Covenant was different to the Abraham Covenant and if we want to understand the way the story unfolds we must try to keep them separate in our minds. The Abraham Covenant was basic and original, the Sinai Covenant was additional and temporary as we have seen previously; *What purpose then does the law serve? It was added because of transgressions, till the Seed should come to whom the promise was made...* Gal 3:19 NKJV.

The tenancy agreement

In spite of all their initial tragic failings that Sinai Covenant had not lapsed and the destiny of this people still awaited them. Although Deuteronomy seems like a re-run of Exodus it isn't. It is Exodus re-applied with a particular end in view. We can see that end in view all through Deuteronomy; the focus is the connection between the keeping of the Covenant and the possession of the Promised Land. The word 'land' or in Hebrew 'eretz' occurs almost 200 times in this book and is often tied to the word 'possess'. The Promised Land was 'given' to the covenant community but they would need to 'take' it and they would only take it as they kept the covenant agreement. We can illustrate the link by moving forward in history to the story of the conquest of Canaan with the tragic story of Achan and the city of Ai. The covenant people had conquered Jericho and the next town was Ai. They presumed that Ai would be an easy exercise but that presumption and the willful disobedience of one man brought a certain victory to a crushing defeat. In the whole story of the conquest of Canaan this is the only battle where it is recorded that the Israelites sustained casualties. The story is fully told in Joshua 7 but we will just focus on the indictment that was brought against the nation and Achan in particular; *Israel has sinned, and they have also transgressed My covenant which I commanded them. For they have even taken some of the accursed things, and have both stolen and deceived; and they have also put it among their own stuff.* Josh 7:11 NKJV. Israel sustained its first defeat because the covenant had been broken.

So back to our story... The conquest of the Promised Land would depend on the covenant people keeping their covenant with God. This principle was to have long-term consequences because only a covenant-keeping people would conquer the land, and only a covenant-keeping people could hold it. Keeping the covenant gave them entrance into their tenancy and keeping the covenant was their tenancy agreement. This is another Bible idea that it is well to keep in mind. The nation of Israel never owned the Promised Land; they were tenants. In English law the purchase of a property may be freehold or leasehold. I might buy my house leasehold, which means I am only 'renting' the land on which the house is sitting. At the end of a fixed period the land and anything I have built on it must return to its owner. If I buy my house freehold I am buying both the building and the land on which it sits. The nation of Israel held their land 'leasehold', the landowner was God himself; *The land shall not be sold permanently, for the land is Mine; for you are strangers and sojourners with Me.* Lev 25:23 NKJV.

This is why, technically, property under the Sinai Covenant could not be 'sold' permanently outside the family. Each generation of the family held the territory in trust for the next generation and the land belonged to God. On entering the Promised Land these territories were entrusted to the different family tribes. Every 50 years each portion of land had to revert to its original family. (Lev 25:30-31) This was an amazing plan to ensure that wealthy landowners did not accumulate vast estates that would have created a permanent underclass of 'farm workers' rather than 'farm owners'. As the years passed this was almost entirely ignored and the property magnates caused great personal hardship to peasant families. The prophet Isaiah would later bring a strong accusation against these property magnates; *Woe to those who join house to house; They add field to field, Till there is no place Where they may dwell alone in the midst of the land!* Is 5:8 NKJV.

So with the keeping of the covenant as a necessary part of the tenancy agreement, failing to keep the covenant put the covenant community in jeopardy of losing their promised land; this was written into the 'deeds'. In spite of the nation's failure to keep the covenant, God graciously permitted them to remain in the land and sent prophetic messengers to remind them of their obligations and of the penalty clauses in the tenancy agreement.

The covenant with David

In the midst of the Sinai Covenant, with its built-in Priestly Covenant, there was later added yet another layer of Covenant; this time a covenant linked with monarchy. The story of how the nation became a monarchy is a tragedy that God transmuted into a blessing. We need to return to our starting point yet again to understand the implications of this. The covenant community-nation was created to be different. They were not just one of many people groups that would develop into nation-states; this nation was different. Its ultimate purpose was not living space or national greatness; its purpose was that it was to be a kingdom of priests serving God. Perhaps it is time to remind ourselves of that foundation; *Now therefore, if you will indeed obey My voice and keep My covenant, then you shall be a special treasure to Me above all people; for all the earth is Mine. And you shall be to Me a kingdom of priests and a holy nation.' These are the words which you shall speak to the children of Israel."* Ex 19:5-6 NKJV.

It would be good to notice too how often the personal pronoun 'me' 'my' or 'mine' is used in this short excerpt. It is a regular failing of human beings that their thinking is man-centred rather than God-centred; they are conscious of the blessings and not so conscious of the obligations. If we read this passage carefully we see that the whole thrust of the Sinai Covenant was that this nation would become 'God's personal possession, or treasure'. The entire world belongs to God but of this nation, in a unique sense, God would be able to say 'you are mine'. They were designed to be different, very different. Their food laws and Sabbath observance would make them conspicuously different. That is why it was such a tragedy that at a point early in their possession of the Promised Land that they began to say; 'we want to be like everyone else'. (1 Sam 8:20)

That story is found in the book of 1 Samuel. Prior to having kings Israel had judges. Judges were individuals whom God raised up at times of particular danger to lead the people in wars of self-defense. It created a cyclic pattern. The covenant nation abandoned its covenant and although God allowed them to continue in their land they could not enjoy it as real tenants. Other nations controlled them and exacted fines and taxes from them that crippled their development. In their distress they called on their covenant God and in his mercy God intervened by raising up a 'Judge'. These Judges had their roots in particular family tribes but they drew other family tribes into their bands and the foreigners were overthrown. In the prosperity that followed the covenant nation generally relaxed their keeping of the covenant and God gave them into the control of yet another foreign oppressor and so the wheel turned another revolution. The solution to the nation's need was staring them in the face. All they had to do was turn to God and keep the covenant and God would have kept the oppressors at bay, but as so often with human beings they decided that the solution was to change the method!

Instead of this hand to mouth dependence upon God why not be 'like the other nations' and have someone who would take the responsibility of leading on his own shoulders? Hence their choice during the time of Samuel, the last of the Judges, to opt for a king; *But the thing displeased Samuel when they said, "Give us a king to judge us." So Samuel prayed to the LORD. And the LORD said to Samuel, "Heed the voice of the people in all that they say to you; for they have not rejected you, but they have rejected Me, that I should not reign over them.* 1Sam 8:6-7 NKJV. That was the essence of it. They were turning their back on God and thought they could limit the damage by imitating the methods of the other nations. Their campaign for change had a simple slogan; *make us a king to judge us like all the nations.* 1Sam 8:5 NKJV.

God, through Samuel, warned them of the consequences of this development but when they were determined to have a monarchy, God permitted it. This too is a sobering lesson.

Apparently some of the things that God does are not Plan A! Their first king began well and ended in tragedy, a familiar pattern for the covenant people's history. Ultimately God rejected the man that he had chosen and provided a second king, David. David is one of the great heroes of the Bible. He was a man of great depths and passions; a soldier-poet, an inspired leader, a man of deep spiritual experience and vision, and a man, in some aspects at least, with a 'heart like God's'.

As we have mentioned earlier by this time the covenant had developed a fault line that would ultimately result in two nations but David brought them all together under his personal rule. It was a great time and marked the greatest fulfillment to date of the nation's control of its own destiny in its own 'leasehold' land. A civil war rumbled on for a while but finally the whole nation rallied to David and proclaimed him their king; *Then all the tribes of Israel came to David at Hebron and spoke, saying, "Indeed we are your bone and your flesh. Also, in time past, when Saul was king over us, you were the one who led Israel out and brought them in; and the LORD said to you, "You shall shepherd My people Israel, and be ruler over Israel.' " Therefore all the elders of Israel came to the king at Hebron, and King David made a covenant with them at Hebron before the LORD. And they anointed David king over Israel.* 2Sam 5:1-3 NKJV. In all he reigned for 40 years and his reign became the golden age in the memory of the nation. This is important; the idea of David reigning over a united nation as a shepherd-king will enter into the nation's psyche and will become part of the language through which God will convey deeper concepts.

Priestly dysfunction

During his reign David began to set things in order for a full return to the prescribed ceremonies in which the nation was to serve God. He lived during a time of severe priestly dysfunction. That ancient ceremony of Yom Kippur required that an animal be sacrificed on the prescribed altar and that its blood be sprinkled on the 'place of propitiation' or 'mercy seat.' However, decades before this the sacred Ark of the Covenant had been lost in battle and when it returned it was not brought back to the now permanently settled Tabernacle but remained separated from the rest of the priestly functions. The implications of this are far reaching. It would seem that for the whole period of Samuel's 'judgeship' and the period of King Saul's reign, and the period of David's reign the Yom Kippur ceremony had not been undertaken in the proper manner. The altar was separated from the 'mercy seat' by a distance of some 20 miles.

As David considered his own increasing prosperity and comfort from his throne within the new palace donated by a neighbouring king, he began to think about making some proper provision for God's throne. He had been accumulating a fabulous store of precious stones and metals with the intention of using this treasure to fund the building of a house 'fit for God'. He even had the plans given to him by divine revelation. However when it came to the moment of beginning the project God blocked it. David had too much blood on his hands to build a 'holy place for God to dwell in'. The account of how David handled this disappointment is another glimpse into the greatness of this man and his willingness to submit his own will and desires to the greater will of God.

But even as God says 'no' he brings a promise that captures David's heart and imagination; *When your days are fulfilled and you rest with your fathers, I will set up your seed after you, who will come from your body, and I will establish his kingdom. He shall build a house for My name, and I will establish the throne of his kingdom forever...* 2Sam 7:12-14 NKJV. The blessing is given even greater detail as God graciously 'turns the tables' on David. David had wanted to build a 'house for God' but God would now build a 'house for David'. There is a play on words here. The house that David wanted to build was a physical house but the house that God was going to build was a dynasty. David's dynasty would last forever; *And your house and your kingdom shall be established forever before you. Your throne shall be established forever.* 2 Sam 7:16 NKJV. That is some promise!

In fact, it is more than a promise it is a covenant. Later in the history of the nation when the Davidic dynasty was under threat we have it spelled out very clearly; *Yet the LORD would not destroy the house of David, because of the covenant that He had made with David, and since He had promised to give a lamp to him and to his sons forever.* 2Chr 21:7 NKJV. So together with the idea of a united kingdom under David we now have the idea of a never ending united kingdom under the Davidic dynasty. This is yet another colour that is being added to the artist's palette.

Three covenants

We now have three interconnected covenants operating at the same time and an often hidden one that continues out of sight. The Sinai Covenant, the Levitical Covenant and the Davidic Covenant became interdependent. However, the original covenant with Abraham's Seed continued unseen working its way through to a culmination in the person of Jesus Christ. We shall need to tread carefully as we try to copy these ideas onto a larger canvas. To go back to our old illustration, each of these covenants will provide different colours on God's palette to enable the painting of a stunning scene, but we still have need of some more colours before that painting can be completed.

In this chapter we saw the link between the Sinai Covenant and the land of Israel. We saw that the people of Israel only ever had a tenancy agreement and never owned the land 'freehold'. We saw the way that the Sinai Covenant began to function as a tenancy agreement and the threat of losing the land if the tenancy agreement was breached. We saw the addition of yet another covenant to the Sinai Covenant, the Davidic covenant of monarchy and added it to our artist's palette in preparation for a final 'masterpiece'.

8: Conflict among the covenants

You may have noticed that there are different kinds of covenants that seem to happily co-exist in the history of the people of Israel. In fact, they didn't always 'happily' co-exist and a tension developed between them. The Abrahamic Covenant seems to be non-conditional; *On the same day the LORD made a covenant with Abram, saying: "To your descendants I have given this land..."* Gen 15:18 NKJV. The Sinai Covenant was clearly a conditional covenant; *if you will indeed obey My voice and keep My covenant, then you shall be a special treasure to Me above all people;* Ex 19:5 NKJV. But the Priesthood Covenant seems to be a non-conditional covenant too; *...Behold, I give to him My covenant of peace; and it shall be to him and his descendants after him a covenant of an everlasting priesthood, because he was zealous for his God, and made atonement for the children of Israel...* Num 25:12-13 NKJV. Then we have the Davidic covenant that also seems to be non-conditional; *And your* *house and your kingdom shall be established forever before you. Your throne shall be established forever.* 2Sam 7:16 NKJV. This will produce an Old Testament version of the Calvinist/Arminian controversy. Is the nation saved 'everlastingly' or can the behaviour of the people ruin everything?

I will not forsake you... I will forsake you...

The last four chapters of Deuteronomy show the last moments of Moses' public ministry and his final ascent into the mountain. They contain a few words that have become a constant source of blessing and encouragement to God's people in all ages. Moses repeats the phrases twice, once to the assembled nation and once to Joshua personally. The words ring with utter certainty; *He will not leave you nor forsake you.* Deut 31:6 NKJV. (See also Deut 31:8) Surely that settles the matter? Well it might have done so if eleven verses later God had not said; *...I will forsake them, and I will hide My face from them...* Deut 31:17 NKJV. There can be no doubt of what is being said, the same Hebrew word is used in both places. Confused? How do we get from "I will not leave you nor forsake" to "I will forsake them and I will hide my face from them" in ten verses?

At the end of Moses' life our first five books of the Bible were committed for safekeeping to the priests, the descendants of Levi. The scrolls were to be kept, as we have seen earlier, by the side of the Ark of the Covenant. These 5 books are known as The Torah, The Law or simply Moses (Deut 31:24-26) and were the foundation of the nation, a kind of Declaration of Dependence! The Covenant had been based on specific words not just on a warm feeling or a decision; *And Moses took the blood, sprinkled it on the people, and said, "This is the blood of the covenant which the LORD has made with you according to all these words.* Ex 24:8 NKJV. The priests became the teachers of the law and the elders of the nation became the upholders of the law. And then Moses taught them a song.

It is a remarkable song. We can find it in Deuteronomy 32 and it was to be memorized by the whole nation. It is a song that predicts the course of history for the covenant community in their promised land. It begins with reminders of God's loving intervention and deliverance. It sketches out God's purpose for the nation and describes it with an unusual title for Israel. God calls the nation 'Jeshurun'; "My Upright One". The title is used only 4 times in the Scripture; Deut 32:15; 33:5, 26; Is 44:2 but it showed God's great desire and destiny for his covenant people. As the song continues the narrative shows the nation becoming 'fat' and complacent. It predicts they will become used to 'blessing' and will forget God and his covenant and turn to other gods. For his part God will 'heap disasters on them' that would result in them being scattered among their enemies. It is a sobering fact that for all the wonderful prospect of the book of Deuteronomy there are more threats of curses in this book than promises of blessing.

I have loved you...

Does this imply that God will run out of patience and withdraw his love from them? Not at all. The biblical history of this covenant nation will begin and end on the same note. Moses declares God's heart in giving the Law; *Now this is the blessing with which Moses the man of God blessed the children of Israel before his death. And he said: "The LORD came from Sinai, And dawned on them from Seir; He shone forth from Mount Paran, And He came with ten thousands of saints; From His right hand Came a fiery law for them. Yes, He loves the people..."* Deut 33:1-3 NKJV. The Law, as we read here, was the gift of his love. We have already seen how the last prophet of the Old Covenant reminds the nation of God's unchanging attitude of heart toward them through centuries of failure and rebellion; *"I have loved you," says the LORD. "Yet you say, 'In what way have You loved us?* Mal 1:2 NKJV.

The priests and elders failed in their God-given responsibility to safeguard and apply the Law and God continued to speak through prophets; men who 'saw' as God 'sees' and were originally known as 'seers'. They brought God's current perspective to the present time. A prophet knows what God is thinking and brings that insight in messages of different kinds. There had always been 'prophets'. Enoch was a prophet, so were Noah and Abraham and many more; some are famous and their names live on, some spoke their words and passed into obscurity. This was how the covenant nation existed for centuries with the word of God in a covenant book and with the words of God constantly breaking into their lives. God's diligence in bringing 'today's message' to his people is expressed in a telling Hebrew idiom. Jeremiah constantly tells us that God was in the habit of 'getting up early and sending his messengers'. (Jer 7:13, 25; 11:7; 25:3–4; 26:5; 29:19; 32:33; 35:14–15; 44:4) The picture is of a king diligently ruling his people with a clear 'hands-on' style.

We have also seen how in time the nation that was united under David split into two separate nations during the reign of his grandson. David's son Solomon was not always wise and in his later years he took the path to idolatry and lavish life style. When his son Rehoboam came to the throne there had already been rumblings of rebellion and a protest meeting was held. The people wanted some assurance of a gentler style of monarchy but Rehoboam rejected their request in favour of a regime that promised to be even harsher than that of Solomon. God's anger with Solomon's idolatry and Rehoboam's arrogance was expressed in God dispossessing Rehoboam of the nation of Israel; he tore it from Rehoboam and gave it into the hand of Jeroboam the son of Nebat. Jeroboam was from the family tribe of Ephraim and the trouble had begun during the reign of Solomon when Solomon had introduced conscription and forced labour for his building projects. (1 Kings 11:26-31) Because Jeroboam was from the tribe of Ephraim, the son of Joseph, the kingdom that Jeroboam created is sometimes known in the Bible as Ephraim, Joseph and even Rachel's children.

More conditional covenants

When the split came it looked as if the Davidic Covenant was over for good, but God did not wholly break the Davidic dynasty. One of those men with God's perspective on things acted out what would take place. A prophet wearing a new garment met Jeroboam and then tore his new robe into 12 separate pieces. He invited Jeroboam to help himself to 10 pieces. He explained that this was prophetic of the nation. As a result of the sin of David's dynasty and its refusal to "walk in My ways to do what is right in My eyes and keep My statutes and My judgments" God would take the kingdom out of Rehoboam's hands leaving only a token tribe loyal so that the Davidic line would not die out. The encounter ended with an astonishing promise to Jeroboam the son of Nebat; *And I will take you, and you shall reign over all that your soul desires, and you shall be king over Israel. And if you will listen to all that I command you, and will walk in my ways, and do what is right in my eyes by keeping my statutes and my commandments, as David my servant did, I will be with you and will build you a sure house, as I built for David, and I will give Israel to you. 1 Kings 11:37-38* ESV. God was duplicating his original promise to David and now making the same promise to Jeroboam.

This is a startling prophecy. God promises Jeroboam a contract that is an equivalent of the Davidic covenant. He promises to give Jeroboam a sure or enduring dynasty 'as I built for David' and then sounds the death knell for the kingdom that had been united under David; *I will be with you and build for you an enduring house, as I built for David, and will give Israel to you.* We now have two covenants running in parallel that seem to be incompatible. How are we to understand this? 'Israel' had been 'given away'; David's dynasty will reign over a mere rump of a nation. Bible readers become fairly familiar with a description of Jeroboam, he is frequently called 'Jeroboam the son of Nebat who caused Israel to sin'. He becomes a new standard for idolatry and false religion so that many a later king is measured against either David or Jeroboam. Jeroboam's 'sure or enduring dynasty' lasted for a very short time. He reigned for 22 years during which he took the northern kingdom further and further away from the Covenant. His son reigned for 2 years and was assassinated in a palace coup. The northern kingdom of Israel was on a flight path to disaster and in spite of God's faithfulness in 'getting up early and sending them messengers' their successive kings stayed on the same bearing and the nation ended 200 years later when the Assyrian super power moved in.

The southern kingdom of Judah under its Davidic dynasty did better, although ultimately they would crash and burn too. The descendants of David were fortified by their assurance that God had promised there would always be a Davidic king on the throne in Jerusalem. The southern kingdom of Judah was also encouraged in its view of ultimate survival and prosperity by the fact that the priesthood was centred in Jerusalem. They had the assurances of two non-conditional covenants and they were sure that ultimately things would 'work out'. The house of David and the Temple were their guarantees of security. Judah survived for about 130 years longer than Israel. God continued to provide prophets to bring his perspective of coming judgment into view but the general population had a different theology with which it sustained itself.

Isaiah, Jeremiah and others said plainly that retribution was coming and that the wholesale ignoring of the Sinai Covenant must ultimately bring Sinai's curses, but their warning was largely ignored. After all, David's everlasting throne was in Jerusalem and so were the Temple and the everlasting Levitical Priesthood. It was unthinkable that God would allow Jerusalem to be conquered. We can almost hear the desperation in Jeremiah's voice; *The word that came to Jeremiah from the LORD, saying, "Stand in the gate of the LORD'S house, and proclaim there this word, and say, 'Hear the word of the LORD, all you of Judah who enter in at these gates to worship the LORD!' " Thus says the LORD of hosts, the God of Israel: "Amend your ways and your doings, and I will cause you to dwell in this place. Do not trust in these lying words, saying, 'The temple of the LORD, the temple of the LORD, the temple of the LORD are these.'* "Jer 7:1-4 NKJV. Earlier he had been saying the same things about their trust in the inviolability of the Sinai Covenant; *"Then it shall come to pass, when you are multiplied and increased in the land in those days," says the LORD, "that they will say no more, 'The ark of the covenant of the LORD.' It shall not come to mind, nor shall they remember it, nor shall they visit it, nor shall it be made anymore.* Jer 3:16 NKJV. It is a sobering moment to imagine. The populace earnestly quoting their Bible verses to assure themselves of utter safety; the Temple and the Ark of the Covenant were their guarantees. They had the Priesthood and the Sinai Covenant what more could they need... and they had Jeremiah pleading with the people that their confidence was misplaced.

Down in the potter's house

But which is true? "I will never leave you, nor forsake you" or "I will forsake you and hide my face from you"? They are both true but there is a vital passage of Scripture in the prophecies of Jeremiah which explains the way in which prophecy works. We rightly say that God's word is utterly reliable and that He will never fail but there are working principles which must be added to that statement otherwise we shall be driven to admit that God's word has not been true. After all, the throne of David is currently not in Jerusalem and, so far as I know, there is not a single identifiable descendant of David alive today on earth. The Temple and its priesthood too are no longer operating although God said both these covenants were 'everlasting'. How can we understand these things? There are two parts to the answer.

Firstly let's hear what Jeremiah has to say in one of those messages from God. It comes from a prophecy in which God was addressing the 'house of Israel' that had gone into captivity some 130 years earlier. That nation had been removed from its land and resettled in various parts of the Assyrian empire. It had vanished and only the memory lingered on, but God had not given up and he sends a message through Jeremiah about a potter having to remake a pot because something had gone wrong while it was spinning on the wheel. For some time I worked as an assistant to a potter at the famous Wedgwood's factory in Staffordshire. It was a never-ending fascination to watch the clay rise and fall under the potter's hands. As long as the clay is in his hands and stays responsive he can remake it, afresh, differently, as the potter desires. Jeremiah uses this picture as an illustration and then draws out a vital unchanging principle about the way in which a prophetic word operates.

The lasting principle comes in two parts; *The instant I speak concerning a nation and concerning a kingdom, to pluck up, to pull down, and to destroy it, if that nation against whom I have spoken turns from its evil, I will relent of the disaster that I thought to bring upon it.* Jer 18:7-8 NKJV. Apparently God's curses are conditional as well as his blessings. Until the very last word is spoken there is always hope. Even if God did not specifically give the 'conditions' and his judgments seemed absolutely final there is still the possibility of him reversing his decision. There are several vivid examples of this in the Scriptures themselves. The story of Jonah ends with a petulant prophet who had wanted God's disastrous judgments to come on the capital city of his enemies. He brought a word of absolute, impending catastrophe. "In 40 days Nineveh will be destroyed". No escape clauses just a single stark sentence. 40 days and it is over. But the Ninevites repented and God spared them and Jonah is angry. We can paraphrase his protest; "I knew you would do that, it's just like you!" (Jonah 4:2)

The nation of Israel had all evil kings but the nation of Judah had some evil ones too. The worst king in Judah was a man called Manasseh. He was easily as bad as any of Israel's kings and suffered his own personal 'captivity'. The Assyrian king took Manasseh off to Babylon which was then ruled by the Assyrians and that was the end of the matter.... Oh, no it wasn't. While in Babylon this most wicked of Judah's kings found genuine repentance; *Therefore the LORD brought upon them the captains of the army of the king of Assyria, who took Manasseh with hooks, bound him with bronze fetters, and carried him off to Babylon. Now when he was in affliction, he implored the LORD his God, and humbled himself greatly before the God of his fathers, and prayed to Him; and He received his entreaty, heard his supplication, and brought him back to Jerusalem into his kingdom. Then Manasseh knew that the LORD was God.* 2 Chr 33:11-13 NKJV. This is one of the great themes of the Bible, God can restore the prodigals. And the Bible is full of them; prodigal kings, prodigal prophets, prodigal wives, prodigal sons, prodigal apostles... almost no end. Each one is proving the validity of this amazing truth that even when God has pronounced the sentence, between the sentence and the execution, there is time to change and when change comes God 'changes his mind' too.

Two way traffic

This is genuine good news and we rejoice in it but this principle works in both directions as Jeremiah makes very plain; *And the instant I speak concerning a nation and concerning a kingdom, to build and to plant it, if it does evil in My sight so that it does not obey My voice, then I will relent concerning the good with which I said I would benefit it.* Jer 18:9-10 NKJV. If God promises blessing and those to whom it has been promised act sinfully then God will 'change his mind' about the blessing that he had promised. There is a sense then in which every promise that God makes is 'conditional' even if he doesn't specify the conditions. As we read Jeremiah 18 we see how God applied this unchanging principle to two separate nations. To the nation of Israel, already in captivity, it becomes a promise of hope. To the nation of Judah relaxing in its complacency it becomes a dire warning.

Jeremiah applies that same principle to the promise of God's blessing or of God's curses. During his day the people of the nation-state of Judah were Bible-sure that God must continue to bless them, but Jeremiah spells out letter by letter the principle. If God promises blessing, but those to whom he promises blessing turn aside into sin, then God will not keep his promise; the blessings will be forfeit. In fact this passage of Scripture is giving us a vital key to the interpretation of all prophecy. It bears repeating; it is telling us that all God's promises are conditional, even those which may appear to be non-conditional.

To many in Jerusalem it became a fight between what God had said and what God was saying and to the last they believed that God would not allow the Davidic monarchy and the Levitical priesthood to end. When the armies of Nebuchadnezzar destroyed Jerusalem, took its king captive and looted the Temple of its most sacred relics the people of the covenant were stunned. As one writer expressed it, 'the battering rams of Nebuchadnezzar's army breached the theology of Israel'.

How long is 'forever'?

And the second thing? That word 'everlasting' needs to be carefully examined to understand its implications; technically it means 'age-lasting'. Sometimes it does mean 'everlasting' in the way in which we generally use it but sometimes it just means 'for the foreseeable future'. Let me illustrate briefly. Under the Sinai Covenant a slave offered his freedom could decide that he would prefer to remain with his master. He was allowed to make that choice. When he made it publicly his ear was bored through as a sign that he was not 'free' but had voluntarily chosen bond-service. As the Scripture records the ceremony; *But if the servant plainly says, "I love my master, my wife, and my children; I will not go out free," then his master shall bring him to the judges. He shall also bring him to the door, or to the doorpost, and his master shall pierce his ear with an awl; and he shall serve him forever.* Ex 21:5-6 NKJV. That word 'forever' is the same Hebrew word that we might translate 'everlastingly' but it is obvious that we have to understand it in its own context. This does not mean, for example, that in heaven...everlastingly... we shall find people who decided to stay with their Hebrew masters 3500 years ago who are still acting as bond-servants.

Tracing through the use of the Hebrew word 'olam' will give a clearer sense of the way in which the word is used. The Temple lamps did not burn 'everlastingly' but throughout that era. The Davidic throne did not remain in Jerusalem 'everlastingly' but for a 'long time'. The priesthood that was given to the Levitical family 'everlastingly' ended finally in AD70. We need to examine the context of the Hebrew word 'olam' as we interpret prophecies.

So we begin to see that the varying co-existing covenants were not mutually exclusive but were part of the way in which God was conveying truth and preparing minds for even greater truth. It is well to be conscious that when we have apparent inconsistencies in the Bible it is not the Bible which needs modification but our own way of thinking.

In this chapter we examined the issues at stake when covenants seem to be contradictory and discovered a vital lesson that all God's promises are conditional even those which seem to be unconditional. We saw the way that Jeremiah struggled to bring the 'current' word of God to a people who were comforting themselves with words that God had said long ago. It is not that God has forgotten or abandoned his promises but often those promises need to be interpreted in the light of the relevant context. We saw too that the word 'everlasting' is context sensitive and that many things said to be 'everlasting' were actually just for fixed periods of time.

9: Why doesn't God do something?

   God continued to 'get up early and send his messengers' and one of his messengers was a man called Isaiah. He lived in the southern kingdom of Judah and brought God's messages to the people for well over 40 years. The first verse of his prophetic writings tell us that he continued to do this through the reign of four 'house of David' kings; Uzziah, Jotham, Ahaz and Hezekiah. That would place him and his work somewhere around 742- 698 BC. Isaiah's prophecies were not written all at once but what we have in the book of Isaiah is the collection of his prophetic writings over his lifetime that was probably preserved by his followers. We need to keep that in mind as we read because there are dramatic 'atmospheric mood swings' in this book as Isaiah swings from threats of devastating judgments to promises of glorious recovery.

Conflicts among the super powers.

Isaiah was writing during a period of international upheaval. Super powers were rising and falling and their client states were being dragged backwards and forwards like a lifeless doll on the turn of the tide. To most people living in those times it must all have seemed chaotic and shapeless, but Isaiah is a 'seer'. He will see things from a different perspective, God's! Try to keep those dates 742-698 BC in mind as we try to catch the flow of God's purposes in history, remembering that dates go forward as numbers get less in the 'Before Christ' half of history. When Isaiah began the northern kingdom of Israel was under the reign of Jeroboam II; not the original Jeroboam who lived some 200 years earlier but another man of the same name. Jeroboam II was a powerful and successful ruler as men judge things. According to the Scripture he was raised up by God to give the house of Israel a respite from their enemies; *So Jehoahaz pleaded with the LORD, and the LORD listened to him; for He saw the oppression of Israel, because the king of Syria oppressed them. Then the LORD gave Israel a deliverer, so that they escaped from under the hand of the Syrians; and the children of Israel dwelt in their tents as before.* 2 Kings 13:4-5 NKJV. The grandson of Jehoahaz was Jeroboam II and for over 50 years the house of Israel had a stable monarchy; first under Joash and then Jeroboam II. They themselves were evil men but God permitted a respite for the northern kingdom.

It was, in fact, the very last chance for the house of Israel. God gave them victories over their enemies and they re-established strong borders. The northern kingdom of Israel was never more 'safe' than under the reign of Jeroboam II, or so it would have appeared to anyone who was not a 'seer'. Isaiah however saw that in spite of its apparent rude health... *The whole head is sick, And the whole heart faints. From the sole of the foot even to the head, There is no soundness in it, But wounds and bruises and putrefying sores...* Is 1:5-6 NKJV. It is not comfortable being a 'seer'. The nation had continued in its idolatry and the house of Israel had squandered its opportunity to get right with God. When Jeroboam II died his kingdom fell to pieces. In the next 20 years the house of Israel had 6 kings, one of whom reigned for just one month. The northern nation-state of Israel was spiraling into disaster.

Intrusion Ethics

Let me introduce you to the idea of 'Intrusion Ethics'. 'Oh help' I hear you cry! Most big ideas are much simpler than they sound. Why did God allow his covenant to be constantly disregarded and the nation of Israel to become more and more pagan? We are raising a question here that surfaces in the thoughts of anyone who takes the Bible seriously or looks at the world in which we live; why doesn't God do something? Long before this time God had promised the land of Canaan to Abraham but gave an interesting reason as to why Abraham would not immediately possess the land. Apparently other factors in the history of other peoples were part of God's synchronizing of events; *But in the fourth generation they shall return here, for the iniquity of the Amorites is not yet complete."* Gen 15:16 NKJV. Abraham's descendants' possession of the land would be synchronized with God's judgments upon the inhabitants of Canaan. Our refusal to bring our lives into line with God's pattern will have consequences; this is an unchanging fact of revelation. And yet so many cruel dictators have died in comfort in their beds and appear to have escaped God's judgments. How can we understand this? Why did God not stop Hitler or Stalin or Idi Amin with an instant judgment?

Paul gives us one answer to this puzzling question in Romans and he almost certainly had Jeremiah in mind; *Does not the potter have power over the clay, from the same lump to make one vessel for honour and another for dishonor? What if God, wanting to show His wrath and to make His power known, endured with much longsuffering the vessels of wrath prepared for destruction, and that He might make known the riches of His glory on the vessels of mercy, which He had prepared beforehand for glory,* Rom 9:21-23 NKJV. In one sense that is an end of the matter. God is God and he will do what he wills. "Intrusion Ethics" is not arguing with Paul's Spirit-inspired words in Romans, but there is an old question that an old 'friend of God' once asked; *Far be it from You to do such a thing as this, to slay the righteous with the wicked, so that the righteous should be as the wicked; far be it from You! Shall not the Judge of all the earth do right?* Gen 18:25 NKJV. There follows a fascinating conversation between God and his friend which we do not have time to pursue other than to remark that this was a conversation between friends and not a bartering encounter in a bazaar, as some have supposed.

In the setting of the Canaanites it seems that God was ever reluctant to visit his judgment on the atrocities that were performed there masquerading as religion. While there is the slightest possibility of repentance he holds back his wrath even though he knows that they will not change. There is a wonderful statement about the nature of God's love in the gospel according to John; *...when Jesus knew that His hour had come that He should depart from this world to the Father, having loved His own who were in the world, He loved them to the end. And supper being ended, the devil having already put it into the heart of Judas Iscariot, Simon's son, to betray Him, Jesus, knowing that the Father had given all things into His hands, and that He had come from God and was going to God, rose from supper and laid aside His garments, took a towel and girded Himself.* John 13:1-4 NKJV. One of those whose feet he washed, having loved him to the end, was Judas Iscariot. If God then is so reluctant to act in judgment why does he ever do so? This is where the idea of "Intrusion Ethics" comes in. At best it is just a 'best fit' answer to the question, it is certainly not the last word on the subject.

"Intrusion Ethics" makes a very clear distinction between the age in which we live in which God allows us to benefit from 'Common Grace' and the coming age of the 'Consummation' or final judgment. The fact that we are still alive in spite of our sinfulness is due to God's 'common grace' towards our race. Even those who have not come into God's 'saving grace' through Christ are benefiting from this time of 'common grace'. Even though we deserve judgment and instant retribution for our sin we are still here because of God's unmerited love towards us, His grace. Why? Well Peter expresses it like this; *The Lord is not slack concerning His promise, as some count slackness, but is longsuffering toward us, not willing that any should perish but that all should come to repentance.* 2 Pet 3:9 NKJV.

There is however another era that is on its way, and here we return to Paul; *He has appointed a day on which He will judge the world in righteousness by the Man whom He has ordained. He has given assurance of this to all by raising Him from the dead.* Acts 17:31 NKJV. So, if God is waiting for 'another day' why does he ever bring judgment now? These judgments are 'intrusions' of the 'ethics' of the coming age of Consummation into our days of Common Grace, or so the idea of "Intrusion Ethics" states it. Some of God's judgments that 'intrude' into this era of common grace are glimpses of a future day. They are 'anticipations' of the era of Consummation. One day this will be the norm and not the exception. These judgments then are examples of another day and a constant warning that the day of the Consummation and Final judgment will arrive. They serve as rare examples of God's character in his attitude to sin and the sinner, an attitude that will be revealed in all its awesome fullness on a coming day. They are Judgment Day in miniature and very rare. Isaiah describes one of these 'out of the ordinary' periods of coming judgment as the 'out of the ordinary' way that God sometimes works; they are God's 'strange works'; *For the LORD shall rise up as in mount Perazim, he shall be wroth as in the valley of Gibeon, that he may do his work, his strange work; and bring to pass his act, his strange act.* Is 28:21 KJV

While we are touching this subject perhaps we should add a word of caution. We need to be very cautious in what we declare to be an act of God's anticipatory judgment. It is folly to try to map specific sins to specific events although many Christians will attempt it. Notice in these following verses the way in which the Lord refuses to link a specific sin with a 'strange act' but insists that the final day of judgment will surely come; *Or those eighteen on whom the tower in Siloam fell and killed them, do you think that they were worse sinners than all other men who dwelt in Jerusalem? I tell you, no; but unless you repent you will all likewise perish.* Luke 13:4-5 NKJV.

So Isaiah and other 'seers' began to declare that God was about to judge the persistent sin of his covenant people. The northern kingdom of the house of Israel would be the first to experience such an 'intrusion' and it would be almost total. He predicted that the super power of Assyria would invade the land and take its people into exile. The process began somewhere around 740 BC when the king of Assyria invaded the areas around Galilee, the tribal settlements of Naphtali, Gad, Reuben and Manasseh and took the inhabitants into exile. (2 Kings 15:29; 1 Chron 5:25-26) And as the book of Chronicles, which may have been written by Ezra some 200 years later, adds they are there 'to this day'; *So the God of Israel stirred up the spirit of Pul king of Assyria, that is, Tiglath-pileser king of Assyria. He carried the Reubenites, the Gadites, and the half-tribe of Manasseh into captivity. He took them to Halah, Habor, Hara, and the river of Gozan to this day.* 1 Chr 5:26 NKJV.

There were a few years of trembling fear and then the Assyrian armies returned and in the year 722 BC the capital city, Samaria, fell to the invading armies. The remainder of the nation was taken into exile and as one writer has said 'pass from history into myth'. The whole nation vanishes into the mists of time and its distinctive peoples, the family tribes of Reuben, Naphtali, Dan, Gad, Asher, Ephraim and Manasseh become inextricably merged into the populations of the lands to which they were exiled. Israel, the northern kingdom, had fallen and would never rise again.

A couple of years before the final exile an invitation arrived from the south. Hezekiah, king of the house of Judah, was organizing a spectacular celebration of the Passover, the feast that had been the beginning of the covenant community's exodus. It was a tremendous spectacle and was meant to provide a new starting point for the covenant people. They could start all over again. Hezekiah sent invitations to the whole northern territory to the families who had not yet been taken into exile. It was God's last invitation to the king's feast and included a promise that even now it was not too late for God to reclaim the exiles. God, said the invitation, is still ready to be gracious. The response was derisory; *So the runners passed from city to city through the country of Ephraim and Manasseh, as far as Zebulun; but they laughed at them and mocked them. Nevertheless some from Asher, Manasseh, and Zebulun humbled themselves and came to Jerusalem.* 2Chr 30:10-11 NKJV.

Just a trickle of people came to the party and seem to have remained and became indistinguishable from the rest of Judah, although we do find one last identifiable descendant of those lost tribes in Jerusalem over 700 years later. When the infant Jesus was taken to Jerusalem for his circumcision an old widow was waiting; *Now there was one, Anna, a prophetess, the daughter of Phanuel, of the tribe of Asher.* Luke 2:36 NKJV. Asher was one of those vanished clans.

Isaiah's warnings were not only for the house of Israel. His prophecies touched all the surrounding nations and the house of Judah. The southern kingdom of Judah had been much more stable than the northern kingdom of Israel. Where Israel had known an unbroken series of disastrous kings who led the people further and further away from the covenant, Judah had been blessed with some godly men and their graph had ups as well as downs; however the trend was clearly downwards. Isaiah and others brought their solemn warnings against Judah; without repentance it would suffer the same 'intrusion ethics' as its sister Israel. As we have seen the southern kingdom felt safely insulated from that possibility, after all they had a promise that a descendant of David would always be on the throne and they had a legitimate priesthood given to the family of Aaron as an 'everlasting covenant'. Things might get a little rough at times but the final outcome was not in doubt, Judah would survive; a sober warning of the dangers of one-eyed, unbalanced, theology.

The remnant comes into view

Even as Isaiah brings his fearsome warnings against Judah another theme begins to emerge... survivors. Perhaps the one-eyed theologians were right after all, Judah would 'make it'. Isaiah, and others, begins to use the language of 'the remnant', the leftovers. It was not the nation that would survive, but a remnant from within the nation would indeed survive. In fact, a remnant from both nations of the house of Israel and the house of Judah would survive and God would restore them and recommence his plans for their destiny.

Could God do this? Could he select a group from within the nation and make this group alone the bearers of the covenant promises? It wasn't the first time that God had said he would do such a thing. To get our example we need to go back again into the nation's history. It is an almost unbelievable story that while the covenant was in process of being established the nation almost lost everything. Moses was in the presence of God receiving the Ten Words on two tablets of stone. While he is alone with God he is informed that the covenant people have already breached the covenant. As repulsive as it may seem this is the equivalent of one of the partners in a marriage being unfaithful during the actual wedding ceremony; it is almost unbelievable but the record stands. Aaron created a golden calf for the people to worship and the people gave themselves to it; *And he received the gold from their hand, and he fashioned it with an engraving tool, and made a moulded calf. Then they said, "This is your god, O Israel, that brought you out of the land of Egypt!" So when Aaron saw it, he built an altar before it. And Aaron made a proclamation and said, "Tomorrow is a feast to the LORD." Then they rose early on the next day, offered burnt offerings, and brought peace offerings; and the people sat down to eat and drink, and rose up to play.* Ex 32:4-6 NKJV. Those sacrifices of burnt offering and peace offerings are the same sacrifices that they had made earlier when they agreed to be God's people. This is betrayal of staggering measure.

Again we will not pursue the story other than to note God's reaction to their behaviour. God declares to Moses that he will wipe out the entire nation and start all over again with just one man, Moses; *And the LORD said to Moses, "I have seen this people, and indeed it is a stiff-necked people! Now therefore, let Me alone, that My wrath may burn hot against them and I may consume them. And I will make of you a great nation."* Ex 32:9-10 NKJV. From the 3 million that had been delivered from Egypt and who are in process of becoming God's special people God will take one man and start all over again. One man will be enough for God to fulfill his promises and his covenant. Please remember that phrase, we shall return to it; "one man is enough for God to fulfill his promises and his covenant". Moses would have been 'a remnant' and from this single-person-remnant God would have begun all over again and fulfilled his purposes. Again the story of Moses' intercession as he offers himself as a substitute for the people is full of wonderful truths but we must move on...

We saw this concept much earlier in the record of the first use of the idea of 'remnant'; the narrative of Noah's flood. So the concept that God can take a remnant and make of it a new beginning is not a new one. Even before Judah's exile takes place, Isaiah is seeing its return, the return of a remnant and he sees it in the language of a second exodus, God is beginning all over again, even in judgment he remembers mercy.

In this chapter we introduced the theological idea of 'intrusion ethics' and suggested this might be part of the answer to the puzzled question 'why doesn't God do something?' We traced the ends of the two nations states of Israel and Judah and reminded ourselves of the concept of a remnant which could be used by God as a kind of survival pod in which his purposes could continue. We saw that on occasion God was ready to wipe out the whole people of Israel and, beginning with Moses as a 'remnant', was ready to start all over again. Just a single seed is all that is necessary.

10: A new start

So the northern kingdom of Israel had tumbled into chaos and a final death and the southern kingdom of Judah wasn't too far behind; about 130 years to be precise. As the northern kingdom tottered to the brink of disaster there was a final flurry of messengers from God: Amos and Hosea in the north and Isaiah and Micah in the south. Their prophecies all have a similar feature, they predict utter disaster and final loss and yet there is an irrepressible bubble of hope that keeps rising from the depths of the woes. It makes the prophecies sound almost schizophrenic; is it the end or isn't it? The answer to both questions is 'yes'.

The end and then...

So the house of Israel, as we know it, has come to its end. The house of Judah as we have known it is also coming to its end but from the ashes of both nation-states something quite different will arise. God's judgments will come but beyond the judgments there is the dawning of another day. This is where the theme of 'a remnant' finds its place. A remnant is just what is left when the larger portion has gone. We saw earlier that the word was introduced in the account of the Flood. *So He destroyed all living things which were on the face of the ground: both man and cattle, creeping thing and bird of the air. They were destroyed from the earth. Only Noah and those who were with him in the ark remained alive.* Gen 7:23 NKJV. Noah and his family 'remained', a remnant. Noah and those who 'shared his baptism' were a remnant, but from that remnant God rebuilt a whole race. If Moses had chosen the offer put to him God would have rebuilt a whole nation from the remnant of the one man, Moses. The fulfillment of the type is Christ as the ultimate remnant. He is the only one of our race to have fulfilled our destiny and from this one man God will rebuild a people for himself.

There is a word that is frequently used by Isaiah; it is the word 'create', in Hebrew 'bara'. 'Bara' is a Hebrew word that usually only has God as its subject; that simply means that only God creates. The word is found in the first sentence of the Bible; *In the beginning God created the heavens and the earth.* Gen 1:1 NKJV. 'Bara' is a word which has a high profile in the book of Genesis as we might expect, then for the greater part it goes underground only to burst out again in profusion in the prophecies of Isaiah; *then the LORD will create above every dwelling place of Mount Zion, and above her assemblies, a cloud and smoke by day and the shining of a flaming fire by night. For over all the glory there will be a covering.* Is 4:5. NKJV. 'Then'! When? If we read the preceding verses we find that this creative activity is going to be preceded by a time of great distress and judgment. After the judgment comes a new creation. The pictures are coming thick and fast now: Exiles, remnants, a new exodus, a new creation. Isaiah is pointing beyond the pain of the judgments to a new beginning. This theme too will create words and ideas which will become part of the nation's vocabulary, words that God will be able to use in another context to convey powerful ideas and truths.

We are back to my familiar theme, Bible words don't have definitions they have histories. Bible words function like this. 77% of the Bible is Old Testament and 40% of the Old Testament is a story line. These ideas and words became embedded in the minds and emotions of generations of Israelites and later God would only need to speak the word to unleash a torrent of emotion and memory. We know how certain smells can powerfully evoke memories of events, so can words. Or to use our earlier illustration, these are the colours that God is adding to the artist's palette so that they are ready for instant use, as the artist requires.

The Bible's story line is not incidental; it is also part of the revelation of God and his character. The covenant people were going to go into exile, their life and culture would come to an end, but God's purposes for them would not. The route is not the one anyone could have expected but the destination is unchanged. Throughout the prophecies of these dark days we hear references to the two nations; the house of Israel and the house of Judah. They have been pursuing different courses for over 400 years and now, after their greatest calamities, their paths are going to rejoin.

Three prophets

The three prophets who have most to say about this are Isaiah, Jeremiah and Ezekiel. It might help to put them into a timeline. Isaiah's prophecies began as the northern kingdom of Israel, the house of Israel, was about to be taken into captivity by Assyria. He lived in the southern kingdom of Judah and as we have seen his prophecies stretched through the reigns of four kings of the house of Judah. In 722 BC the northern kingdom of Israel finally came to an end and the people were taken into exile into the Assyrian empire. Their land was then repopulated with other captive nations. In the next super-power struggle Babylon rose to be top dog and around the 600s Babylon began a series of incursions into the remaining southern kingdom of Judah, the house of Judah. Initially, somewhere around 597BC, the Babylonian army attacked Jerusalem and took hostage all the sons of the nobility and important players in the national scene. A young man named Daniel was taken at this time and we shall consider his contribution separately. And another young man, from a priestly family, named Ezekiel. Ezekiel spent the rest of his life in Babylon and his prophetic activity all takes place in the Babylonian empire. Jeremiah was from a priestly family too but was not taken captive by the Babylonians so most of his prophetic activity takes place in and around Jerusalem. There was another deportation of people from the kingdom of Judah in 587 BC and a third in 582 BC. During the 587 deportation Jerusalem and its Temple was destroyed and the priests and their ceremonies ended.

These three prophets were working in very different contexts and as far as we know never met each other, but their prophecies follow the same lines. Their language is different and so are the pictures they use to communicate to the people but their theme is one. They are all looking past the current judgment to something 'new'. Isaiah the earliest of these men brings a message that people are not to think about the old ways in which God had worked in the past; *Do not remember the former things, Nor consider the things of old. Behold, I will do a new thing, Now it shall spring forth; Shall you not know it? I will even make a road in the wilderness And rivers in the desert.* Is 43:18-19 NKJV. He is using the language of the exodus to describe the future but is making it clear that what God is planning is not simply a repeat of their escape from captivity in Egypt. God, he says, is going to do a 'new thing'.

Jeremiah is saying the same thing but using a different vocabulary when he says; *Behold, the days are coming, says the LORD, when I will make a New Covenant with the house of Israel and with the house of Judah— not according to the covenant that I made with their fathers in the day that I took them by the hand to lead them out of the land of Egypt, My covenant which they broke, though I was a husband to them, says the LORD.* Jer 31:31-32 NKJV. This is an especially important prophecy and we shall return to it later but in passing we should notice that it was addressed to both of the separate nations "the house of Israel" and to "the house of Judah" and declares that God is going to make a New Covenant. Using the same pattern of contrast we have just seen in Isaiah he says "not according to the covenant that I made with your fathers in the day that I took them by the hand to lead them out of the land of Egypt." Isaiah's 'new thing' was not to be compared to the 'former days' and now Jeremiah says this 'New Covenant' is not going to be like the Sinai Covenant.

When Ezekiel's turn to prophesy comes he also declares the same truths but uses yet another different vocabulary; *I will give you a new heart and put a new spirit within you; I will take the heart of stone out of your flesh and give you a heart of flesh.* Ezek 36:26 NKJV. He says much more than this but for the time being and at the risk of repetition we will just gather these key points together. The old ways, the Old Covenant and the old heart were all to be left behind and in their place there would be a new thing, a New Covenant and a new heart.

Who were going to be the recipients of these new blessings? At first glance it seems the answer is obvious, the house of Israel and the house of Judah. After all are they not the nations to whom Jeremiah addressed his prophecy? Yes, they are. He needed to gain the attention of 'the house of Israel' now in captivity and 'the house of Judah' also in captivity but when he has their attention he makes a significant statement. If we extend our quotation from Jeremiah we may see the apparent discrepancy; *Behold, the days are coming, says the LORD, when I will make a New Covenant <u>with the house of Israel</u> and with <u>the house of Judah</u>— not according to the covenant that I made with their fathers in the day that I took them by the hand to lead them out of the land of Egypt, My covenant which they broke, though I was a husband to them, says the LORD. But this is the covenant that I will make with <u>the house of Israel</u> after those days, says the LORD: I will put My law in their minds, and write it on their hearts; and I will be their God, and they shall be My people.* Jer 31:31-33 NKJV. Verse 31 says God is going to make a 'New Covenant' with both 'the house of Judah' and 'the house of Israel'. In other words, those two ancient and separate nations. However in verse 33 he declares the nature of the covenant that he is going to make with 'the house of Israel'. What has happened to the 'house of Judah' previously mentioned in verse 31? Is this New Covenant with both or only one? In the previous chapter,

Jeremiah 30, God says that he will bring back both nations from captivity; *The word that came to Jeremiah from the LORD, saying, "Thus speaks the LORD God of Israel, saying: 'Write in a book for yourself all the words that I have spoken to you. For behold, the days are coming,' says the LORD, "that I will bring back from captivity My people Israel and Judah,' says the LORD. 'And I will cause them to return to the land that I gave to their fathers, and they shall possess it.'"* Jer 30:1-3 NKJV. So just who is it that will enter into this 'New Covenant' with God and be 'His people'? The house of Israel AND the house of Judah or just the house of Israel?

A forgotten miracle

We shall find the answer in a miracle. In Ezekiel 37 God commands the prophet, to take two separate sticks. On the first stick Ezekiel is to write the words; *For Judah and for the children of Israel, his companions.* Ezek 37:16. On the second stick he is to write the words; *For Joseph, the stick of Ephraim, and for all the house of Israel, his companions.* Ezek 37:16 NKJV. The northern kingdom is not only described in the Bible as 'the house of Israel' but also as 'Ephraim' and 'Joseph'. Its first king Jeroboam I was from the family tribe of Ephraim and Ephraim was its largest single clan, while Ephraim was the son of Joseph. It is also called 'Samaria' after the name of its capital city. So Ezekiel has two sticks, two separate sticks. Then he receives further instructions; *Then join them one to another for yourself into one stick, and they will become one in your hand. "And when the children of your people speak to you, saying, 'Will you not show us what you mean by these?'— say to them, "Thus says the Lord GOD: 'Surely I will take the stick of Joseph, which is in the hand of Ephraim, and the tribes of Israel, his companions; and I will join them with it, with the stick of Judah, and make them one stick, and they will be one in My hand."' And the sticks on which you write will be in your hand before their eyes.* Ezek 37:17-20 NKJV. A miracle would take place. In the hand of Ezekiel these two quite separate sticks would become one. I wonder if Ezekiel brought to mind a much older Bible verse? *Therefore a man shall leave his father and mother and be joined to his wife, and they shall become one flesh.* Gen 2:24 NKJV.

Just in case there was any doubt as to the significance of this miracle God spelled it out clearly for any who were puzzled by it all; *Thus says the Lord GOD: 'Surely I will take the children of Israel from among the nations, wherever they have gone, and will gather them from every side and bring them into their own land; and I will make them one nation in the land, on the mountains of Israel; and one king shall be king over them all; they shall no longer be two nations, nor shall they ever be divided into two kingdoms again.* Ezek 37:21-22 NKJV. God was going to re-unite the nation... *they will be one in My hand.* They would become one nation again under one king. It would no longer be 'the house of Israel' AND 'the house of Judah' but simply, as Jeremiah expressed it 'the house of Israel'. They would become a 'new Israel' as a result of a new thing, a New Covenant and a new heart. The two would be reconstituted as a single nation, a single entity. Covenants can do that! It was going to be a 'new creation'. God, who alone can bara-create, was committed to the project.

However, we do need to remind ourselves of the Isaiah factor. Is 10:21-22; 11:11, 16. This return would not be every single individual from the house of Israel and the house of Judah but a remnant from both houses. When the apparent outworking of these wonderful promises began to take place, it was indeed a remnant that returned, a tiny remnant. Out of an original population of 7 million less than 50,000 would return as a remnant but when the 'remnant' returned in the time of Ezra he calls it 'Israel' and records that 'all Israel' were back in their cities (Ezra 2:70) Slightly more than one half of one percent 'remained' to become the start of a new nation; the remnant was tiny but this remnant was enough and was now 'all Israel'.

We read of this promise to reunite the people under one king earlier in the prophecies of Ezekiel but this time the manner of expression is breathtaking; *therefore I will save My flock, and they shall no longer be a prey; and I will judge between sheep and sheep. I will establish one shepherd over them, and he shall feed them—My servant David. He shall feed them and be their shepherd. And I, the LORD, will be their God, and My servant David a prince among them; I, the LORD, have spoken.* Ezek 34:22-24 NKJV. Again we ought to remind ourselves that David had been dead and buried for almost 400 years when God gave Ezekiel this prophecy. Did it just mean some kind of return to the family of David, the Davidic dynasty, or did it mean that which was far beyond their comprehension at this time? The scene was being set for a fulfillment of these promises that would be more complete than anything they could imagine. Surely Christ had these words and colours in his mind some 500 years later when he declared himself to be 'the good shepherd'. *And other sheep I have which are not of this fold; them also I must bring, and they will hear My voice; and there will be one flock and one shepherd.* John 10:16 NKJV. He is consciously using the language/colours of Ezekiel. The New Covenant would reconstitute the separated peoples of Israel and Judah in a 'new Israel' and over that one flock 'David' would reign. But who are the 'other sheep' that will also find their place in this new setting and become part of the one flock? Now, can you keep a secret? ...so can God.

In this chapter we revisited the new thing, New Covenant, and new heart themes of the prophets who spoke of the restoration. We began to see that this is not just a reclamation or a salvage attempt but that out of this Assyrian/Babylonian exile something quite new would come to birth. We saw that a new Israel would be constituted with a different covenant and we saw that Christ had these prophecies in mind in some of his most famous New Testament sayings. We also asked, but did not answer, who Christ's 'other sheep' might be.

11: The Remnant Returns

The northern kingdom of Israel never returned from exile. A remnant of the southern kingdom returned some 70 years later and began the process of re-colonizing the land. During their exile they were encouraged with the prophecies that had promised a triumphant return. Unlike the escape from Egypt, the escape from Babylon was going to be one glorious step after another. This time they would not journey through a hostile wilderness but through a garden paradise until they reached their promised land. *I will bring the blind by a way they did not know; I will lead them in paths they have not known. I will make darkness light before them, And crooked places straight. These things I will do for them, And not forsake them.* Is 42:16 NKJV. It was a powerful prospect. The desert would blossom like a rose for them; *...Then shall the lame man leap as an hart, and the tongue of the dumb sing: for in the wilderness shall waters break out, and streams in* *the desert. And the parched ground shall become a pool... Is* 35:6-7 KJV

The once and future flock

Micah's pre-captivity promises had been just as breathtaking; *I will surely assemble all of you, O Jacob, I will surely gather the remnant of Israel; I will put them together like sheep of the fold, Like a flock in the midst of their pasture; They shall make a loud noise because of so many people.* Mic 2:12 NKJV. This, it appeared, was going to be a grand production that would put the original Exodus in the shade. In fact, other than that trickle that joined the house of Judah before the captivity, none of the house of Israel returned. How are we to understand these prophecies? Could there still be a future return of the vanished family tribes of the house of Israel? As I write these words we are 2500 years further down our timeline and extracting 'the house of Israel' from the nations of the world is going to pose some unique problems.

A remnant of the house of Judah did return. Their story is found in the books of Ezra and Nehemiah. Somewhere around 535 BC an upstart nobody toppled the mighty empire of Babylon; his name was Cyrus and he had been predicted by Isaiah 180 years earlier! An historian once wrote eloquently of Cyrus; "The tapestry of history has no point at which you can cut it and leave the design intelligible. Yet the sudden rise to Empire c.550 of Cyrus the prince of a petty Persian tribe is almost such a point. Herodotus saw the event as the turning point of all Greek history." Kingdoms tumbled one after another under Cyrus' conquering army and in the first year of his reign he began a policy of returning exiled peoples to their original homelands. His royal decree targeted the exiles of Judah and the book of Ezra includes a copy from the royal archive; *Now in the first year of Cyrus king of Persia, that the word of the LORD by the mouth of Jeremiah might be fulfilled, the LORD stirred up the spirit of Cyrus king of Persia, so that he made a proclamation throughout all his kingdom, and also put it in writing, saying, Thus says Cyrus king of Persia: All the kingdoms of the earth the LORD God of heaven has given me. And He has commanded me to build*

Him a house at Jerusalem which is in Judah. Ezra 1:1-3 NKJV. That wasn't the end of it, Cyrus returned much of the looted Temple treasure to the exiles, although some key pieces like the ark of the covenant were never retrieved.

Less than 50,000 people returned under the governorship of a prince of Judah named Zerubbabel or to give him his Persian name, Sheshbazzar. Part of this group is described as 'the whole congregation'; the Greek translation of the Bible used the word 'ekklesia', this was the recovered 'Church of Jehovah'. The new immigrants struggled to maintain their life and culture but they made the establishing of worship a priority and laid the foundations of a new temple. People's feelings were somewhat mixed; *But many of the priests and Levites and heads of the fathers' houses, old men who had seen the first temple, wept with a loud voice when the foundation of this temple was laid before their eyes. Yet many shouted aloud for joy,* Ezra 3:12 NKJV. Part of the reason for the sorrow of the older generation was that they remembered the glories of Solomon's temple and these foundations were on a much more modest scale. Perhaps the words of Micah were haunting them... *I will surely assemble all of you, O Jacob, I will surely gather the remnant of Israel; I will put them together like sheep of the fold, Like a flock in the midst of their pasture; They shall make a loud noise because of so many people.* Mic 2:12 NKJV.

Greater glory

The rebuilding of the temple dragged on and finally came to a stop. The reasons were many but one was sheer discouragement. God reached out to them again, rising up early and sending his messengers. His messengers on this occasion were the prophets Haggai and Zechariah. We need to remember how tenuous the covenant nation's grasp on destiny was at this time. They could so easily have become just another scrap of history, buried and forgotten, like so many before them. Haggai and Zechariah brought a series of encouraging prophecies and the people received the word of God enthusiastically; *Then Haggai, the LORD'S messenger, spoke the LORD'S message to the people, saying, "I am with* you, says the LORD." So the LORD stirred up the spirit of Zerubbabel the son of Shealtiel, governor of Judah, and the spirit of Joshua the son of Jehozadak, the high priest, and the spirit of all the remnant of the people; and they came and worked on the house of the LORD of hosts, their God, Hag 1:13-14 NKJV. For the besieged returnees it was just the word they needed and they set to again to complete the building of the Temple. These prophecies had the same soaring themes as much older prophecies; "According to the word that I covenanted with you when you came out of Egypt, so My Spirit remains among you; do not fear!' "For thus says the LORD of hosts: 'Once more (it is a little while) I will shake heaven and earth, the sea and dry land; and I will shake all nations, and they shall come to the Desire of All Nations, and I will fill this temple with glory,' says the LORD of hosts. "The silver is Mine, and the gold is Mine,' says the LORD of hosts. "The glory of this latter temple shall be greater than the former,' says the LORD of hosts. 'And in this place I will give peace,' says the LORD of hosts." Hag 2:5-9 NKJV. The link to 'when you came out of Egypt' continues the theme of the return from Babylonian captivity as another Exodus that we find in Jeremiah 31.

As they laboured to build their smaller, more modest sized temple, a prophecy is received which declared that the 'glory of this latter temple' would be 'greater than the former'. If that were not enough, Haggai's prophecies include some words for Zerubbabel the prince of Judah; Speak to Zerubbabel, governor of Judah, saying: "I will shake heaven and earth. I will overthrow the throne of kingdoms; I will destroy the strength of the Gentile kingdoms. I will overthrow the chariots And those who ride in them; The horses and their riders shall come down, Every one by the sword of his brother." "In that day," says the LORD of hosts, "I will take you, Zerubbabel My servant, the son of Shealtiel," says the LORD, "and will make you like a signet ring; for I have chosen you," says the LORD of hosts. Hag 2:21-23 NKJV. This sounds very much like the promise to restore the Davidic dynasty in the person of Zerubbabel. What amazing promises, the little temple would exceed Solomon's temple in glory and their struggling governor would become like a signet ring stamping God's will on the nations.

These prophecies were never fulfilled... or were they? Were these some of the promises of God that he withdrew because of the continued disobedience of his covenant people? Ezekiel prophesied that David would return to the throne, Haggai prophesies that Zerubbabel would rule the nations. What are we to make of these things? At this point sincere Christians divide. Some believe that these physical prophecies will be physically fulfilled at a future day and that there will yet be a physical throne in Jerusalem with the heir of David's dynasty sitting upon it, that is a future physical reign of Christ over this territory. Others see these physical prophecies lifting off into a realm of spiritual fulfilment. For the latter group they see the prophecies 'transposed' into a higher key, not just 'fulfilled' but 'over filled'. They see the promises of Haggai finding their fulfilment and overflowing fulfilment in Christ and the temple they see as his church; not the mixed multitude of modern day Christendom but the true 'New Covenant' people, a new Israel of God. Some others hold parts of both of these views at the same time believing in a spiritual fulfilment in the Church of Christ and a future physical fulfilment at some point in the future.

In our whistle-stop tour of Old Testament history that only leaves us with the book of Malachi. My own estimate for the dating of the book of Malachi is somewhere around 400 BC. The Second Temple had been rebuilt, sacrifices have been restarted... and the nation is reverting to type. Although they have not re-established primitive idol worship, their worship of God has become routine and superficial. The nation and its priests are 'going through the motions' but there is no heart in their worship and God has to make do with the leftovers of their lives. It begins with those words which we considered earlier; *"I have loved you," says the LORD. "Yet you say..."* Mal 1:2 NKJV. It is a phrase which captures the mood of an earlier complaint spoken by Isaiah and repeated by Paul; *But to Israel he says: "All day long I have stretched out My hands To a disobedient and contrary people."* Rom 10:21 NKJV. There were notable exceptions of course, men and women who served God with all their hearts, but in summary it expresses the temperament of the nation; disobedient and contrary.

The Messengers

There is an abundance of messengers in the book of Malachi. Malachi means 'my messenger'. His prophecy declares that the Levitical priesthood was intended to be God's messenger but had failed; *"For the lips of a priest should keep knowledge, And people should seek the law from his mouth; For he is the messenger of the LORD of hosts.* Mal 2:7 NKJV. They had received their sacred and 'everlasting' stewardship partly as a result of wholehearted service of God that allowed nothing, not even close family, to impede obedience to the will of God. They had been forbidden alcohol so as to keep their minds sharp and able to discern clearly in teaching and matters of judgment. They had been given no land so that they could concentrate on the unique service that they were to perform for God. Their privilege had been turned into license and their service of God had become a feeble chore. A modern Bible version captures one of the great groans from the heart of God; *"Oh that there were one among you who would shut the doors, that you might not kindle fire on my altar in vain! I have no pleasure in you, says the Lord of hosts, and I will not accept an offering from your hand."* Mal 1:10 ESV.

In the third chapter of Malachi we meet another messenger, in fact we meet two more messengers. The first is the promise of the man we know as John the Baptist; *Behold, I send My messenger, And he will prepare the way before Me.* Mal 3:1 NKJV. This was John's own testimony. When pressed as to just who he was and what role he was taking John made things very clear; *Then they said to him, "Who are you, that we may give an answer to those who sent us? What do you say about yourself?" He said: "I am The voice of one crying in the wilderness: 'Make straight the way of the LORD,' as the prophet Isaiah said."* John 1:22-23 NKJV. That was John's destiny. By descent he was one of the priestly family tribe, his father was a functioning priest. John, however took on the style of Elijah and brought a piece of audacious innovation to the days in which he lived; he preached repentance in preparation for the arrival of someone else and encouraged his hearers to start again with a baptism of repentance. The Jews of his day were not unfamiliar with baptism in water, it was part of the process of a non-Jew becoming a Jew. They patterned their practice on the account of one of the most famous proselytes of all, Naaman. John's innovation was that he was not baptising non-Jews into Judaism but baptising Jews as a sacrament of repentance and new beginning.

The coming of John Baptist fulfilled the last great promise of the Old Testament; *Behold, I will send you Elijah the prophet Before the coming of the great and dreadful day of the LORD. And he will turn The hearts of the fathers to the children, And the hearts of the children to their fathers, Lest I come and strike the earth with a curse."* Mal 4:5-6 NKJV. In many ways John really was the Sinai Covenant nation's last chance. Christ bore witness to John's faithful work when he told his enquirers that John had 'restored everything'; Then He answered and told them, *"Indeed, Elijah is coming first and restores all things. And how is it written concerning the Son of Man, that He must suffer many things and be treated with contempt?* Mark 9:12 NKJV. John Baptist's light is quickly outshone and we seldom do justice in our thinking to the work of this remarkable man. He was in many ways like an early morning glimpse of Venus, the morning star; his brilliance is disturbing but the brightness of the rising sun quickly causes it to vanish in greater brilliance. John knew that was his destiny and he had no complaints; *...this joy of mine is fulfilled. He must increase, but I must decrease. He who comes from above is above all...* John 3:29-31 NKJV.

In fact John is not the last messenger in the book of Malachi; there is one more. It is impossible to mistake who we are reading about because of the way in which it makes clear that the work of John was to prepare the way for this last messenger. He is described, wonderfully, by Malachi; *"And the Lord, whom you seek, Will suddenly come to His temple, Even the Messenger of the covenant, In whom you delight. Behold, He is coming,"* Says the LORD of hosts. Mal 3:1 NKJV. This is one of the titles of Christ that is often forgotten. John came to introduce another messenger, and that 'final' messenger came to introduce another covenant. The title was not forgotten in John Newton's great hymn, "Join all the glorious names..."; (in both Hebrew and Greek the original words can be translated 'messenger' or 'angel').

> Arrayed in mortal flesh
> This Covenant Angel stands,
> And holds the promises
> And pardons in His hands;
> Commissioned from His Father's throne
> To make His grace to mortals known.

The Covenant Angel/Messenger, of course, was none other than Christ himself.

So we have come to the end of the Old Testament with the promise of the last Sinai Covenant messenger who would serve as a herald to the one who would bring God's last word. This great Messenger of the Covenant was promised to come 'suddenly to His temple'. Was that Zerubbabel's temple? No, that temple was superseded by a much more glorious temple, a temple whose stones took away the breath of the disciples. But even Herod's temple was not the temple in mind when this promise was made. The temple that would be God's new residence was not going to be made with human hands as Stephen and Paul and Peter pointed out; this temple to which he would come would be a new residence and constructed of living stones; *Coming to Him as to a living stone, rejected indeed by men, but chosen by God and precious, you also, as living stones, are being built up a spiritual house, a holy priesthood, to offer up spiritual sacrifices acceptable to God through Jesus Christ.* 1 Pet 2:4-5 NKJV.

There are four hundred years of silence between the end of Malachi and the birth of Jesus in Bethlehem. For all that time the last lingering word was that God would send an Elijah. Four hundred years later a priest of the Levitical priestly family became a prophet and spoke these words over his son John about the man his son would serve; *Blessed is the Lord God of Israel, For He has visited and redeemed His people, And has raised up a horn of salvation for us In the house of His servant David, As He spoke by the mouth of His holy prophets, Who have been since the world began, That we should be saved from our enemies And from the hand of all who hate us, To perform the mercy promised to our fathers*

And to remember His holy covenant, The oath which He swore to our father Abraham: To grant us that we, Being delivered from the hand of our enemies, Might serve Him without fear, In holiness and righteousness before Him all the days of our life. Luke 1:68-75 NKJV. Certainly John would restore all things and prepare the covenant nation for the arrival of God's promise.

In this chapter we saw that the return of the exiles during the times of Ezra and Nehemiah does not do justice to the soaring prophecies that had been given. We saw that the prophecies of Haggai and Zechariah only had a token fulfilment in these days and we examined the 'last word' of the Old Testament, a promise that the LORD himself would come as the Messenger of the Covenant. We saw too that these 'last words' echoed in the hearts of the people for over 400 years before their fulfilment in Christ.

12: Final Preparations

As we pass from the Old Testament to the New Testament we soon find a unique time of preparation is under way. In all of the gospel accounts the work and life of John the Baptist is the focus of the earlier chapters. This extraordinary man was in many ways the culmination of the Old Covenant. He preached repentance and he warned those who listened of the dangers of relying on their perceived destiny. In some ways he was doing exactly what earlier prophets had done. Earlier prophets warned the covenant nation of the dangers of a complacent reliance on an inevitable destiny; *Do not trust in these lying words, saying, "The temple of the LORD, the temple of the LORD, the temple of the LORD are these."* Jer 7:4 NKJV. That is to say, don't put your trust in blank cheque promises. The promises of an 'everlasting' covenant with the priestly family of Levi and with the royal family of David had become a source of false comfort to them. John also strikes at this root; *Therefore bear fruits worthy of repentance, and do not begin to say to yourselves, "We have Abraham as our father.' For I say to you that God is able to raise up children to Abraham from these stones.* Luke 3:8 NKJV. It is hard now to imagine the impact of this radical message of John. The whole nation prided itself on its descent from Abraham and the whole nation was sure of its destiny simply because they were the children of Abraham. Being 'children of Abraham' was what made sense of their history and their future. Imagine then the effects of someone who arrives on the scene declaring that this is no longer of any significance! The amazing thing is that John's message received very wide acceptance and thousands submitted to his baptism of repentance. (Matt 3:5)

Baptism and the Kingdom of God

Let's take a brief detour. There had always been the possibility of non-Hebrews joining the covenant nation. This is often a surprise to Christian folk but many non-Jews did and do convert to Judaism. Orthodox Judaism allows this but insists on three criteria; circumcision, offering and baptism. Any male wishing to become a Jew must submit to physical circumcision, this marks him as a member of Abraham's household; this is based on the account of Abraham's own circumcision that included that of his physical descendants and male members of his household servants. (Gen 17:9-14) Traditionally the convert was also required to make an offering at the Temple but, since the destruction of the Temple, the spirit of this is usually carried out in a charitable gift. Finally the convert must be baptised, usually by self-baptism. Where did this idea of self-baptism originate? There are no specific instructions concerning these things in the Sinai Covenant. The answer is, it comes from the record of one of the most famous converts to Judaism, a Syrian field-marshall named Naaman. (2 Kings 5)

There is a specific reason why Naaman was often seen as the model for a convert. When he saw the power of God in his own personal healing he exclaimed; *"Indeed, now I know that there is no God in all the earth, except in Israel; now therefore, please take a gift from your servant."* 2Kings 5:15

NKJV. To the Jewish Rabbis this set Naaman, as a convert, even above Jethro the father-in-law of Moses. When Jethro saw the power of God in the deliverance of the nation he exclaimed; *"Now I know that the LORD is greater than all the gods; for in the very thing in which they behaved proudly, He was above them."* Ex 18:11 NKJV. For Jethro, Jehovah was the most powerful of all the gods, to Naaman he was the only god and all the others were fakes. Naaman clearly had a much more definite testimony and becomes the archetypal convert.

They also saw Naaman's self-dipping in the Jordan River as a parallel to the Israelites experience at the Red Sea and 40 years later at the river Jordan. When the Israelites crossed over the Jordan into their promised land they gathered in the land in a place called Gilgal and there all the males who had not been circumcised during the wilderness wanderings were circumcised. This was clearly a new beginning for the covenant people and provided a great model for people wishing to become part of the covenant people of God; circumcision and a 'baptism'. When the story of Naaman was translated from Hebrew into Greek some two centuries before Christ the translators used a key Greek word to express Naaman's self immersion, they used the word 'baptism'. Naaman baptised himself. This is the word 'baptizO' that we encountered back in Chapter 2.

When a convert undertook to take upon himself the yoke of the law and submitted to circumcision, offering and baptism he was regarded as a thorough member of the covenant nation. These converts were sometimes known as full proselytes. There were other proselytes who were attracted to Jewish morality and who only worshipped one God but these did not become part of the covenant people; Cornelius in the Acts was one of these. Cornelius was a devout man, who prayed and gave alms, but he had not submitted to circumcision, offering and baptism; he was still outside the covenant; a Gentile.

The Rabbis used extravagant language to describe the full converts who became part of the covenant nation. They borrowed part of the language from the account of Naaman. When Naaman submitted himself to self-baptism and 'baptised himself' seven times his leprous skin became as the skin of a child. He was, said the Rabbis, 'born again'. This 'baptismal regeneration' changed everything, it changed the laws of inheritance and some Rabbi's went so far as to say that technically he was so completely a new person that he could legally marry his own sister! They did not allow this in fact because of the impact that such an action would have on the testimony of Jewish morality, but technically he might!

Preaching revolution

Consider now the impact of John the Baptist preaching repentance and the coming of the King and insisting upon 'baptism'. What did it all mean? Did Jews who could trace their ancestry back to Abraham need to start all over again and be 'born again' just like a proselyte? Did their family history and connection to the original root mean nothing? John again uses very deliberate language in his preaching; *And even now the ax is laid to the root of the trees. Therefore every tree which does not bear good fruit is cut down and thrown into the fire.* Matt 3:10 NKJV. As a boy scout I learned to cut down trees and learned to take careful aim by 'laying the axe' to the point where I intended to strike. The danger of imminent severance from Abraham and his blessing was staring the nation in the face.

John's influence was very widespread; *Then Jerusalem, all Judea, and all the region around the Jordan went out to him and were baptized by him in the Jordan, confessing their sins.* Matt 3:5-6 NKJV. This is the context to the famous conversation between a leading Jewish Rabbi named Nicodemus and Jesus in the gospel according to John. Nicodemus begins his gentle probing with a word of acknowledgement as to the divine origin of Christ's mission, but Jesus 'cuts to the chase' and tells him that entrance into the Kingdom of God must be by a sovereign work of God's Spirit; to water baptism must be added Spirit baptism to ensure new birth. As regards the shadow and type Jewish ceremonies of baptism were not too far from the mark, but the reality to which the shadow bore testimony could only be accomplished by a birth that was of water and Spirit.

The religious leaders of the day hardly knew what to do about John. They objected to this 'unnamed' phenomena who had influenced the whole nation but did not dare oppose him publicly in case they lost the support of the ordinary people who regarded John as a prophet. You can hear their exasperation a little earlier in John's gospel; *And they asked him, "What then? Are you Elijah?" He said, "I am not." "Are you the Prophet?" And he answered, "No." Then they said to him, "Who are you, that we may give an answer to those who sent us? What do you say about yourself?"* John 1:21-22 NKJV. John had no doubt as to his mission, quoting the Old Testament prophet Isaiah he declared himself to be...*The voice of one crying in the wilderness: "Make straight the way of the LORD," as the prophet Isaiah said.* John 1:23 NLKV His quotation from Isaiah 40 is very significant; Isaiah is a book of two halves. The first half predicts terrible retributions which are about to fall upon the nations around Israel and upon Israel itself, but the second half, which begins at Chapter 40, is a brand new beginning for the remnant of the house of Israel and the house of Judah. John understands his mission in terms of the beginning of the restoration of the covenant people. If he had continued his quotation he would have said; Behold, *the Lord GOD shall come with a strong hand, And His arm shall rule for Him; Behold, His reward is with Him, And His work before Him. He will feed His flock like a shepherd; He will gather the lambs with His arm, And carry them in His bosom, And gently lead those who are with young.* Is 40:10-11 NKJV. We are back to the language of restoration and a single shepherd caring for a single flock. The artist is using those colours he prepared earlier on his palette.

John knew that his part was only the preparation. On another occasion he expressed this very plainly; *"Behold! The Lamb of God who takes away the sin of the world! This is He of whom I said, "After me comes a Man who is preferred before me, for He was before me.' I did not know Him; but that He should be revealed to Israel, therefore I came baptizing with water."* John 1:29-31 NKJV. That puts John's baptism into a clear perspective; his job was to clear the ground, and to set the stage for the arrival of the main act. Isaiah's language, in Isaiah 40, describes the way in which ancient kings would make their triumphal entrance into conquered territories. On occasion they would literally fill in the valleys, flatten the hills and straighten the roads so that the people could get a clear uninterrupted view of the coming king. This was John's work, destruction and construction in preparation for the arrival of the king. It was vital that the one who would be the world's Sin Bearer should be clearly seen. Later this same gospel describes Christ's death in terms of another ancient story when the covenant nation was in danger of imminent annihilation and the remedy was to get a clear view of a bronze snake on a pole. (John 3:14-19. Num 21) John must remove every distraction, every impediment so that when the Remedy arrived they could get a saving view.

To appreciate John's work we can turn to the words of Christ as he later explained John's role; *And they asked Him, saying, "Why do the scribes say that Elijah must come first?" Then He answered and told them, "Indeed, Elijah is coming first and restores all things.* Mark 9:11-12 NKJV. The 'Elijah' that he had in mind, of course, was the 'Elijah' that Malachi had promised. That was the man who was to prepare the way for the coming of 'the Messenger of the Covenant'; that Elijah was John the Baptist.

The messenger of the covenant

Before we look at the life of Christ in the gospel account let's take a moment to consider this title that Malachi gives prophetically to Jesus Christ. If we read the preceding verses we can see the link to John Baptist's essential work of preparation; *"Behold, I send My messenger, And he will prepare the way before Me. And the Lord, whom you seek, Will suddenly come to His temple, Even the Messenger of the covenant, In whom you delight. Behold, He is coming," Says the LORD of hosts.* Mal 3:1 NKJV. This puts the ministry of John Baptist and that of Christ into a very specific relationship. The 'My Messenger' of this verse is John Baptist, but the 'Messenger of the Covenant' is Christ himself. In what sense is Christ a messenger? Again we can see this theme unfolding in John's gospel.

One of the themes of John's writings in his gospel, epistles and the Revelation is the theme of the witness. The first eight verses of the gospel introduce two men and both are witnesses. The pattern is instructive. John begins with a revelation as to the nature of eternal godhead in which he refers to the Word of God. He is referring to a person when he used this phrase at this point. What is a word? Well it is a means of communication. The words you are reading here are designed to give you an insight into the way I am thinking. They are a means of expression. My imperfect thoughts are being expressed in imperfect words in order to communicate ideas. In Jesus Christ we meet God perfectly expressed in a language that is designed to perfectly communicate God himself to people who are not god. The Word, says John, became flesh. Flesh or human-ness is the language in which the Word has expressed himself so that human beings could know what God is really like.

John, the gospel-writer, says that the Word always existed and that the Word was always with God and that the Word was God. John's gospel helps us to distinguish the persons without separating them. John then speaks of the creation and says the Word was the agent in creation. God 'spoke' the creation. The Word created everything. Everything that exists, exists partly to communicate some truth about God to us. He is, says John, the source of Life and that life has shone on human beings. He is talking, of course primarily, about the incarnation, God becoming Man. In a single sentence he then describes the career of the Word, this is the English Standard Version rendering; *The light shines in the darkness, and the darkness has not overcome it.* John 1:5 ESV. We should notice the tenses, we might paraphrase that as "the light continues to shine in the darkness and the darkness did not overcome it". The Word then is the source of Life and that Life was the light or the way that God has illumined our race. That Light continues to illumine our race even though at a point of time our race tried to extinguish it. The revelation of who God is can be seen, in its fullness, only in Jesus Christ.

Then John the gospel-writer introduces John the Baptist and describes John's mission; *There was a man sent from God, whose name was John. This man came for a witness, to bear witness of the Light, that all through him might believe. He was not that Light, but was sent to bear witness of that Light.* John 1:6-8 NKJV. First of all we must see a clear separation between these two men; John was not that Light. So who was he and what was his mission? His mission was to act as a witness. He came, says John's gospel, for the purpose of 'witness' and specifically to bear witness to that Light. In the familiar Old English style of our Bibles John's real work was to say 'Behold' - 'Look'. John's task was to turn the eyes of all who heard him away from John himself and onto the person of Jesus Christ. John Baptist is only fulfilled when his converts leave him and follow Christ. This alone gave him joy. "He must increase and I must decrease" was his life's motto.

Jesus Christ was the Word made human and was the true, or real, Light coming into the world to illumine the whole race so that no one would remain in darkness as to what God was really like. Jesus Christ as the incarnate Word of God is the real witness; John is just a witness *to* the witness, John's real message is 'the messenger is coming', the true messenger. Many years after John's ministry the writer to the Hebrews gave his own explanation of what was happening; *God, who at various times and in various ways spoke in time past to the fathers by the prophets, has in these last days spoken to us by His Son,* Heb 1:1-2 NKJV. Jesus Christ is God's Last Word to our race; he is the final Witness, the Ultimate Messenger. We will discuss this later in Appendix 1 but it will be important to understand that the purpose of John Baptist's ministry and of every authentic messenger since that time is to get people to listen to the Messenger. Ultimately it is not our response to the Message but our response to the Messenger that will determine our personal destiny.

Did you get my message?

Who were the people best placed to recognise the voice of the Messenger? Well, the people of the covenant. They had been prepared over hundreds of years to respond to the Messenger. God had blessed them with many earthly blessings, land, priesthood, covenants, promises, the service of God but Paul was in no doubt as to the covenant nation's greatest blessing; *What advantage then has the Jew, or what is the profit of circumcision? Much in every way! Chiefly because to them were committed the oracles of God.* Rom 3:1-2 NKJV. An oracle was a place where pagans believed they would hear the voice of God. Israel's greatest treasure was the archive of God's spoken word to them. As they read these holy Scriptures and obeyed them their minds would be prepared to recognise 'God's accent' or to use our old analogy, they would recognize the old colours and make the connections. This is Israel's supreme tragedy described in the words that follow in John's gospel; *That was the true Light which gives light to every man coming into the world. He was in the world, and the world was made through Him, and the world did not know Him. He came to His own, and His own did not receive Him.* John 1:9-11 NKJV. This latter part of this passage has an implication that is difficult to convey in an English translation, we could translate it "he came to his own place and his own people did not receive him'.

In what way did they 'not receive him'? They did not receive his testimony; they rejected both the Message and the Messenger. They heard him using accents that ought to have awoken powerful national memories that in turn would have brought them to genuine repentance and faith. Initially some 'heard him gladly' but, as time went by and the message became plainer, they rejected 'Him' and because they rejected the Messenger their ears were deaf to the message. Not all of them, of course, there were exceptions to the general pattern of things. Some did 'receive him'. This is language that is frequently used to describe personal faith in Christ as it is expressed in a moment of decision to follow Christ but originally it has to do with people's response to the Messenger. (See Appendix 1, Receiving Christ)

Do people still have that responsibility of responding to the Messenger? Yes they do and their destiny will depend upon their response to the Messenger. The Messenger may speak today through a preacher or a Bible verse or by any means he chooses, but it is not my response to the human messenger that is most important but my response to the Messenger. The Light is still shining, Christ is still bearing witness. It is our response to him as a person and not our response to a theology that changes our destiny. Listen to the way Paul spoke in the letter to the Ephesians; *But you have not so learned Christ, if indeed you have heard Him and have been taught by Him, as the truth is in Jesus:* Eph 4:20-21 NKJV. Paul believed that men and women were still able to 'learn Christ' by 'hearing him and being taught by him'. This letter was written over thirty years after Christ had returned to heaven and His father's side, but Paul still expected men and women to 'hear' him and 'be taught by him'. He is still the Messenger of the Covenant.

If we read John's comments carefully we discover that those famous verses at the beginning of his gospel are not really speaking about an evangelistic meeting or a counselling room. They are recounting history. The historical fact is that 'most' rejected him, but 'to those who received him' a new potential opened up, to those who received him, to those he gave the right to become the children of God. It was true then and it is true now that those who receive his witness, to those who receive him as God's Messenger, to those he holds out the prospect of a new birth and a new destiny.

In this chapter we passed from the Old Testament to the New and saw how John Baptist set about clearing away any debris that might obstruct our view of Jesus Christ. We saw that the language of 'new birth' was not foreign to the people who first heard it but that Christ made it clear that no ceremonial rite, on its own, can achieve new birth. The earthly response of water baptism is entirely appropriate but without Spirit baptism it is incomplete. We also saw the importance of personal response to the Messenger of the Covenant who even today still 'teaches' those who will receive his testimony.

13: The King has come

One day John Baptist received an unexpected candidate for his baptism, Jesus of Nazareth. Unexpected because John's was a baptism of repentance and this candidate had nothing of which he needed to repent. John protested and was told that it was appropriate to fulfil a righteous requirement by this action. John's protest is significant and we shall need to return to it later, but his main objection was that far from Jesus being an appropriate candidate for John's baptism, John himself was a ready candidate for Jesus' baptism; *And John tried to prevent Him, saying, "I need to be baptized by You, and are You coming to me?"* Matt 3:14 NKJV.

Baptists and their baptisms.

What did Christ mean when he said 'this will fulfil a righteous requirement'? Baptism is a symbol of death and new beginning. In John's baptism it was a symbol of death to an old way of life and a new beginning. Christ took the symbolism of John's baptism but used it as a means of public acknowledgment that his own mission would bring a new beginning but only through a death. It was his public acceptance of the work he had come to do. The life and words of Jesus are a wonderful testimony to the fact that he was God's authentic messenger and that the Father was endorsing his words with signs and wonders. His teaching was thrilling and disturbing. His standards went deeper than the external obedience to the Sinai Covenant to an insistence that it was the inward response to God's will that was required. In this his standards were far more exacting that the 'do-s and don't-s' of Moses, but his real commission was to 'pay the price' by his own death and in his baptism by John he publicly embraces that mission.

John had waited for this meeting but when it came it took him by surprise. He claimed that he 'had not known him'. In fact, on the human, side John was related to Jesus of Nazareth and it would be surprising if they had never spent some time in each other's company, but in terms of his true identity John was being quite truthful when he said he had not known him. John had been given a sign by which he would recognise the coming king but in the meantime he continued his work of preparation. The sign that John had been given was very clear; *I did not know Him, but He who sent me to baptize with water said to me, "Upon whom you see the Spirit descending, and remaining on Him, this is He who baptizes with the Holy Spirit.' And I have seen and testified that this is the Son of God."* John 1:33-34 NKJV. This moment of the Spirit of God descending and resting upon the person of Jesus of Nazareth is highly significant and is recorded by all four gospel writers. Luke's account says the Holy Spirit descended in bodily form like a dove. And... a voice was heard publicly acknowledging that the one upon whom the Spirit had settled was none other than God's own beloved Son.

Much later when Peter recounted this event he used another image; *...God anointed Jesus of Nazareth with the Holy Spirit and with power, who went about doing good and healing all who were oppressed by the devil, for God was with Him.* Acts 10:38 NKJV. It was an anointing. The pouring of oil upon the head of significant people was part of the history of the covenant community. They had anointed priests, prophets and kings. It was symbolic of God's approval and empowering and identified those who were anointed as set apart for unique service under God's specific authority. These anointings did not change a man's character, they simply acknowledged that this was a man under authority, God's authority. It is important to distinguish between the picture of anointing and the picture of baptism. Some have identified this moment as the time when Jesus was 'baptised in the Holy Spirit' but the Scripture never refers to this event as a 'baptism in the Holy Spirit' and to fail to distinguish between a baptism and an anointing will cause inevitable confusion. The Hebrew word for an 'anointed one' is Messiah, and the Greek equivalent is Christ. At this moment Jesus of Nazareth stepped publicly into the role for which he had come to earth; the long awaited Messiah, Jesus the Christ.

Up until this moment Jesus of Nazareth had led an exemplary life and had lived in relative obscurity in the Galilee town of Nazareth working in the family carpentry business. He had spoken no word as God's messenger nor performed any authenticating miracles. He had lived out his life for some 30 years under God's scrutiny and had developed through the normal stages of life and in intellectual and spiritual measure too; *And Jesus increased in wisdom and stature, and in favor with God and men.* Luke 2:52 NKJV. No doubt his personal piety and behaviour set him apart but there were no other signs of the destiny that awaited him; not until the Holy Spirit anointing. So was he anointed as a prophet, a priest or a king? In some measure as all of these, although the full revelation of some of these roles was some year's away. However, it is in the words spoken at his water baptism and Spirit anointing that we find our real answers.

Servant and Son

As he emerged from the waters of the Jordan and stood praying, heaven was opened and the Holy Spirit descended upon him in bodily form like a dove. This is Luke's description of the event, to which he adds the words; and a voice came from heaven which said, *"You are My beloved Son; in You I am well pleased."* Luke 3:22 NKJV. This is a short message from heaven but its inference is very great. In the messages of those prophet-servants that God 'got up early and sent' there were many themes and some of them apparently contradictory. Sometimes they spoke of suffering and pain and sometimes of great glory. They are like two different coloured threads in an elaborate embroidered tapestry. We might call them the 'red thread' for the passages that spoke of suffering and pain, and the 'purple thread' for those that spoke of kingship and glory. Naturally the people of Israel preferred to dwell on the purple passages.

The red passages were complex. Sometimes the prediction of suffering seemed to be as a punishment and sometimes as a necessary preparation. In some of the passages in Isaiah the prophet continued to speak of the destiny of the covenant people and described them as both Jehovah's Servants and Jehovah's Witnesses; *"You are My witnesses," says the LORD, "And My servant whom I have chosen, That you may know and believe Me, And understand that I am He. Before Me there was no God formed, Nor shall there be after Me."* Is 43:10 NKJV. That seems to be clear enough but as those prophecies continue the idea of a nation which is God's Witness and God's Servant begins to morph into the idea of a single person who would become God's Witness and God's Servant. In an earlier passage we read; *"Behold! My Servant whom I uphold, My Elect One in whom My soul delights! I have put My Spirit upon Him; He will bring forth justice to the Gentiles.* Is 42:1 NKJV. Now who is in focus here? The covenant nation or an individual? When Jesus first spoke publicly, after his Jordan baptism and Spirit anointing, it was in a synagogue in his home town of Nazareth and at that time he boldly claimed that in himself there was now a fulfilment of the ancient prophecies of Isaiah; *"The Spirit of the LORD is upon Me, Because He has anointed Me To preach the gospel to the poor; He has sent Me to heal the brokenhearted, To proclaim liberty to the captives And recovery of sight to the blind, To set at liberty those who are oppressed; To proclaim the acceptable year of the LORD."* Luke 4:18-19 NKJV. In his own mind there was no doubt. He himself was the long awaited 'anointed one'; the Servant of Jehovah, Jehovah's True Witness, and he had come to fulfil God's ancient purpose. (See Appendix 2. Jesus the Witness)

But the observant reader may have noted that the voice from heaven switched a word. Instead of referring to the anointed one as a 'servant' that heavenly voice identified him as the 'beloved Son'. That single sentence brings together the red and purple threads. The red thread of suffering will be fulfilled in the destiny of the suffering servant of Jehovah, but the purple thread of majesty and glory is included in the switch to the word 'Son'. Another ancient prophecy would find its fulfilment in the man who had emerged from the waters of his baptism; *The kings of the earth set themselves, And the rulers take counsel together, Against the LORD and against His Anointed... "Yet I have set My King on My holy hill of Zion... I will declare the decree: The LORD has said to Me, 'You are My Son...* Psa 2:2,6-7 NKJV. The words heard on Jordan's riverbank were God's confirmation that the one upon whom the Spirit had come to rest was the one who had come to fulfil the will of God as the Servant/Witness of Jehovah and that he was, in truth, not just another servant or witness but none other than God's own Son.

The times are changing

This event marks a change in relationship. It was customary in ancient cultures for the king to publicly display his heir and from this moment we can discern a change in Christ's relationship to Mary. Luke tells an earlier story of Jesus' visit to the Temple in Jerusalem when he was around 12 years of age. He lingered in the Temple courts and amazed the learned Rabbi's with his questions and answers but the time had not come for him to be publicly displayed as the Son of God so he returned, submissively, to his hidden life in Nazareth. Mary and Joseph had much less understanding of 'his Father's business' than the teenage Jesus but the record continues; *Then He went down with them and came to Nazareth, and was subject to them, but His mother kept all these things in her heart.* Luke 2:51 NKJV. He was greater and wiser than they but he returned to Nazareth as a dutiful son.

However, from the day of his public acknowledgment as the 'Son of God' at the Jordan he will never again be 'subject' to his mother; now his time has come to be 'about his Father's business'. It is a pattern that is continued in those who become sons by genuine regeneration; *For as many as are led by the Spirit of God, these are sons of God.* Rom 8:14 NKJV. They become those who are 'taught by God' and the purpose is to please him alone.

As a Son, the Spirit led him... right into the teeth of a fierce battle; *Then Jesus was led up by the Spirit into the wilderness to be tempted by the devil.* Matt 4:1 NKJV. It was his sonship that was put to the test in the wilderness. He has received heaven's witness, God's Spirit bearing witness with his own spirit, that he was the Son of God, but now that revelation will be sorely tried. These stories are well known to us but we can pause just to note how specifically the first temptation targeted what that voice had spoken by the Jordan; *Now when the tempter came to Him, he said, "If You are the Son of God, command that these stones become bread." But He answered and said, "It is written, 'Man shall not live by bread alone, but by every word that proceeds from the mouth of God.' "* Matt 4:3-4 NKJV. His answer is also very significant. He had been challenged to prove a point by behaving like the 'Son of God', but he refused the temptation determining instead that he would live as a 'man' dependent upon what he heard his Father saying to him. This would be his pattern for the rest of his earthly ministry; *I can of Myself do nothing. As I hear, I judge; and My judgment is righteous, because I do not seek My own will but the will of the Father who sent Me.* John 5:30 NKJV.

His words were wonderful and so were his mighty acts but there is something even more wonderful that John draws attention to in his gospel. In that first chapter when he has introduced the Word who became human, he adds this comment; *And the Word became flesh, and dwelt among us (and we have contemplated his glory, a glory as of an only-begotten with a father), full of grace and truth;* John 1:14 DARBY. That translation expresses a truth we shall find throughout the whole of John's gospel. The glory that Christ displayed and which so amazed the witnesses was that he behaved like 'an only son *with* a father'. His words and miracles were wonderful but what gripped John was Christ's relationship with his Father. It is this relationship that is one of the great themes of John's gospel. When John later wrote his letters he recalls the impact that the life of Christ had upon him, and 60 years after the event we can still feel that impact. John never 'recovered' from what he saw; *That which was from the beginning, which we have heard, which we have seen with our eyes, which we have looked upon, and our hands have handled, concerning the Word of life— the life was manifested, and we have seen, and bear witness, and declare to you that eternal life which was with the Father and was manifested to us—* 1 John 1:1-2 NKJV. John had seen a revelation of eternal life in a human being and there is an interesting partial definition of eternal life in one of the prayers that John records; *And this is eternal life, that they may know You, the only true God, and Jesus Christ whom You have sent.* John 17:3 NKJV. Eternal life, prayed the Son of God, is a relationship with God.

The New Covenant appears

Why are we pursuing this line? Let's remind ourselves of the way that Jeremiah described the New Covenant; *I will put My law in their minds, and write it on their hearts; and I will be their God, and they shall be My people. No more shall every man teach his neighbour, and every man his brother, saying, "Know the LORD,' for they all shall know Me, from the least of them to the greatest of them, says the LORD.* Jer 31:33-34 NKJV. This is not the whole of the prophecy but it will suffice to make the point. Did you ever know anyone who lived like this, I mean consistently, all the time? Did you ever know anyone who had God's will written in his heart and mind? Anyone who never betrayed that relationship? Anyone who really 'knew the Lord'? I only know one person in whom the New Covenant found its perfect expression, Jesus Christ. Let's do the same with the prophecy of Ezekiel: *I will give you a new heart and put a new spirit within you; I will take the heart of stone out of your flesh and give you a heart of flesh. I will put My Spirit within you and cause you to walk in My statutes, and you will keep My judgments and do them. Then you shall dwell in the land that I gave to your fathers; you shall be My people, and I will be your God.* Ezek 36:26-28 NKJV. Again this in not the whole passage but again we can ask our questions. Did you ever know anyone who was perfectly, caused to walk in God's statutes? Anyone who kept all his judgment faithfully? Yes, we do know someone who lived this kind of life. John the gospel-writer had seen this kind of life and he never forgot it.

Jesus Christ is a human embodiment of the New Covenant. In him the perfect relationship between God and man is perfectly maintained. This is the life that was lived, not far away in heaven, but here on earth in the person of Jesus Christ. This is the life that John witnessed. As a demonstration of life it is glorious but if that is all it is it must leave me in hopeless discouragement. Is it possible for the life that was in Christ to be communicated to other human beings so that they could begin to become partakers of it? There is an old phrase which God had given to the covenant people; yet another colour for the palette. He was preparing their minds for an idea that would be truly astonishing. When he spoke of death or sacrifice he used the phrase 'the life is in the blood'. The value of the blood is the value of the life. What was the value of Christ's life? It was in his blood and his life was another definition of the New Covenant. Listen again to his words in the upper room shortly before that life was poured out in blood; *Likewise He also took the cup after supper, saying, "This cup is the New Covenant in My blood, which is shed for you.* Luke 22:20 NKJV. The New Covenant was in his blood, in his life. His life was the display of a relationship between a Father and a Son and the value of that life would be poured out in death.

Was Calvary just a demonstration of God's love or was it an essential step in the miracle of bringing a New Covenant within the reach of ordinary men and women? How does a man or a woman gain access to this covenant? The only way possible for this to be achieved would be for that same life to be reproduced on the inside and Christ made it plain how we might access that life; *Then Jesus said to them, "Most assuredly, I say to you, unless you eat the flesh of the Son of Man and drink His blood, you have no life in you. Whoever eats My flesh and drinks My blood has eternal life, and I will raise him up at the last day. For My flesh is food indeed, and My blood is drink indeed. He who eats My flesh and drinks My blood abides in Me, and I in him.* John 6:53-56 NKJV. What I eat and drink becomes part of me. To eat the flesh and to drink the blood is Bible language for receiving the life. The salvation that God had planned is not to be gained by the imitation of Christ's life but by imbibing it. The life that was poured out is the life that is now poured in. The New Covenant that was 'in his blood' becomes my own as I receive his life into my inner man. The emblems have no power to impart life; it is the Spirit that brings life. (John 6:63)

In this chapter we saw how Jesus of Nazareth publicly embraced the commission of Messiah, a commission that included the giving up of his own life in the pouring out of his blood. We distinguished between the Bible pictures of 'anointing' and 'baptism' and showed that at the river Jordan Christ was 'anointed' with the Holy Spirit. We also saw that in the Bible idiom shed blood represents the value of the life and we introduced the idea that Christ's life, in its relationship with his Father, is the price that was paid to achieve redemption. We saw that in the terms used by Jeremiah and Ezekiel Christ was an embodiment of the New Covenant and that this life was in his blood. Finally we began to explore how this New Covenant that he lived out might be communicated to others.

14: Heaven touching earth

The King had come, the Light had shined, but in the main, the Messenger of the Covenant had not been received. In the way that a country might refuse to receive or recognise an ambassador from another country so, in the main, the covenant people refused to recognise his role and authority.

A true temple

At the beginning of his public ministry John the gospel-writer records that Christ visited the Temple in Jerusalem during the time of the Passover. He discovered that the court of the Gentiles had been wholly given over to a market and the scene was one of bellowing oxen and bleating sheep. The officials who changed foreign currencies into temple currency had set up their stalls and the whole atmosphere was of a bustling oriental bazaar, and this in the area that had been set apart for Gentiles who were seeking to worship the God of

Israel. Some have seen this as an outburst of rage and consequently sin but it was not uncontrollable rage but deliberate action. He took the time to fashion a small whip with which to herd the animals and then went into action. His war-cry was "This is my Father's House". He drove out those who had turned the house into a market and later when they considered these things the disciples remembered an ancient Psalm which seemed to explain it all; *I have become a stranger to my brothers, And an alien to my mother's children; Because zeal for Your house has eaten me up, And the reproaches of those who reproach You have fallen on me.* Psa 69:8-9 NKJV. He had been aroused to this action out of a sense of the disgrace that was being brought upon His Father by the behaviour of the covenant people.

When the authorities protested at his own behaviour and demanded some evidence of his right to do such a thing he replied that the sign of his authority would be his resurrection, but not nearly so plainly as that; Jesus answered and said to them, *"Destroy this temple, and in three days I will raise it up." Then the Jews said, "It has taken forty-six years to build this temple, and will You raise it up in three days?" But He was speaking of the temple of His body.* John 2:19-21 NKJV. He knew that initially his words would be misunderstood by everyone who heard them but he took the opportunity of sowing a seed in the minds of those who would later witness his resurrection. We are so familiar with these words and John's explanation of them that we easily miss the significance of the fact that Christ was regarding himself as a Temple, and temples in Jewish history were the 'residence of God'.

It is a theme that begins earlier in John's record. A devout Israelite had become convinced of the identity of Jesus of Nazareth and expressed his conviction in a remarkable confession; *Nathanael answered and said to Him, "Rabbi, You are the Son of God! You are the King of Israel!"* John 1:49 NKJV. These two titles are impressive in themselves. Nathaniel saw clearly who he was and what he had come to do. To these amazing revelations Jesus added another; *And He said to him, "Most assuredly, I say to you, hereafter you shall see heaven open, and the angels of God ascending and descending upon the Son of Man."* John 1:51 NKJV. Perhaps that is a little obscure until we realise the story that Jesus had in mind when he said it. In the very beginnings of God's dealings with Abraham, Isaac, and Jacob, God revealed himself to these men, spoke to them and entered into personal covenants with them. At one point God revealed himself to Jacob in a dream. The dream terrified Jacob. He saw a connection between heaven and earth with free access to and fro. He saw a place where heaven touched earth and where the free intercourse between the two was expressed in a powerful image; *Then he dreamed, and behold, a ladder was set up on the earth, and its top reached to heaven; and there the angels of God were ascending and descending on it.* Gen 28:12. Jacob's terror was caused by the sense that he had fallen asleep on God's doorstep and the record states; *Then Jacob awoke from his sleep and said, "Surely the LORD is in this place, and I did not know it." And he was afraid and said, "How awesome is this place! This is none other than the house of God, and this is the gate of heaven!"* Gen 28:16-17 NKJV. We see here a combining of ideas, the house of God is marked by the presence of angels ascending and descending upon it.

Nathaniel was a devout Israelite and these words of Jesus would have spoken to him much more clearly than they might speak to us today. Christ was saying 'I am the house of God.' I am the place where God has chosen to take up residence. I am not only the Messiah of your expectations, I am the access point to heaven itself'; I am the 'heaven-gate'.

A house for God

The four gospel accounts and particularly John's record have many layers of truth running through them. John's account has been called 'Love's Remembrance of Love's Story'. This account was written after some 60 years of loving meditation and every sentence is pregnant with deeper significances. This is not a biography in the usual sense of that word, but a devotional in which the reader is invited to pause and contemplate the lasting significance of what may have seemed, initially, to be just passing events. Let's look backwards over our shoulder for a moment.

The covenant people of Israel were chosen to be a kingdom of priests for God, a set-apart nation with a unique destiny. When the nation had confirmed their willingness to embrace the Sinai Covenant God began to open out to them a larger plan, God was going to take up residence among them. In their desert wanderings and for some 300 to 400 years after that 'God's Residence' was a simple shrine. Simple, that is, to outwards appearance. On the inside it was a revelation of gold and silver and glory. The tabernacle or tent that was known as the Holy Place was created by a framework of gold-plated wooden frames. (It is almost certain that these were not solid planks of gold-plated wood but more in the style of window frames.) When this framework was erected the splendid first covering was draped over the frame. That first covering was elaborately embroidered with the forms of cherubim, angelic beings who are God's personal attendants. The result was that for the priests who were allowed into this Holy Place, which was the antechamber to the throne room, it was a vision in gold and silver and blue and red and purple of a room surrounded by angels. Every wall was filled with angels, and if they looked upwards they would see the same serried ranks of angelic hosts. Looking towards the wall and the ceiling would have given the impression of countless angelic beings. This was God's residence and the angels of God were 'ascending and descending' upon it.

During the reign of Solomon this portable palace was transformed into a magnificent palace for the King, God himself. It was David who had received the revelation and who became the architect for this wonder of the world and David's feelings about it are very plain; *the house to be built for the LORD must be exceedingly magnificent, famous and glorious throughout all countries.* 1Chr 22:5 NKJV. It is interesting to see that David was not only thinking about the covenant people when he designed the Temple that Solomon built. There is a little cameo of the way this magnificent building might have worked in the story of the Queen of Sheba. She had heard rumours of the greatness of Solomon and his kingdom and she abandoned her kingdom for a pilgrimage to Jerusalem. Solomon answered her questions about the God of Israel but it was what she saw that, literally as the record runs, took her breath away; *And when the queen of Sheba had seen the wisdom of Solomon, and the house that he had built... there was no more spirit (breath) in her.* 2 Chr 9:2-5 NKJV.

That Temple was made of wood and stone, but the symbolism of the old Tabernacle was faithfully reproduced; *Then he carved all the walls of the temple all around, both the inner and outer sanctuaries, with carved figures of cherubim, palm trees, and open flowers.* 1 Kings 6:29 NKJV. The priests who entered into the Holy Place were still surrounded by cherubim, the angels of God 'ascending and descending'.

Almost a thousand years later Herod launched on an elaborate and expensive building programme. He built magnificent mini-Romes like Caesarea on the Mediterranean, and he rebuilt the Temple to replace the smaller building that had been constructed during the time of Zerubbabel, Haggai and Zechariah. It was a magnificent building and might even have been considered one of the wonders of the world but it was never occupied, not by God. Zerubbabel's temple had never been occupied by God either. The essential missing feature that never returned from the Babylonian exile was the Ark of the Covenant, God's throne. When the original Tabernacle was erected God took up residence in such splendour and glory that even the priests were not able to minister there. The same thing happened when Solomon's Temple was built; God took up residence in such splendour and glory that again the priests were unable to go about their ordinary work. But of Zerubbabel's and Herod's Temples there is no such record. They both remained like empty palaces awaiting the arrival of the King. The centuries passed and still the covenant people waited for the fulfilment of the prophecies; *"Behold, I send My messenger, And he will prepare the way before Me. And the Lord, whom you seek, Will suddenly come to His temple, Even the Messenger of the covenant, In whom you delight. Behold, He is coming,"* Says the LORD of hosts. Mal 3:1 NKJV.

Then in private conversation with Nathaniel and in public confrontation with the religious leaders Jesus of Nazareth, plainly declared himself to be not only the Christ, but also the place of God's residence. In him they would see, if they would allow him to open their eyes, the splendour and the glory of Immanuel; this was God himself now 'with them'.

An abandoned house

The better part of three years of public ministry followed and in the last days of his earthly life he returned to the Temple in Jerusalem and found that it had simply slipped back into its old ways. In spite of his 'cleansing' everything had reverted to its original condition and the Court of the Gentiles was once again a bellowing, bleating, market. Earlier that day he had viewed the city of Jerusalem and wept over it, sorrowing most of all because they had not known the day of God's visitation. (Luke 19:44)

When he entered the Temple and found that they had gone back to their old ways, he repeated his action and drove out the market traders. This time his war-cry was different; *saying to them, "It is written, "My house is a house of prayer,' but you have made it a 'den of thieves.' "* Luke 19:46 NKJV. It is a quotation that combines the words of two prophets, Isaiah and Jeremiah... *Even them I will bring to My holy mountain, And make them joyful in My house of prayer. Their burnt offerings and their sacrifices Will be accepted on My altar; For My house shall be called a house of prayer for all nations."* Is 56:7 NKJV. *Has this house, which is called by My name, become a den of thieves in your eyes? Behold, I, even I, have seen it," says the LORD.* Jer 7:11 NKJV. The Jeremiah quotation is particularly ominous, it was first declared some 10 years before Solomon's beautiful Temple was sacked and burned to the ground. There is a saying that says that history repeats itself because no one listens the first time!

On this second occasion of cleansing Christ refers to the Temple as *'My* house'. Later he will go on to predict the destruction of Herod's masterpiece in which not one stone of the Temple itself would be left standing on another. But in the order of Matthew's gospel before he pronounced the death sentence for Herod's Temple he said something much more chilling; *"O Jerusalem, Jerusalem, the one who kills the prophets and stones those who are sent to her! How often I wanted to gather your children together, as a hen gathers her chicks under her wings, but you were not willing! See! Your house is left to you desolate; for I say to you, you shall see Me no more till you say, "Blessed is He who comes in the name of the LORD!" "* Matt 23:37-39 NKJV. "My Father's House", "My House", but now "Your House"... he has disowned it. It fitted the pattern of an earlier parable in which the tenants had said; *"This is the heir. Come, let us kill him, that the inheritance may be ours.'* Luke 20:14 NKJV. The inheritance became 'Theirs', but it was not 'taken' by them but 'left' to them. God had left it abandoned.

What can we make of all those promises of an everlasting covenant made with Levi, and Lamps that would burn everlastingly? In AD 70 the Roman armies under Titus were engaged in a bloody battle at Jerusalem. The nation had revolted and Rome's iron boot was stamping down firmly. In July of 70 AD the final sacrifice was offered and it was all over. The writer to the Hebrews writing just 5 years or so before the event linked it to the promise of Jeremiah's New Covenant and declared; *In that He says, "A New Covenant," He has made the first obsolete. Now what is becoming obsolete and growing old is ready to vanish away.* Heb 8:13 NKJV. For the writer to the Hebrews the 'writing was on the wall' and the end of the Temple an inevitability.

The Tabernacle/Temple and its sacrifices were an essential part of the Sinai Covenant and not an optional extra. They were, what earlier we called, its 'maintenance element'. The elements of covenant people, covenant law and covenant priesthood are inseparable; they create an integrated entity. If one of these elements fails the whole structure comes tumbling down. Perhaps we can illustrate with a less well-known passage of Scripture, the sacrifice of the red heifer. The sacrifice of the red heifer is mentioned in passing in Hebrews but you will search for it in vain in the list of sacrifices in the book of Leviticus. It appears in the book of Numbers and that is significant. (Num 19:1-13) The book of Numbers takes its name from the census that was taken when the covenant people were about to start their brief march and conquest of Canaan. How is the sacrificial system of the Sinai Covenant going to be kept in 'good order' while the nation is on the march and engaged in battle? Each time they move they will have to dismantle and then reassemble the Tabernacle before the sacrificial system can be up and running again. And there is another issue; only 'clean' priests can operate the sacrificial system. What happens if a priest is 'defiled' by coming into contact with a dead body; an almost inevitable event in the time of war? Well, a 'clean' priest could perform the necessary sacrifices and the defiled priest could be cleansed, but what if they were all defiled by contact with a dead body, now what? Enter, the sacrifice of the red heifer!

The cycle is broken

The sacrifice of the red heifer is a unique kind of sin offering. The writer to the Hebrews puts it in that context. (Heb 9:13) In this sacrifice a red heifer, without blemish, was taken outside the camp, as the main sin offering was, and there the animal was slaughtered. Some of the blood was kept and some of the blood was then sprinkled in front of the Tabernacle precincts. The heifer was then burned in its entirety and to its ashes were added various other ingredients. The priest who officiated, a clean priest, was now regarded as ceremonially defiled and he and his clothing were thoroughly washed. Next another 'clean' man gathered up the ashes of the mingled sacrifice and other ingredients and preserved them in a safe and 'clean' place outside the main camp. This created a reserve sacrifice, a kind of 'instant sacrifice' that could be quickly reconstituted in a time of emergency. It seems that the preserved sacrifice could be instantly reconstituted simply by adding fresh or living water, hence an 'instant sin offering'.

In later times this sacrifice was used for the cleansing of defiled priests and the priest once cleansed could recommence his ministry and the cycle was active again. It works wonderfully... as long as there is a reserve of 'red heifer ashes' kept somewhere safe. It works because the priest cleansed by the instant sacrifice can now create more 'instant red heifer' ashes and so the supply can be replenished. It is a wonderful system but perhaps you have seen the catch? What happens if all the priests are ceremonially unclean, having been in contact with dead bodies or something similar and if there is no reserve of 'red heifer ashes' available? We can see that the whole system grinds to a halt. There is no clean priest to create the 'red heifer ashes' and there are no 'red heifer ashes' to cleanse the priest. Once this cycle was broken it is impossible to get it up and running again; no red heifer ashes and the whole system quickly grinds to a halt. The law and its sacrificial system was a perfectly integrated institution but once any element is broken the whole machine falters. The sacrifice of the red heifer may seem obscure to our modern eyes but it is a telling illustration of the way in which once broken 'it could not be put together again' simply by human determination.

The Sinai Covenant was originally initiated by Moses. It was attended by miracles of God's presence. A wind that divided between the Egyptians and the Israelites and a fiery presence on Sinai itself. It was then maintained by a series of sacrifices and ceremonies. To reconstitute the Sinai Covenant it would be necessary to have another mediator and another infusion of wind and fire. The production of the raw materials themselves, of red heifer and other ingredients, could not in themselves be sufficient. It would require a new mediator and a new priest and essentially a complete repeat of the events of Sinai; it would require nothing less than a 'New Covenant'. The Sinai Covenant, once halted, can never be restarted by human agency, it would need to be a new beginning instituted by God and not the rekindling of an old fire. The Sinai Covenant will never be restarted; there is no need. God has promised and provided a New Covenant, with a new mediator and a new High Priest and that covenant is 'up and running'.

Judaism regards, quite rightly, the Sinai Covenant as the beginning of the nation's unique identity. Judaism also regards the Jewish feast of Weeks, or Pentecost, as the anniversary of the giving of the Law. It is called the feast of weeks because it takes place after 7 times 7 days after Passover. Christians know it better as the 'fiftieth day' or in Greek, Pentecost. Christ died at the time of Passover, and fifty days later "when the day of Pentecost had fully come..." there was an amazing event which included fire and wind, those ancient attendants of the Exodus, and God arriving in the person of the Holy Spirit to take up residence in his new temple. The same God who had been resident in the Person of his Son had come to take up residence in a New Covenant people. Initially it would be a remnant of the house of Israel and the house of Judah but soon it would include a unique and secret ingredient; ...*the mystery of Christ), which in other ages was not made known to the sons of men, as it has now been revealed by the Spirit to His holy apostles and prophets: that the Gentiles should be fellow heirs, of the same body, and partakers of His promise in Christ through the gospel,* Eph 3:4-6 NKJV. The new temple of the Church was created to fulfil God's desire that his house would be a house of prayer for all nations.

In this chapter we examined the references in which Christ referred to himself as 'the Temple' and saw the significance as he claimed to be the place where God was in residence. We saw the dreadful finality with which he disowned the physical Temple of his day and that once 'broken' the Sinai Covenant could never be restarted. We examined the special emergency measure of the sacrifice of the 'red heifer' and saw that once 'broken' this pattern too could never be restored. And we saw the significance of the Day of Pentecost as the anniversary of Sinai and the plain declaration that the New Covenant was now 'up and running' and that God was again 'resident' in his Temple.

15: The Calvary Baptism

But we have overrun our storyline and we need to look at Christ's covenant making work on the cross. The Scriptures use many images and metaphors to speak of the achievements of Calvary. It was a Day of Atonement in which the victim carried away the sin, not of one nation alone, but of the whole world. It was a lifting up of God's cure for the plague that was destroying the people in the metaphor of Moses' bronze snake. It was a propitiation in which a price was paid to remove the cause of the offence and pave the way for reconciliation. In this chapter we will consider a cluster of Bible metaphors and images that were used by Christ himself.

Shortly before Christ's final entrance into Jerusalem Matthew and Mark record one of those persistent topics of discussion which seem to have broken out at fairly regular intervals among the disciples; when the kingdom comes which of us will be the most important? This occasion was Christ's opportunity to speak about the true nature of authority and responsibility in his kingdom but it is the language he uses to introduce the subject that catches our attention. He referred to his death as 'a baptism' and as a 'cup'; *But Jesus said to them, "You do not know what you ask. Are you able to drink the cup that I drink, and be baptized with the baptism that I am baptized with?"* Mark 10:38 NKJV. The eager response of the disciples only goes to show how little they understood what he was asking. What is the significance of this language? Why did he not just say 'Are you able to suffer as I am going to suffer?'

There are complex layers of threads to unpick in this tapestry but we shall see that they are each perfectly consistent with his view of his coming death. The inevitability of his death had been an established fact of life for Christ from the moment of his water baptism in the Jordan, if not before that time. His water baptism had been a symbolic acceptance of the inevitability of another baptism that must be accomplished for his task to be completed. As we have seen he used John's public baptism for a different purpose to the rest of John's candidates. Christ had no sins to confess but the baptism was an opportunity to fulfil all righteousness; it was an act of simple obedience to God pointing to his acceptance of the messianic mission in all its consequences. One of those consequences was that he must fulfil the role of the Suffering Servant and submit to an overwhelming experience that he describes, in Mark 10:38, as a baptism. His physical water baptism in the Jordan is a signpost to this Calvary baptism.

Isaiah's baptism

In the Greek version of the Old Testament known as the Septuagint or the LXX, with which Christ was familiar, the Greek word 'baptise' or 'baptism' is used on two separate occasions. The first as we saw in Chapter 12 was a reference to Naaman's self-immersion into the Jordan river, the second instance of the word occurs in the prophecy of Isaiah. In the earlier chapters of Isaiah we have lists of coming retribution against the nations that surrounded the covenant nation. Those nations and city-states included Tyre, Philistia, Syria-

Damascus, Moab, Assyria and others. The list also included Babylon. The vision that Isaiah saw of the ferocity of Babylon's destruction overwhelmed him. It seems that none of the other predictions moved him as profoundly as his vision of Babylon's coming judgment. There are two separate visions given in Chapters 13 and 21 and it is in the latter chapter that we shall find our word 'baptism'. Isaiah uses the language of the intense pains of child-birth and declares; *Therefore my loins are filled with anguish; pangs have seized me, like the pangs of a woman in labor; I am bowed down so that I cannot hear; I am dismayed so that I cannot see. My heart staggers; horror has appalled me; the twilight I longed for has been turned for me into trembling. Is 21:3-4* ESV. In the Greek Old Testament the phrase "my heart staggers, horror has appalled me" includes the word for 'baptise'. The word 'appalled' signifying that horror had overwhelmed him, is the Greek word 'baptised'; horror had baptised/overwhelmed him.

This is quite consistent with the way in which the word was used in ancient times. Ships were overwhelmed, or baptised, in storms and as we have already seen vegetables were marinated, or baptised, in pickling vinegars. A baptism was a life-changing event. When we recall that both Noah's flood and Moses' Red Sea crossing are described in the New Testament as 'baptisms' we begin to see a deeper significance to the word. When Paul speaks of 'baptism' in his epistle to the Romans he refers to a 'baptism into death'. There is an important sense in which all baptism is a baptism into death. It marks the death of the old state and is frequently linked with the idea of judgment. Even water baptism, seen in this light, is an embracing of the death of the old way of life. In this sense there is no way back from a real baptism.

When Christ spoke of baptism then he was speaking of his death. But baptism does not only mark the end of the old it also marks the beginning of something new. Noah's flood overwhelmed the old order and marked the beginning of something new. Moses' Red Sea crossing overwhelmed the pursuing Egyptians and marked the beginning of something new. In each case there is a powerful end and a new beginning. This is wonderfully expressed in the account of Naaman and his self-baptism that brought his old religious ways to an end and marked a new beginning as a proselyte. When Christ spoke of his death as a baptism, what was being brought to an end? And what new beginning was there in prospect?

Baptism into Adam?

In his epistle to the Roman's Paul speaks of being baptised into Christ's death and then explains one of the purposes behind Christ's death. First he speaks of the uniting power of a baptism into death and then adds; *Therefore we were buried with Him through baptism into death, that just as Christ was raised from the dead by the glory of the Father, even so we also should walk in newness of life. For if we have been united together in the likeness of His death, certainly we also shall be in the likeness of His resurrection, knowing this, that our old man was crucified with Him, that the body of sin might be done away with, that we should no longer be slaves of sin.* Rom 6:4-6 NKJV. We have all the signs here of a true baptism. The old patterns have come to an end and the entrance of a new way of life has appeared. This prospect is the consequence of his death and our baptism into it. Christ's death as Sin-bearer united him with the full condition of mankind in its separation and rebellion against God. This 'community' of the human race in alienation from God is referred to in the older, more literal, versions of the New Testament as 'the old man'.

This is a sometimes-difficult concept but it is a vital one. The 'old man' is the result of a single man and his sin. This Paul makes plain in the previous chapter of Romans; *Therefore, just as through one man sin entered the world, and death through sin, and thus death spread to all men, because all sinned—* Rom 5:12 NKJV. Even though technically we might say that Eve sinned before Adam it was Adam's sin that had this devastating effect on the race. Eve's sin had no direct impact upon Adam, but Adam's sin impacted the whole human race and, in fact, the whole created order of things; *For the creation was subjected to futility, not willingly, but because of Him who subjected it in hope;* Rom 8:20 NKJV. This act of rebellion by the federal head of the human race affected the human constitution. It created a condition which the Bible refers to as being 'in Adam' and the Bible makes it plain that by first, natural birth, every human being is 'in Adam' and consequently a constituent part of 'the old man'.

The human race, in Adam, is a deadly force. This is not to say that every incident in life is deadly but only that this instinct for rebellion has penetrated the whole race and every individual within it. The full animosity of this destructive spirit has only ever been seen once, at Calvary. For the most part a constraining grace restrains the full expression of this nature, but just once all the restraints were taken away and we see it in its true colours. Frequently throughout his earthly ministry Christ spoke of 'a coming hour'. The gospel narrative tells us that some attempts to kill him prematurely were divinely prevented 'because his hour had not come'. On occasion he referred to it as 'my hour'. There is a telling detail in the account of his arrest in the garden of Gethsemene that shows things in a somewhat different light. When those who had wanted to arrest him were finally allowed to do so he reminded those who arrested him that they had had more than one opportunity to arrest him. But now something had changed. God's restraining hand on 'the old man' had been removed and the race begins to be seen in its true nature; *When I was with you daily in the temple, you did not try to seize Me. But this is your hour, and the power of darkness.* Luke 22:53 NKJV. The word 'your' is emphasised in the original language. 'My hour' and 'your hour' were to meet in the climax of the ages.

When God gave his law to the covenant community of the nation it served several different purposes. The law itself was good, as was that Sinai Covenant, and the Scriptures never suggest otherwise. God's New Covenant was to be brought in not because there was intrinsically anything lacking in the Old Covenant but because, as we read in the epistle to the Hebrews, he found fault with 'them'. The weakest link was not God, not the Sinai Covenant itself but the people who received it. In his letter to the Galatians Paul described the Law as a child-conductor or *paidogogus*. This was not an actual teacher but a boy's personal policeman that wealthy Roman families engaged to ensure that high-spirited boys actually got to their lessons. There were lots of potential distractions between the home and the school but the task of the *paidogogus* was to ensure that none of them drew him off course. Paul refers to the Law as the *paidogogus* of the Old Covenant. It's purpose was to close them in and narrow their path to make sure they arrived in the presence of the true teacher, Christ himself.

Measuring the Old Man

The Law had another purpose, it made it possible to some extent to measure the 'old man' in each individual. "Hope", says the proverb, "springs eternal" and our race has an amazing capacity to believe what it wants to believe in spite of any evidence to the contrary. On one famous occasion Christ declared the route to genuine freedom; *Then Jesus said to those Jews who believed Him, "If you abide in My word, you are My disciples indeed. And you shall know the truth, and the truth shall make you free."* John 8:31-32 NKJV. The response of the 'believers' was to launch a stinging attack. No one likes to be told that he is a slave or an addict and they remonstrated with Christ. "We are Abraham's seed" they protested " and were never in bondage to any man." This is an amazing assertion of aspiration over reality. Throughout their long history as the covenant nation they had frequently been in bondage to Egyptians, Philistines, Moabites, Midianites, Babylonians, Persians, Greeks and now the Romans. Their refusal to face the facts is a striking example of the 'don't confuse me with the facts, I have made my mind up' philosophy of life. Christ refused to give way on the matter; *Jesus answered them, "Most assuredly, I say to you, whoever commits sin is a slave of sin. And a slave does not abide in the house forever, but a son abides forever. Therefore if the Son makes you free, you shall be free indeed.* John 8:34-36 NKJV.

Part of the purpose of the Law had been to disillusion them in these things. (If we have illusions about our spiritual health it is a mercy to be 'dissed' of our 'illusions'!) If we are able, in our own strength, to fulfil all the righteous requirements of the law, then the Law would be a sure means of salvation. By it a man or woman might accumulate solid proof that he was fit for God and heaven, but the law was not given for that purpose.

Rather it was given as a means of revealing the true inward nature of the 'old man'. Paul is speaking about the law when he makes this exact point; *Has then what is good (the law) become death to me? Certainly not! But sin, that it might appear sin, was producing death in me through what is good, so that sin through the commandment might become exceedingly sinful.* Rom 7:13 NKJV. It has an old-fashioned ring to it in the 21st century but this is simply declaring that part of the purpose of the law was so that "sin, might appear sin", in other words, that 'sin' the inward constitution of the 'old man' might be seen as it really is. Through the work of the commandment, the law, sin was seen to be not a mere aberration in the human psyche but 'exceedingly sinful'. The law was designed to show sin in its true light.

The way God made this so abundantly clear was to establish a covenant community who would be provided with a clear account of God's will, and given a covenant law and priesthood. A people who would be reinforced in their calling by prophets and leaders and have God himself resident in their midst. The covenant community of the nation was the world in microcosm and a perfect test-bed for demonstrating the true nature of human beings. No one who understands this can ever be anti-Semitic. The nation was taken 'out of' the other nations and quarantined for the purpose of this unique destiny, but it was not in essence any worse than or any better than any other nation.

Tailor-made covenants

If we see this clearly we begin to understand that the covenants, the Old and the New Covenants are tailor-made covenants. The Old Covenant was designed expressly for 'the old man', and the New Covenant was designed expressly for 'the new man'. A member of the 'old man' can never live in the provisions of the 'New Covenant' and a member of the 'new man' ought not to try to live in the provisions of the 'Old Covenant; alas both attempts are part of the confusing pattern of much that is called Christianity.

Christ's death, as a baptism, united him to what the race had become. He was baptised, we might say, into our death;

our spiritual deadness which is one of the consequences of being 'in Adam'. Being united into that death he took it down into death with him, turning Satan's own weapons on him; *he also himself likewise took part of the same; that through death he might destroy him that had the power of death, that is, the devil;* Heb 2:14 NKJV. That Calvary baptism united him with the essence of our rebellion against God. In a stark statement Paul makes a bold claim; *For He made Him who knew no sin to be sin for us, that we might become the righteousness of God in Him.* 2 Cor 5:21 NKJV. The identification with the human race which began in Mary's womb was completed on the cross when he was joined to, or baptised into, Sin, the inner deadly dynamic of the human heart.

And while 'joined' he 'drank the cup' that he had been offered by the Father. In simple terms, he experienced the reality of sin and then took the punishment for it. The 'cup' in God's hand is another older image from the God-given history of the covenant people; *For in the hand of the LORD there is a cup, and the wine is red; It is fully mixed, and He pours it out; Surely its dregs shall all the wicked of the earth drain and drink down.* Psa 75:8 NKJV. and again from Isaiah; *Awake, awake! Stand up, O Jerusalem, You who have drunk at the hand of the LORD The cup of His fury; You have drunk the dregs of the cup of trembling, And drained it out.* Is 51:17 NKJV. The 'cup' in the hand of the Lord is the metaphor of judgment poured out to its last drops. As Isaiah says, until the cup is 'drained'. 'Baptism' with its pictures of judgment and union and the ending of things is combined with the 'cup' in its picture of a personal acceptance and drinking of all that it contained.

In the garden of Gethsemene prior to his statement about 'your hour and the power of darkness' Christ had reached out and received what was offered to him. The horror of that impending baptism took him to the edge of sanity. In fact, the language used has been used in ancient times to describe insanity. The prospect of the cross and the sin-bearing overwhelmed him and three times he prayed using the same words; *And He said, "Abba, Father, all things are possible for You. Take this cup away from Me; nevertheless, not what I will, but what You will."* Mark 14:36 NKJV. When the Temple guard moved in to arrest him and Peter began his defence, the matter was already settled, the final choices had been made. From this point on he would fly as an arrow to its target. He had taken the cup, Calvary was the moment when he drank it; *So Jesus said to Peter, "Put your sword into the sheath. Shall I not drink the cup which My Father has given Me?"* John 18:11 NKJV.

The moment that broke the power of the 'old man', the human race under the wrong head, was the moment that the Old Covenant too came to its end. The Old Covenant had served its purpose; *What purpose then does the law serve? It was added because of transgressions, till the Seed should come to whom the promise was made;* Gal 3:19 NKJV. The Seed had come, the mission accomplished. The way was open now for the creation of a 'new man' and that new creation would have its own New Covenant.

In this chapter we examined Christ's work on the cross in the language of 'a baptism' and saw how he became 'united' with the inner rebellious dynamic of the 'old man'. We saw some of the purpose of the Law and the Sinai Covenant in alerting the original covenant people to the deadly power of inward sin. We saw Calvary as the final act in identification with the human race in its separation from God and the moment when Sin is dealt its deathblow.

16: In that day

Somewhere around 150 AD a Christian by the name of Tatian had a good idea. He decided that it would be helpful to create a composite of the four gospel records. By interleaving verses from Matthew, Mark, Luke and John he created a story line that gives a kind of biography of the gospel. Others have copied the idea over the years and these 'Harmonies', as they are usually called, can be very helpful in gaining an overview of events and teaching in the life of Christ. Of course, no 'harmony' is inspired and different writers have reached different conclusions at times. Technically there is only one gospel but in four accounts. So we have 'the gospel' according to Matthew, and the same 'gospel' according to Mark and so on but sometimes it helps to have the different accounts gathered together into a single chronology.

One of the consequences of such a harmony is that we can see how much time the 'gospel' gives to certain events.

Approximately 20% is given over to the last 24 hours of Christ's earthly life and 20% of John's entire gospel account seems to take place in the upper room. As we mentioned at our beginning some have questioned the Bible's sense of proportion. But this is God's sense of proportion and it shows a very great focus on the events that mark the culmination of Christ's life and ministry. This, in one sense, is the heart of the gospel. Without committing ourselves too rigidly to one 'harmony' we can see that the meal occupied the whole evening and that during the meal Jesus paused to wash the feet of his disciples. He gave the sweetest morsel to Judas who then left the room. It was at this point that he instituted what is usually known as the Holy Communion celebration, or Breaking of Bread.

The backward glance

The meal itself was the traditional Jewish Passover with its various cups of wine and blessings but it seems that at the end of that meal Christ began a new tradition. Do we need to remind ourselves of the context of the Passover? It was the meal that celebrated the redemption of a people from slavery. Instituted by Moses before the Sinai Covenant itself it marked a necessary step in God's plans for the people. Each family unit, in essence, took a lamb and slaughtered it. The blood of the lamb was then daubed on the doorposts and lintel of the house where the meal was being eaten. It is one of the details so easily overlooked that not only was blood daubed on the doorposts but the lamb itself was to be eaten. This meal prepared them for their exodus. They ate it in a state of readiness, when the moment came they must move without delay. As we saw earlier this process prevented judgment coming upon the first-born sons of the Hebrews, but its absence put the first-born of the Egyptians on a death list.

They left that same night and crossed the Red Sea in an event that we have seen Paul call 'a baptism into Moses' and assembled themselves at the foot of Sinai three months later. Moses began his several journeys to and fro as the mediator and the covenant itself was 'enjoined'; from that time everything changed for this people. They became God's special people, a kingdom of priests, a holy nation. They became God's covenant community with the promise of God being resident in his own tent in their midst. When Moses sprinkled the blood of other sacrifices upon the people, the altar and the book he declared that the covenant was 'in force'; *And Moses took the blood, sprinkled it on the people, and said, "This is the blood of the covenant which the LORD has made with you according to all these words."* Ex 24:8 NKJV. In fact, it was a full nine months before the Tabernacle and the priesthood could be established and become a working reality but legally it was now 'signed and sealed'.

At the annual celebration of these events, in the upper room, Christ fulfilled the traditional pattern and then added to it a unique event. He took the bread and broke it and declared that it represented his body that would be broken for them. Then... *Likewise He also took the cup after supper, saying, "This cup is the New Covenant in My blood, which is shed for you.* Luke 22:20 NKJV. He is consciously repeating the words of the mediator of the Sinai Covenant. This is a conscious re-enactment of the event that created a covenant community but he is not re-enforcing the Sinai Covenant but rather initiating a New Covenant. It is not only a repetition of the words of Moses but of Jeremiah too; *"Behold, the days are coming, says the LORD, when I will make a New Covenant with the house of Israel and with the house of Judah—* Jer 31:31 NKJV. From Moses we have the idea of 'the blood of a covenant', from Jeremiah the idea of a 'New Covenant'.

What did those remaining 11 disciples make of it all? Something implied in this account moves me whenever I read it. I presume that the 11 shared the broken bread with him and took their drink of the cup. They can have had only a vague idea of all that it signified and yet they took the bread and the cup too. As far as it lay in them they committed themselves to this 'New Covenant by blood'. They must have understood that it meant suffering and death and yet they 'signed up' for it. Perhaps later Peter spoke in some measure for all of them when he declared his 'to the death' allegiance to Christ.

The last supper or the first?

John does not record the 'New Covenant in my blood' saying but a 'harmony' of the gospel accounts will usually put it immediately before the long section of John 14-16. We usually read John and the other recorders separately but if we unite them in a 'harmony' we can recreate the scene pretty well. The sayings about 'blood' and the 'New Covenant' are still hanging in the air. What can all this mean? He adds a statement that he will not share in this celebration until a future day; *Then He took the cup, and gave thanks, and gave it to them, saying, "Drink from it, all of you. For this is My blood of the New Covenant, which is shed for many for the remission of sins. But I say to you, I will not drink of this fruit of the vine from now on until that day when I drink it new with you in My Father's kingdom."* Matt 26:27-29 NKJV. The atmosphere is now charged with anticipation and foreboding. This is a farewell meal. It is in this atmosphere with words of blood and New Covenants ringing in their ears and with the solemn assertion that this shared meal will be their last for some time that the story line passes onto John; *"Let not your heart be troubled; you believe in God, believe also in Me. In My Father's house are many mansions; if it were not so, I would have told you. I go to prepare a place for you. And if I go and prepare a place for you, I will come again and receive you to Myself; that where I am, there you may be also. And where I go you know, and the way you know."* John 14:1-4 NKJV. The celebration will continue but not here and not now.

The pattern of the section of John which runs from Chapter 14 to Chapter 16 reminds me of some of those Old Testament passages where the prophet's gaze looked beyond the immediate calamity to a better time to come. There is the introduction, unique to John's account, of an amazing promise. Christ was leaving, but the disciples would not be left orphaned; *And I will pray the Father, and He will give you another Helper, that He may abide with you forever— the Spirit of truth, whom the world cannot receive, because it neither sees Him nor knows Him; but you know Him, for He dwells with you and will be in you.* John 14:16-17 NKJV. Bible translators struggle with the word translated here as 'Helper'.

It is a technical term used to describe someone called alongside to provide support. When John uses this word in his first letter most Bible versions have it translated as 'Advocate' - a legal representative. Christ was leaving the scene of earth but his personal agent, his Advocate, would take his place. This agent would be authorised to speak on Christ's behalf. In fact he would speak Christ's own words to those left behind.

The Greek language can be very precise and it is here. Biblical Greek has two words for 'another'; one means another of a different kind, the other means another of the same kind. If the first term had been used we might have expected the coming agent to be very different to the one who is leaving, but if the second term is used it means the agent will be of exactly the same kind as the one who is leaving; it is this word signifying 'another of the same kind 'that is used here. There is no possibility of confusing the identity of the agent as he is named quite clearly; *the Spirit of truth, whom the world cannot receive, because it neither sees Him nor knows Him; but you know Him, for He dwells with you and will be in you.* John 14:17 NKJV. The great theme of these next chapters is a simple one; Christ is leaving but the Spirit is coming, and the Spirit will be to them all that Christ has been to them... and more.

Union

How did we get from 'New Covenant' to the 'coming of the Spirit'? It is in the coming of the Spirit that the 'New Covenant' will become operational. There is one sense in which these verses apply particularly to the disciples and we see this clearly in Chapter 17 (John17:20) but there is an application for every individual too. One consequence of the coming of the Spirit would be a sure conviction of spiritual union with Christ himself; In *that day ye shall know that I am in my Father, and ye in me, and I in you.* John 14:20 ASV. This is a simple verse with simple words but the implications are very great. Christ used the formula of 'I am in the Father, and the Father is in me' earlier in the same passage to describe the intimate relationship that existed between the Father and the Son. Try this do-it-yourself illustration. Let your hands represent the Father and the Son; the Son is the left hand and the Father the right hand. Put the left hand inside the right hand; the Son is in the Father... but the Father is not in the Son. Reverse hands. Now the Father is in the Son... but the Son is not in the Father. Now interleave your fingers and squeeze tight... now the Father is in the Son and the Son is in the Father. It is only an illustration but this statement of the Father being in the Son and the Son being in the Father is a statement of the utmost intimacy and communion. It does not surprise us to read it, after all the whole of John's gospel has this relationship as its theme. But what are we to say about the later statement? Now you will need a friend to lend a hand to interlock the fingers of another hand into your two. Again, it is only an illustration but that Christ should take the language of his relationship with his Father and apply it to his relationship with human beings is truly breathtaking; *In that day ye shall know that I am in my Father, and ye in me, and I in you.* John 14:20 ASV.

When would the disciples become conscious of that union with the Christ who is united with his Father? "In that day" said Christ. What day? The day that the Spirit comes. Now lets read the words of Ezekiel speaking over 500 years earlier; *I will give you a new heart and put a new spirit within you... I will put My Spirit within you...* Ezek 36:26-27 NKJV. The metaphors are different but we see the same expression of intimacy. Ezekiel does not speak of a 'New Covenant' but of a new heart and a new spirit... and of God's own Spirit indwelling. The consequence of the coming of the Spirit would be that men and women were joined 'in spirit' to Christ. The coming of the Spirit would bring into being the union from whence the comm-union could develop.

It is in this promise of 'that day' that we have another expression of the glories of another covenant; *the Spirit of truth, whom the world cannot receive, because it neither sees Him nor knows Him; but you know Him, for He dwells with you and will be in you.* John 14:17 NKJV. Those simple words mark the ultimate distinction between the two covenants; "for He dwells with you and will be in you." What a world of difference is expressed in those two small prepositions. These men had received power and authority to cast out demons, heal the sick and raise the dead. They were not novices in things relating to the power of God. They had been commissioned to teach through the villages and to demonstrate that the kingdom had drawn near. And all this is summed up in the phrase you know Him, for He dwells with you, but beyond all that there is a new era on its way, an era in which he will be *in* you.

Let's make sure we are thinking clearly here. Christ who said these things was *with them* when he made these statements. Their relationship with him had been close. They had seen and examined and handled him, as John says in his first letter. They *knew* him. There can be no doubt of that. Christ was *with* them. When they had gone about their itinerant preaching the Spirit had been *with* them. We might say they were familiar with the experience of Christ and the Spirit being *with* them. What then might they expect from this promise that on that day they would know Christ was *in* them and this promise that on that day the Spirit would be *in* them? The Christian teaching of an indwelling Christ through the power and presence of the Holy Spirit is greatly cherished but it could only begin on that day that the Spirit came.

Truth on the inside

The inwardness of the New Covenant is one of the main themes of Jeremiah and Ezekiel. Jeremiah specifically contrasted the promised New Covenant with the covenant that God had initiated at Sinai; *"Behold, the days are coming, says the LORD, when I will make a New Covenant with the house of Israel and with the house of Judah— not according to the covenant that I made with their fathers in the day that I took them by the hand to lead them out of the land of Egypt,* Jer 31:31-32 NKJV. To be led by the hand is an external guidance, to be led by the Spirit is internal. It is difficult to imagine how this could be stated any more clearly. Some have taught that the New Covenant is substantially the same as the Old Covenant and that only the outer forms are different, but this passage states the opposite. The coming 'New Covenant' would not be according to the pattern or substance of the Old Covenant and the key difference would be its inwardness; *But this is the covenant that I will make with the house of Israel after those days, says the LORD: I will put My law in their minds, and write it on their hearts;* Jer 31:33 NKJV. The Sinai Covenant did not put God's law into men's minds, it wrote them on stone. We find this same emphasis on inwardness in Ezekiel; *I will give you a new heart and put a new spirit within you; I will take the heart of stone out of your flesh and give you a heart of flesh. I will put My Spirit within you and cause you to walk in My statutes, and you will keep My judgments and do them.* Ezek 36:26-27 NKJV. The writer to the Hebrew's surely had these kinds of truths in mind when he declared; *But now He has obtained a more excellent ministry, inasmuch as He is also Mediator of a better covenant, which was established on better promises.* Heb 8:6 NKJV.

The better promises just get better and better. Christ promised that the coming of the Spirit would affect their understanding of spiritual truth; *But the Helper, the Holy Spirit, whom the Father will send in My name, He will teach you all things, and bring to your remembrance all things that I said to* you. John 14:26 NKJV. Again, this passage would have a unique application to the disciples in matters of doctrine but there is a personal and local application too. The better promises continue; *However, when He, the Spirit of truth, has come, He will guide you into all truth; for He will not speak on His own authority, but whatever He hears He will speak; and He will tell you things to come.* John 16:13 NKJV. This is not a mere academic appreciation of truth but a journey into truth itself with a personal, indwelling guide. These things can easily be abused with each man becoming his own authority but the danger of abuse should not rob us of the blessings of right use. After all this too was one of the promises of the New Covenant; *No more shall every man teach his neighbor, and every man his brother, saying, "Know the LORD,' for they all shall know Me, from the least of them to the greatest of them, says the LORD. For I will forgive their iniquity, and their sin I will remember no more."* Jer 31:34 NKJV.

Twice more Christ pinpointed the day when things would change dramatically with that same simple pattern of words, *in that day...* John 16:23, 26 These instances speak again of amazing intimacy with God in prayer. Did the disciples connect the coming of the Spirit with the inauguration of the New Covenant? Probably not while they were in the upper room, but when the day came and the promises began to be fulfilled they saw plainly that Christ had done a new thing in inaugurating a New Covenant. They saw that the two covenants were mutually exclusive and that the beginning of the new was the death knell to the old. During their vigil in prayer they surely recalled the things that he had said and looked forward to *that day*.

In the Upper Room the ten-day countdown had begun and the days followed one upon another until... *When the Day of Pentecost had fully come, they were all with one accord in one place. And suddenly there came a sound from heaven, as of a rushing mighty wind...* Acts 2:1-2 NKJV. The 'day' had arrived; the New Covenant was in force. Peter stood to answer the question 'what does it mean?' and took his cue from the prophecy of Joel; But this is what was spoken by the prophet Joel: *And it shall come to pass in the last days, says God, That I will pour out of My Spirit on all flesh;* Acts 2:16-17 NKJV. 'That' distant day had arrived, as the older version declared... *this is that...*

In this chapter we made the connection between the promised New Covenant and the promised coming of the Spirit. We noted the distinctive 'inwardness' of the New Covenant and the way in which Christ emphasised this in his teaching about the coming Spirit. We marked the key distinctive in the comparison of the prepositions 'with' and 'in' and saw that this is the essence of the New Covenant that has a better mediator and is based on better promises.

17: To you first

For the forty days between his resurrection and his ascension Christ demonstrated the reality of his triumph over death in a series of appearances to his disciples, and he talked to them. The topics of his conversation were two; the Kingdom of God and the Coming of the Spirit... or is that one topic with two parts? Wouldn't you love to have been present at those times? What did he have to say about the Kingdom of God? And what was the connection between the Kingdom of God and the coming of the Spirit that caused the disciples to ask their question; *And being assembled together with them, He commanded them not to depart from Jerusalem, but to wait for the Promise of the Father, "which," He said, "you have heard from Me; for John truly baptized with water, but you shall be baptized with the Holy Spirit not many days from now." Therefore, when they had come together, they asked Him, saying, "Lord, will You at this time restore the kingdom to Israel?"* Acts 1:4-6 NKJV. What is the connection between 'the Kingdom of God' and 'restoring the kingdom to Israel' and a 'baptism in the Spirit'? That could be another book! The reply they received is probably the conclusion we would come to in such a book; it is the Father's business and not ours.

Sit! Wait!

In times of war, information is often published on a 'need to know' basis. Sometimes God's truth comes to us on the same basis. Sometimes to know too much would only distract us from the work in hand and these who were gathered together certainly had a work to do. Their work was to spread into all the nations bearing witness to Christ himself. This 'you shall be witnesses to me' is not strictly speaking a command or even a promise, it is a simple statement of fact. This is what is going to happen and the enabling power will be the consequence of the Holy Spirit coming upon them; *and you shall receive power, the Holy Spirit having come upon you.*

In both his gospel account and the Acts of the Apostles the historian Luke makes a strong point that the disciples were not to begin their mission until the promise of the Father had been fulfilled and the Holy Spirit had come. It might be profitable to pause to consider this. The apostles and the other disciples represented here were well qualified to be witnesses to Christ. Many had witnessed his life for more than three years. Some had received profound experiences in which they had seen Christ in a blaze of glory; they had heard voices from heaven. They had seen his ministry of power throughout the land and they had witnessed his death and resurrection. Some had been told to rejoice because their names were written in heaven. Some had received an enduement of the Spirit that opened their understanding to the truth of the Scriptures. These are impressive qualifications and yet they were not sufficient; *And He opened their understanding, that they might comprehend the Scriptures. Then He said to them, "Thus it is written, and thus it was necessary for the Christ to suffer and to rise from the dead the third day, and that repentance and remission of sins should be preached in His name to all nations, beginning at Jerusalem. And you are witnesses of these things. Behold, I send the Promise of My Father upon you; but tarry in the city of Jerusalem until you are endued with power from on high."* Luke 24:45-49 NKJV. They must 'tarry', literally 'sit down and wait', in Jerusalem until the promised Spirit arrived. Why? They had preached the gospel, healed the sick, cast out demons, why must they wait?

You shall receive power... but they had already known power. The Greek word for power used in Acts 1:8 is the word *'dunamis'*. It has a verb and a noun form and means power not in the sense of authority alone or muscular strength but inherent power. The kind of power a thing has by virtue of its nature. The power of an army might be said to be a force of 1000 men; that would be the inherent power of that army. *dunamis* is life-force demonstrated. It is not power bolted-on as an accessory but power which flows from the very nature of a thing. This is why they must sit still and wait, the coming Spirit would bring about a change in their nature. In some senses there was little added to them in terms of miracles that they had not experienced before. The quantity might increase but there was no essential difference in the way they healed the sick when Christ had sent them out as apostles and the way they healed the sick later in the Acts. It is a sobering thought to consider that Judas Iscariot had also been given power to heal the sick, cast out demons and raise the dead but there had clearly been no change in his nature.

No, this coming of the Spirit was not merely to add something but to change something, radically. We can gather the clues together. According to Luke, they were to be 'endued with power from on high'. Luke has used this kind of language before. When Mary asked how she could bear a child while being virgin, the angel replied; *"The Holy Spirit will come upon you, and the power of the Highest will overshadow you; therefore, also, that Holy One who is to be born will be called the Son of God."* Luke 1:35 NKJV. A few months later Zacharius, the father of John Baptist, had spoken of the incarnation in these words; *Through the tender mercy of our God, With which the Dayspring from on high has visited us;* Luke 1:78 NKJV. 'Power' coming from 'on high'? It is the language used to describe a life that has a heavenly origin, and that will lead us to our next clue.

Regeneration and the rabbis

Nicodemus was a leading Rabbi in Israel. He is a man of integrity and some humility as we see from the way that the senior rabbi is willing to consult with a much less senior rabbi, Jesus of Nazareth. One of the contexts of the early chapters of John is, as we have already seen, that context of water baptism. John Baptist was raising a lot of interest and a mass of questions. The rabbis had a theology of regeneration in terms of proselytes or Gentile converts to Judaism. They patterned their practice and their theology on the story of Naaman and his self-baptism in the Jordan. Naaman was a very acceptable proselyte and such proselytes were considered to have become a true member of the Kingdom of God if they fulfilled the conditions of taking on the burden of the law, making a sacrifice at the temple and baptism.

'Full proselytes' or 'proselytes of righteousness' became 'children of the covenant,' 'perfect Israelites,' Israelites in every respect, both as regarding duties and privileges. The rabbis taught that as he stepped out of these waters the proselyte was considered as 'born anew' - in the language of the Rabbis, as if he were 'a little child just born' as 'a child of one day'. The proselyte was to regard himself as a new man in reference to his past. Country, home, habits, friends, and relationships were all changed. The past, with all that had belonged to it, was past, and he was a new man - the old, with its defilements, was buried in the waters of baptism. We commented earlier this was carried out with such relentless logic as not only to determine such questions as those of inheritance, but that it was declared that, except, for the sake of not bringing proselytism into contempt, a proselyte might have wedded his own mother or sister!

If we understand the theology of Nicodemus and the other rabbis of his day we have understood why John's baptism was so perplexing to them. Baptism, according to the rabbis, brought a convert into the covenant community and made him (or her) a full partner in the kingdom of God. How, then, were they to understand John's baptism of 'Israelites', people who were already in that covenant? It was no doubt with these perplexing questions in mind that Nicodemus respectfully greeted the younger rabbi, Jesus of Nazareth; *"Rabbi, we know that You are a teacher come from God; for no one can do these signs that You do unless God is with him." Jesus answered and said to him, "Most assuredly, I say to you, unless one is born again, he cannot see the kingdom of God."* John 3:2-3 NKJV. It was, as we sometimes say, a conversation stopper! Christ, knowing Nicodemus' puzzlement cuts short the question and goes immediately to the answer... and what an answer.

We have seen that the word translated 'again' here would better be translated 'from above'. Entrance into the kingdom of God is by a birth that has a heavenly origin. It is not baptism in water that brings in this new birth. John's baptism of repentance was a necessary point in the journey and in that sense men and women would need to be 'born of water' but in itself such a watery baptism could never achieve entrance into the kingdom of God. The birth necessary for entrance into the Kingdom of God would require another baptism; such men and women would need to be 'born of the Spirit' too; *Jesus answered, "Most assuredly, I say to you, unless one is born of water and the Spirit, he cannot enter the kingdom of God. That which is born of the flesh is flesh, and that which is born of the Spirit is spirit.* John 3:5-7 NKJV. We can see from the narrative just how devastating this was to Nicodemus' theology. Christ then expounds the bold statements of a birth that has a heavenly origin. There is no way to progress from the natural to the spiritual. Natural birth can never evolve into spiritual birth; there must be a brand new beginning. And this will always have an element of the mysterious within it. The Spirit is like the wind, you feel the impact but cannot map the route it took to get to you, nor predict where it will lead.

He struggles to get a hold on the concept and we can almost hear the pain in his voice; *Nicodemus answered and said to Him, "How can these things be?"* John 3:9 NKJV. He has already received his answer. To the profound questions of 'how' a man comes to regeneration there is a simple but sometimes frustrating answer... the Holy Spirit. Mary had asked a similar question of the angel messenger and received a very similar answer; *Then Mary said to the angel, "How can this be, since I do not know a man?" And the angel answered and said to her, "The Holy Spirit will come upon you, and the power of the Highest will overshadow you; therefore, also, that Holy One who is to be born will be called the Son of God.* Luke 1:34-35 NKJV. It might well be frustrating to human intellect that loves to enclose things in boxes with clear labels, but this is the true explanation and the only one God will give.

Suddenly from heaven...

I have repeated these truths so that we can carry forward with us these Bible concepts of 'birth with a heavenly origin' and its link with 'entrance into the kingdom of God' as we move back to the Acts of the Apostles. They sit and wait and pray. They knew 'that day' was approaching although almost certainly they did not fully appreciate all that would transpire in it. The count-down continued until ...*suddenly there came a sound from heaven, as of a rushing mighty wind, and it filled the whole house where they were sitting. Then there appeared to them divided tongues, as of fire, and one sat upon each of them. Acts 2:2-3 NKJV.* That was the outward manifestation to illustrate the inward reality that now took place; *And they were all filled with the Holy Spirit and began to speak with other tongues, as the Spirit gave them utterance.* Acts 2:3-4 NKJV. They praised God in languages that were intelligible to thousands of pilgrims who were visiting Jerusalem for the feast of Pentecost, but which they had never learned. It was a phenomenon which demanded an explanation; "what does it mean?" they asked. Peter's Spirit-inspired message then expounds the event.

The explanation is that what has happened in Jerusalem is the earthly consequence of something which has happened in heaven. It is a fulfilment of ancient prophecy in which God had promised to send his Spirit, but it is more than that. It is the heavenly proof that Christ's earthly mission has succeeded. This day was only possible because the rejected Jesus of Nazareth, King of the Jews, had taken his place at the right hand of God in heaven, a place of supreme authority and power. The nation had rejected him but God had acknowledged him and given him the throne. The events of this day were proof positive of the finished work of Calvary and had now made it possible for the promise of the Father to be fulfilled. And the Father's promise had been fulfilled through the Son, and Jesus having left the earth had sent his Advocate as he promised; *This Jesus God has raised up, of which we are all witnesses. Therefore being exalted to the right hand of God, and having received from the Father the promise of the Holy Spirit, He poured out this which you now see and hear.* Acts 2:32-33 NKJV.

Of those who heard, 3000 received Peter's witness to the Christ and were baptised in expectation of release from their sins and a personal receiving of this Spirit that Christ had poured out from heaven's throne. This day marked the beginning of a New Covenant community; it is frequently referred to as the 'birthday of the church' and so it was. The church that Christ had promised he would build is now under way and men and women can be 'added' to it. The pattern of life of that New Covenant community is expressed simply; *And they continued steadfastly in the apostles' doctrine and fellowship, in the breaking of bread, and in prayers. Then fear came upon every soul, and many wonders and signs were done through the apostles. Now all who believed were together, and had all things in common, and sold their possessions and goods, and divided them among all, as anyone had need. So continuing daily with one accord in the temple, and breaking bread from house to house, they ate their food with gladness and simplicity of heart, praising God and having favor with all the people. And the Lord <u>added</u> to the church daily those who were being saved.* Acts 2:42-47 NKJV. This coming, descent, filling of the Holy Spirit is also called a baptism. It is the baptism that John Baptist had referred to years earlier, not in water but in Spirit. A birth, not from earth, but from heaven.

A New Covenant community in Jerusalem

In the same way that Moses had inaugurated the Old Covenant the Mediator of a New Covenant had now begun the building of a Temple not built with hands, constituted of living stones, and designed to be a place where God could take up residence. The crossing of the Red Sea had baptised that covenant people into Moses, this event baptised a new people into a new Mediator and laid the foundations for a New Covenant community. The new community expressed their common life in an earthly expression of heavenly life. They lived in perfect harmony and instinctively moved to relieve those of their community who were in any distress. The sense of individualistic ownership was consumed in the fires of a passionate love for each other. Charles Wesley wrote a beautiful hymn describing these days;

> Happy the souls that first believed,
> To Jesus and each other cleaved;
> Joined by the unction from above,
> In mystic fellowship of love.

This was too good to keep to themselves and the instinctive witness to Christ began to fill Jerusalem. One key event was the healing of a congenital cripple who begged daily at one of the entrances to the Temple. God healed the man through Peter and the moment attracted an enormous crowd of curious onlookers. Peter took the opportunity to bear witness to Christ in whose name and power the miracle had taken place and then pressed on his hearers their need to respond to the 'miracle worker', Christ himself. He spoke of Christ's death and resurrection and called the nation to repentance. Even after their rejection of their Messiah God was still willing to pour out 'seasons of refreshing from the presence of God'. Christ, said Peter, was the central theme of all the prophets and then proved his case by a key reference to Moses.

Moses had predicted another prophet *like himself. For Moses truly said to the fathers, "The LORD your God will raise up for you a Prophet like me from your brethren. Him you shall hear in all things, whatever He says to you. And it shall be that every soul who will not hear that Prophet shall be utterly destroyed from among the people.'* Acts 3:22-23 NKJV. The early church frequently returned to this prophecy as being a prophecy of Christ himself. Moses was the Mediator of a covenant that brought into existence a covenant community over which he was the head. Now God had repeated the exercise with a new mediator of a New Covenant that had brought into existence a New Covenant community over which Christ was the head.

In spite of their rejection God was still at work to fulfil his promises. Peter concluded with a ringing statement; *To you first, God, having raised up His Servant Jesus, sent Him to bless you, in turning away every one of you from your iniquities.* Acts 3:26 NKJV. "To you first..." Paul repeats this truth in his epistle to the Christians in Rome; *For I am not ashamed of the gospel of Christ, for it is the power of God to salvation for everyone who believes, for the Jew first...* Rom 1:16 NKJV. There is, in the word 'first', the bud of another truth. The apostles, at this time, were not clear as to the extent of those who would profit from Christ's death and resurrection but as Peter preaches under the inspiration of the Spirit we see here clear clues to a divine order... to you first... and then?

We recall from Jeremiah 31 that in its earliest introduction the New Covenant was promised to the separate nations of Israel and Judah. The northern nation of Israel had long vanished in obscurity with its peoples and only the southern nation of Judah was to return from its captivity, and even then only a remnant. Nevertheless God had not, could not, forget the northern nation of Israel. As Jerusalem stood under the impending destructions of Babylon Jeremiah had prophesied; *Behold, the days are coming, says the LORD, when I will make a New Covenant with the house of Israel and with the house of Judah— not according to the covenant that I made with their fathers in the day that I took them by the hand to lead them out of the land of Egypt, My covenant which they broke, though I was a husband to them, says the LORD.* Jer 31:31-32 NKJV. Both nation states are recognised in this introduction but when the promise itself is stated we read; *But this is the covenant that I will make with the house of Israel after those days, says the LORD: I will put My law in their minds, and write it on their hearts; and I will be their God, and they shall be My people* Jer 31:33-34 NKJV. The separate nations of the house of Israel and the house of Judah become merged in the promise of the New Covenant under the single designation of 'the house of Israel'. As with Ezekiel's two sticks, the two have become merged into one in God's future purposes.

The 'Israel' that heard Peter speak was the nation partially reconstituted under the label of 'Israel' and was being offered 'first' the personal blessing of Christ himself in turning each individual away from his own iniquities. It is as Peter said earlier in his message; *You are sons of the prophets, and of the covenant which God made with our fathers, saying to Abraham, And in your seed all the families of the earth shall be blessed.* Acts 3:25 NKJV. The nation of Israel was destined for blessing from the time of God's call to Abraham and now Peter repeats the promises. In spite of their rejection of the Messiah all they need do is... *Repent therefore and be converted, that your sins may be blotted out, so that times of refreshing may come from the presence of the Lord, and that He may send Jesus Christ, who was preached to you before,* Acts 3:19-20 NKJV.

The invitations have gone out. Even now the Lord of the feast was inviting them to share in the celebrations of the marriage of his Son. But God's plans were never exclusively for the nation of Israel and that phrase 'to you first...' tells us that at the right time God's plans would be fully revealed. For the time being, on a need to know basis, all they had to do was say 'yes' to the invitation.

In this chapter we began to make the connections between the Kingdom of God that is entered by new birth and the coming of the Spirit on the Day of Pentecost. We saw that *'dunamis'* is inherent and not 'bolt on' power; power intrinsic to a new inward 'dynamic'. We also saw that God was continuing to reach out to the 'remnants' of the 'house of Israel' and 'the house of Judah' and that the foundations were being laid, in a New Covenant, for a New Covenant people.

18: And to the end of the earth

During the time of the Babylonian exile the prophet Daniel had several visions and prophecies that outlined future events. In one such message there is the only direct reference to the Messiah in the Old Testament. It reads: *And after threescore and two weeks shall Messiah be cut off, but not for himself: and the people of the prince that shall come shall destroy the city and the sanctuary; and the end thereof shall be with a flood, and unto the end of the war desolations are determined. And he shall confirm the covenant with many for one week: and in the midst of the week he shall cause the sacrifice and the oblation to cease,* Dan 9:25-27 NKJV. The interpretation of this passage has divided Christians for the last 150 years in their understanding of future events. The units that Daniel uses are 'weeks of years' i.e. seven year blocks. The nation had been sentenced to 70 years exile and as Daniel prays God gives him an outline of 70 times 7 years in units of seven years each.

In the final 'week' Daniel refers to Messiah being 'cut off', seemingly a clear pointer to Calvary and then predicts that a foreign nation will destroy both the city and the sanctuary. It is clear that this was future when Daniel received it as the city and the sanctuary were already in ruins at that time. He has the prophet's gift of looking over the valleys and seeing the mountain peaks.

Daniel's 70 weeks

There is a reference here to a covenant being confirmed or strengthened with 'many' for one 'week' i.e. for seven years. And that half way through that period he would cause 'sacrifice and the oblation to cease'. By this he seems to mean the temple ceremonies. It is not easy to interpret all these details. As Charles Spurgeon once said 'only fools and madmen are certain in their interpretation of the Revelation' and perhaps we should extend that comment to include the prophecies of Daniel. But here is my 'best fit' of which I am not 'certain' but at least 'comfortable'. Christ's public ministry to the covenant nation was approximately three and a half years, or half a 'week'. During that time he concentrated on the people of the covenant, confirming God's plan and word to them. He strictly forbad his disciples to widen this focus saying that his role was to reach the lost sheep of the house of Israel; language which links with the promises of God to restore his exiled flocks and bring them together under a single shepherd. The days of his public ministry were as though all the promises were coming true. Their days were as the days of heaven upon earth, as Moses had once promised Israel. Like a second Joshua he conquered the land and brought God's kingdom in wherever the sole of his foot was placed. Storms, sicknesses, demons.. all came under his rule. The kingdom was at hand, within reach.

After three and a half years he was violently 'cut off' and his death effectively made 'sacrifice and oblation' redundant. Christ was raised from the dead and continued his ministry through his Agent or Advocate, the Holy Spirit. The second period of three and a half years would seem to culminate with the death of Stephen as the first martyr. The sense of continuity can be heard in the opening phrases of the Acts;

The former account I made, O Theophilus, of all that Jesus began both to do and teach, Acts 1:1 NKJV. Luke's gospel is the 'beginning'; the Acts is the 'continuation' of the 'doing and teaching' of Christ. For the earliest part of the Acts the scene is set in Jerusalem and the circles then begin to widen. For the first period Christ, in the person of the Holy Spirit, continues his labours among the original covenant people. This was their destiny and he would honour his promises. He confirmed the covenant with many, with very many. In fact, the chief priests complained that the Christians had filled Jerusalem with this teaching and great crowds of people numbering thousands came to genuine faith in Christ. However it was this vast increase in the numbers of the believers that precipitated an action by the religious leaders that had far reaching consequences.

The conflict ultimately focused on one man, Stephen. Stephen was a Hellenist-Jew. He was thoroughly Jewish but his mind-set and his mother tongue was Greek. There were thousands like him in Jerusalem and throughout the Mediterranean world. The Christians now numbered so many thousands that they could be thought of as yet another group within Judaism. There had already been Pharisees, Sadducees, Essenes and others and now there was a large and vigorous group known as The Nazarenes; the followers of Jesus of Nazareth. Their patterns were increasingly different and would have given the appearance of a 'church within a church'. We must not forget that the covenant people were already regarded as 'the church'. Now however, we have another church within the church and it is outside the control of the religious leaders and they become increasingly agitated.

The 'church within a church' began to function as a separate community. They had their own times of prayer and teaching and had adopted a simple ceremony of the Lord's supper in which they remembered the Christ and the cross and looked forward 'till he come' to his return and kingdom in all its fulness. They began their own 'community care' programme and the needy widows received a daily allowance. However, because the majority of Nazarenes were from a Hebrew-Jewish background and the apostles too were from this background the simple organisation tended to function best among the

Hebrew-speaking Jews. There was a complaint that the Greek-speaking widows in the community were being neglected. Seven men were chosen to administer the allowance specifically to this group. Men who were clearly part of that Greek-speaking community; we have the list of their names and each name is Greek. One of these men was a fiery evangelist, a man full of the Spirit and faith and one who could not be silenced. It seemed he would be the perfect 'test-case' for the authorities to show their muscle. He was arrested and brought before the Sanhedrin, the official Jewish authority in the land, and the charges were brought.

The evidence against Stephen

If it is true that 'there is no smoke without fire' we may get a fairly accurate idea of the messages that Stephen had been preaching. The charges all have to do with Stephen's attitude to Moses, the Sinai Covenant and the Temple; *Then they secretly induced men to say, "We have heard him speak blasphemous words against Moses and God." And they stirred up the people, the elders, and the scribes; and they came upon him, seized him, and brought him to the council. They also set up false witnesses who said, "This man does not cease to speak blasphemous words against this holy place and the law; for we have heard him say that this Jesus of Nazareth will destroy this place and change the customs which Moses delivered to us."* Acts 6:11-14 NKJV. As with any mob the story line becomes a little confused but we can identify some clear elements of Stephen's preaching.

It seems that Stephen was making a clear distinction between Moses and Jesus of Nazareth. He made statements about the Sinai law and the Temple that caused people to say he is 'against' the Temple and the Law, and he seemed to have claimed that Jesus of Nazareth would bring the Temple ceremonies to an end and change the customs that Moses had instituted. For the religious rulers of the day this man was instigating revolution. For us as we read the record we can see that Stephen was putting 'clear blue water' between the Old and the New Covenants.

Stephen's answer to the charge is to launch on a mini-history of the covenant people from their physical beginnings in Abraham, through the time of their captivity in Egypt and through to Moses' first abortive attempt to bring them deliverance. The council must have wondered where all this was going. He finds the point he wants to make in the protest of a fellow Israelite captive in Egypt who asked Moses; *"Who made you a ruler and a judge over us?* Acts 7:27 NKJV. We are back to the old question of authority. During his earthly ministry this question was frequently asked about Jesus of Nazareth; *"Tell us, by what authority are You doing these things? Or who is he who gave You this authority?"* Luke 20:2 NKJV. But the link with Moses is especially telling because Moses prophesied that God would send a prophet like himself; *This is that Moses, which said unto the children of Israel, A prophet shall the Lord your God raise up unto you of your brethren, like unto me; him shall ye hear. This is he, that was in the church in the wilderness with the angel which spake to him in the mount Sina, and with our fathers: who received the lively oracles to give unto us:* Acts 7:37-38. KJV. I have reverted to the old King James version here where the Greek word *ekklesia* is translated as it is in most of the New Testament by the word 'church'.

Stephen is building his case. Moses was the mediator of a covenant. That covenant brought a covenant people into being and that people was required to give absolute obedience to the mediator of the covenant or suffer the penalty of death. And Moses predicted that God would perform an action-replay but with another man. God would raise up another prophet with a like destiny; another who would lead the people to freedom. Another who would bring them into the presence of God and establish a covenant in which they would become the covenant people of God. Another whose word would be law in their midst. And tragically the action-replay was being repeated in every detail; *...whom our fathers would not obey, but rejected. And in their hearts they turned back to Egypt...* Acts 7:39 NKJV. Stephen now turns the tables and suddenly it is the nation's leaders who are in court under trial; *"You stiff-necked and uncircumcised in heart and ears! You always resist the Holy Spirit; as your fathers did, so do you.* Acts 7:51 NKJV.

At the time of the first outpouring of the Spirit Peter had brought a similar accusation against the people; *Him, being delivered by the determined purpose and foreknowledge of God, you have taken by lawless hands, have crucified, and put to death;* Acts 2:23 NKJV. And their response is recorded too; *Now when they heard this, they were cut to the heart, and said to Peter and the rest of the apostles, "Men and brethren, what shall we do?"* Acts 2:37 NKJV. Peter was able to continue in offering free forgiveness and the promise of the Spirit to all who surrendered to Christ. It gives a tragic backdrop to the events recorded in Acts 7. When the religious leaders heard Stephen they too were 'cut to the heart' but with a very different response; *When they heard these things they were cut to the heart, and they gnashed at him with their teeth.* Acts 7:54 NKJV. They threw Stephen out of the city and stoned him to death. As the old evangelists used to say 'it is the same sun which melts the butter and hardens the clay'. They heard, essentially, the beginnings of the same message but, as the people had rejected Moses and refused to obey him, now they rejected the word of Christ through Stephen. This was the last recorded national opportunity for the original covenant nation to enter into its destiny and submit to the man at God's right hand.

It is not possible to measure the time exactly, but did this fill up the last half-week, three and a half years, of God's unique faithfulness to the covenant people? Whether that is so or not the rejection of Stephen's testimony and his stoning mark a watershed in the Acts. Up until this time the focus has been Jerusalem but from this point on the focus will shift, slowly but surely, to the ends of the earth. There can surely be no accident that this is the exact moment that Luke brings another character into his account of Christ's continuing mission through the agency of the Spirit. This is the moment that we first read of Paul or Saul as he was known then; *Then they cried out with a loud voice, stopped their ears, and ran at him with one accord; and they cast him out of the city and stoned him. And the witnesses laid down their clothes at the feet of a young man named Saul.* Acts 7:57-58 NKJV.

In the next three chapters the gospel moves South, North and West. North towards the land of the Samaritans. South in the life of a court official from Ethiopia. North towards Damascus and West towards the Roman centre and chief garrison town of Syria, Caesarea. Saul was one of the young Jewish leaders of his day. A man of boundless energy and determination and the worst enemy the Nazarenes would ever have. He used the death of Stephen as the ripe moment to launch a programme of persecution against the Nazarenes and the saints were scattered by his activities. All except the apostles, who stayed with the harassed flock in Jerusalem, fled from the city. Peter's 'running away' days were over.

One of Stephen's colleagues in the distribution of the Hellenist's widows' allowance was another powerful evangelist, Philip. Philip went north and came to the city of Samaria. The city of Samaria had once been the capital of the northern 'house of Israel' and had been captured in 722BC by the armies of Assyria. It then underwent its own special history. As we have seen earlier, the Assyrians not only deported the house of Israel into the far reaches of their empire but they repopulated the land with foreign groups who intermarried with the dregs of Israel that had been left behind. Life was difficult for the new immigrants. They were attacked by wild animals and decided they must placate the god of their new homeland. They managed to get some renegade Jewish priests who taught them some basics from the books of Moses and the people became known as Samaritans from their new homeland. They were a mongrel people and theirs was a mongrel religion.

When the remnant of Judah returned to the ruins of Jerusalem and began to rebuild their temple the Samaritans wanted to join in but they were banned by the returned people of Judah and animosity burned between the two peoples. At one time the Samaritans built their own temple on the sacred site of Gerizim but the Jews burned it down in the years between the Old and New Testaments. As John's gospel expressed it many years later... *Then the woman of Samaria said to Him, "How is it that You, being a Jew, ask a drink from me, a Samaritan woman?" For Jews have no dealings with Samaritans.* John 4:9 NKJV. We need to carry John's comment with us into Philip's visit to the city of Samaria; the Jews have no dealings with the Samaritans, but one Jew did and revealed to them that he was the Saviour of the World. Even though Judaism had excluded them Christ had included them in his itinerary and brought a promise of living waters to the people. With the arrival of Philip the time has come for the promise to be fulfilled.

Philip preached Christ to them. It is a simple statement. God confirmed the preaching with wonderful signs and the joy was city-wide. There were some notable converts, among them a local wonder-worker whose name was Simon. We are told that *Philip preached the things concerning the kingdom of God and the name of Jesus Christ, and that many believed, were baptised* and 'continued earnestly' with Philip. But for all these wonderful events there was something incomplete about the experience of these believers and it is very informative to observe the logic of the early Christians in action; *Now when the apostles who were at Jerusalem heard that Samaria had received the word of God, they sent Peter and John to them, who, when they had come down, prayed for them that they might receive the Holy Spirit. For as yet He had fallen upon none of them. They had only been baptized in the name of the Lord Jesus.* Acts 8:14-16 NKJV. When Peter and John arrived in Samaria, and John remember had once wanted to bring down a very different kind of fire on the Samaritans (Luke 9:54), they laid hands on the converts and they received the Holy Spirit.

We are not told exactly what happened but Simon saw enough to make him want to be able to have the same power of giving the Spirit. Peter's rebuke declares that Simon, who had believed, been baptised and continued in company with Philip, was still in the grip of sin and that his heart was not right. The Samaritans have believed but the promise made to some of their countrymen that they would drink and never thirst again has not yet been fulfilled. These passages have perplexed Christian commentators as they have tried to explain why things happened as they did here in Samaria. In simple terms the kingdom is expanding and non-covenant community people are being drawn into it. There is a strong connection, as we have seen, between the kingdom of God and the coming of the Spirit and a strong connection between the coming of the kingdom and the commencement of the New Covenant.

In that upper room where Christ had spoken about the New Covenant and where later he said so much about the coming Spirit, he ended the New Covenant commemorative meal by connecting the New Covenant with the coming kingdom; *Then He said to them, "With fervent desire I have desired to eat this Passover with you before I suffer; for I say to you, I will no longer eat of it until it is fulfilled in the kingdom of God."* Luke 22:15-16 NKJV. The Old Covenant community first celebrated Passover just once before they were joined in covenant with God at Sinai. Their first Passover was not commemorative but looked forwards. In the upper room the same pattern emerges. Before the New Covenant is established, they celebrate not a commemorative meal but a meal in which they anticipate the New Covenant and its blessings. It was, as we have seen, during this same evening that Christ gave the most explicit promises of the coming Spirit. A coming covenant, a coming kingdom, a coming Spirit all come together in this final hour of fellowship with his followers.

Simon in Samaria had responded deeply to what he had heard but he has not come into union with Christ. The Spirit has been manifested all around him but not in him. In heart he remains what he had always been... a man outside the New Covenant.

Breakthrough!

The kingdom continued to spread and in Acts 10 it soon engulfs the home of a Roman centurion. We quickly forget things that we do not understand and Peter had not yet understood the full implications of the New Covenant. It had been promised to a reconstituted Israel and events in Jerusalem had fitted his expectations. We cannot be sure of his thinking in regards to the Samaritans. Perhaps he thought there was sufficient pure blood in these mongrels to qualify them for a place in the kingdom and a part in the New Covenant community, but what was he to make of a request to visit the home of a thoroughgoing Gentile with not a drop of Israelite blood in him. He had seen implications of a wider truth but he had not understood them and so had forgotten them.

Cornelius, the centurion from Caesarea has a wonderful character reference. He was part of an occupying army and yet highly regarded by some of his household who were Jews. He gave charitable gifts regularly and generously. Cornelius' servants said that Cornelius' reputation was known throughout Judaism and they pleaded with Peter to journey to Caesarea to instruct him. Peter had received a vision in which God had told him not to call unclean what God has cleansed and travelled to Caesarea with six companions. The thrilling story is well known but we should point out Peter's diffidence. He is really not sure what he is doing in this home. He is unsure as to what is expected of him and begins to speak. It appears that Cornelius already had a good grasp of the public ministry of Christ as Peter puts it "you already know these things." (Acts 10:37) Peter begins to expound the consequences of the cross declaring that 'whoever believes in Christ will receive remission of sins'. His message was interrupted by a powerful visitation of the Spirit. The language is vital and dynamic; "the Holy Spirit fell upon all those who heard the word..."

Even though Peter has still not quite fitted all this into his theology he is convinced, as were his colleagues; *And those of the circumcision who believed were astonished, as many as came with Peter, because the gift of the Holy Spirit had been poured out on the Gentiles also.* Acts 10:45 NKJV. This is a repeat of the day of Pentecost and Peter recognises it as such. He slowly grasps the truth; God is including the Gentiles, people outside the Sinai Covenant community in this New Covenant. And seeing the clear implications he instructs them to be baptised in water in submission to the person of Jesus Christ. This, incidentally, is the only time that 'baptism' was 'commanded' in the record of the Acts.

When Peter returned to Jerusalem he is cross-questioned by a strongly Jews-only contingent within the gathering and explains what has occurred. He tells the story in terms of his own experience on the day of Pentecost. He gathers together a whole bundle of words, outpouring, the Spirit falling, Spirit-baptism used to describe the day of Pentecost and applies them to the household of Cornelius. His questioners demand an explanation of his behaviour and Peter's only defence is that *"the Holy Spirit fell on them, as upon us at the beginning"*. Acts 11:15 NKJV.

How could they argue against such a thing? We have a description of their final response to Peter's testimony in the words; *When they heard these things they became silent; and they glorified God, saying, "Then God has also granted to the Gentiles repentance to life." Acts 11:18 NKJV. It is hard today to recapture the almost incredulous gasp of the people who heard... "then God has included the Gentiles". Events often occur before their explanations and we ought to be generous in our judgments as we observe the theological struggles of these early Christians. Isaiah had said; *"Do not remember the former things, Nor consider the things of old. Behold, I will do a new thing."* Is 43:18-19 NKJV. But that is often easier said than done. The things that were happening represent a genuine paradigm shift. They had no points of reference from which to understand what was happening. What they needed was someone who could grasp the implications of the events and express them by the Spirit in a way that made all the right connections. God had just the man in mind. The last time many of them saw him he had been holding the coats of those who stoned Stephen; his name was Paul.

In this chapter we suggested a fulfilment of Daniel's 70 Weeks prophecy in Christ's reaching out to the people of the Old Covenant during his life and in the first years of the New Covenant. We traced the widening circle of those who were responding to the message and see as each group has their own conscious event of the 'coming of the Spirit'. We tried to be generous in understanding Peter's struggles with the whole concept of the New Covenant and introduced the man to whom God would give the definitive explanation; Paul.

19: The Mystery is Unveiled

Paul introduced himself to his readers in Rome with this brief explanation; *Paul, a bondservant of Jesus Christ, called to be an apostle, separated to the gospel of God* Rom 1:1-2 NKJV. It is a very revealing self-description. The self-assertive, confident rising star of Judaism has become a bond-slave to the man he persecuted most of all. As an individual he has relinquished all his rights to self-development and prospects. His life is now at the beck and call of a new master. In Roman culture bond-slaves had no rights. They were, according to one philosopher, to be regarded as a tool, used, and when worn out, discarded. But this 'tool' is also an 'apostle', an emissary and herald of a king and a man whose word is as though the king himself had spoken. It is this combination of self-humbling and a sense of enormous and authoritative responsibility that explains this man in all his moods and actions. For himself he would not raise a finger in self-defence, for his mission he would take on the might of Rome if need be. A single moment had separated him forever from the ordinary and the mundane and given him a commission that absorbed his whole life.

The chosen man

He was different to the others; of that there was no doubt. The original apostles were judged to be 'unlearned and uneducated' and men wondered at their understanding and power of expression. Paul, on the other hand, was once rebuked by a senior representative of Rome with the words 'your great learning has made you mad'. The others were, in the main, ordinary working men and they came from an area of heavy immigrant domination, Galilee of the Gentiles. Speaking of their master the question was once asked; 'can anything good come out of Nazareth?' Paul came from a privileged background. His father was a Roman citizen which points to the fact that he had either bought that honour at a high price or had provided some significant service for Rome and had been rewarded with citizenship. He almost certainly came from a wealthy family. He was also highly educated, having spent some years as a pupil of one of Israel's greatest rabbis, Gamaliel. He was a front-runner in his personal piety and had outstripped all his contemporaries in his devotion to his faith. His pedigree was exemplary. He was not a Hellenistic Jew with a Greek mind-set but a 'Hebrew of the Hebrews'; Hebrew speaking, Hebrew thinking. He traced his genealogy back to the family of Israel's first legitimate king. Perhaps that is where he got his name. As regards the keeping of the law he lived in good conscience and was surely on target for blessing and influence and high regard... until the day he took the road to Damascus.

In a single encounter with the risen Christ his whole life tumbled in on him. Later he testified that he regarded all of these natural qualifications as of no value; 'offal' was the word he used. He also testified that not only did he not put any value on any of these qualities and achievements but that he had actually 'suffered/experienced the loss' of them. It seems that Paul's conversion 'lost him' his family, his wealth and his high standing in the community, perhaps even his wife. He had been trained as a rabbi and all rabbis were required to have a physical trade. The idea was that it taught them the dignity of labour and kept them 'down to earth'. Paul, or Saul, as he was known at that time, was a cloth-worker or tent-maker and this trade was something he took up again on occasion.

All that Paul was, suffered a fatal blow on the road to Damascus. The account is so well known that even unbelievers will use the language of 'a Damascus Road experience' to signify a radical change of mind and direction. The account is punctuated by two simple questions that Paul asked. The first "who are you Lord?" and the second might well have become his lifetime's motto; "Lord, what do you want me to do?" From that time he became a 'bond-slave of Jesus Christ', his whole life was based on the simple theme that Jesus Christ was his lord and master and Paul's life was dedicated to ascertaining his master's will and doing it with all of his considerable energy.

It was in that encounter, even before he had received the Holy Spirit, that Paul received his commission. He was to go wherever he was sent as a personal representative of his master. From this time forward his days could never be divided into secular and holy, his whole life became 'separated to the gospel of God'. As a king's representative he will stand before kings. He will take the king's proclamations into market place and synagogues. His mission and commission were burned into his being; "woe unto me", he said, "if I do not preach the gospel". (1 Cor 9:16)

Getting a grip on the truth

With his extensive knowledge and traditional understanding of the Jewish Scriptures it is inevitable that Paul would need to consider very deeply the implications of what had happened to him. His theology had been turned up-side-down in a matter of moments and Paul was the kind of man who would have to try to understand what had happened. When he started his journey all the parts were neatly labelled and sitting in their boxes, by the time he arrived in Damascus his theology was a shambles.

In the first flush of his experience he kept his appointment with the synagogues in Damascus but his agenda had changed. He had been commissioned by the religious authorities to chase the heretics as far as they could be found. As a high-profile opponent of the Nazarenes, as the early Christians were known, and their teaching his visit would be awaited with anticipation in Damascus. The expectant listeners were stunned by his messages; *Immediately he preached the Christ in the synagogues, that He is the Son of God. Then all who heard were amazed, and said, "Is this not he who destroyed those who called on this name in Jerusalem, and has come here for that purpose, so that he might bring them bound to the chief priests?"* Acts 9:20-21 NKJV.

By combining the accounts in the Acts and in Paul's letter to the churches in Galatia we can put together an outline of his next movements. He spent 2 years in apparent solitude in 'Arabia', most likely the Trans-Jordanian desert and then seems to have returned to Damascus. His visit caused a furore among the people in Damascus who were so incensed that they determined to assassinate him and he had to be smuggled out of the city over the wall in a donkey pannier. He then made a brief visit to Jerusalem where he met up with a few of the leaders of the Nazarenes but his presence there aroused suspicion among the believers and violent opposition among the Jews and he was put on a boat en route for Asia Minor and finally arrived in his old home city of Tarsus. He next surfaces in our account over 10 years later when Barnabas finds him and brings him to the church in Antioch.

Paul is the kind of high profile, highly intelligent and energetic person that many contemporary Christians would love to see converted. "What an impact" they say, "this famous individual would have if he were converted". His name would be on all the banners and his preaching tours would take him far and wide. God's strategy with Paul was somewhat different. Other than for brief appearances he vanishes from the public gaze for about 14 years. The Public Relations gurus had missed their moment. He was no longer a 'hot item'. In fact, after 14 years people may well have been saying..."Who is Paul?"

But those 'hidden years' have not been wasted. As he worked at his cloth Paul opened his heart and his mind to God and sought to understand the implications of what had happened to him. We need to re-emphasise something. By natural ability and position Paul was perfectly placed to be the 'systematic theologian' of the new movement. His knowledge of the Old Testament Scriptures and Jewish tradition would have been almost encyclopaedic. He was a trained theologian, well versed in the language and culture of the original documents. If anyone was going to 'work it all out' Paul would have been the man, but there is a persistent element in Paul's testimony that says this is not how it happened. Paul claimed to have 'received' truth and frequently used the word 'revelation'. His mind and heart were open and he was not afraid to think but the truth he preached was not the consequence of his own logical digestion, it was revelation.

Truth on the loose

A revelation is an unveiling, the drawing aside of a curtain to un-veil, or re-veal, what has been hidden. Paul did not invent the theology; it was unveiled to him. The other apostles were aware of this extra dimension in the life and ministry of Paul. Peter comments of the occasional difficulty of understanding Paul's writing but he is in no doubt as to where Paul's insights have come from; *and consider that the longsuffering of our Lord is salvation—as also our beloved brother Paul, according to the wisdom given to him, has written to you, as also in all his epistles, speaking in them of these things, in which are some things hard to understand, which untaught and unstable people twist to their own destruction, as they do also the rest of the Scriptures.* 2 Pet 3:15-16 NKJV. In this strong recommendation Peter states that Paul's writings were the result of 'wisdom given to him' and then goes on to equate Paul's writing with 'the rest of the Scriptures', a clear statement that Peter regarded Paul's letters themselves as 'scripture'. When we consider how a Jew regarded the authenticity and sacredness of the ancient Scriptures this statement from Peter that Paul's epistles have equal authenticity and sacredness is remarkable.

Can we recreate Paul's thinking process and the revelation that brought it all together? Not really, but we can consider some possibilities. In 1 Corinthians 11 Paul quotes the words used by Christ at the last supper; *For I received from the Lord that which I also delivered to you: that the Lord Jesus on the same night in which He was betrayed took bread; and when He had given thanks, He broke it and said, "Take, eat; this is My body which is broken for you; do this in remembrance of Me." In the same manner He also took the cup after supper, saying, "This cup is the New Covenant in My blood. This do, as often as you drink it, in remembrance of Me."* 1 Cor 11:23-25 NKJV. He knew that Christ had regarded his own death as the means of bringing in 'the New Covenant'. He would have known where the reference to 'the New Covenant' had its beginnings in the prophecy of Jeremiah; *"Behold, the days are coming, says the LORD, when I will make a New Covenant with the house of Israel and with the house of Judah— not according to the covenant that I made with their fathers in the day that I took them by the hand to lead them out of the land of Egypt, My covenant which they broke, though I was a husband to them, says the LORD. But this is the covenant that I will make with the house of Israel after those days, says the LORD: I will put My law in their minds, and write it on their hearts; and I will be their God, and they shall be My people."* Jer 31:31-33 NKJV. He also knew that men and women who could claim no descent from either the house of Israel nor the house of Judah were receiving the Spirit and entering the kingdom. How could these things be?

When we first introduced Jeremiah's prophecy we drew attention to the way in which the original promise of a New Covenant 'with the house of Israel' and 'with the house of Judah' narrows in the next verses to focus just on 'the house of Israel'; *But this is the covenant that I will make with the house of Israel after those days.* We also saw that Isaiah had redefined the 'house of Israel' and the 'house of Judah' to mean a 'remnant' of those peoples. Isaiah had promised a remnant would return. We also saw that Ezekiel performed a miracle in which two sticks became one. In these Old Testament passages we discover that God will restore his people who have been taken into captivity. We also see that God will not restore the whole nation but a remnant from 'the house of Israel' and 'the house of Judah'. In the 'two' becoming 'one' we discover that this 'one' will continue to be the bearer of the ancient promises and, in effect, a new Israel. We also saw that the prophets used the language of two different flocks coming together under a single shepherd, of David's dynasty.

Paul also knew that a 'New Covenant' spoke of a new beginning. He would have known of what happened to Peter and the others at their 'beginning'. And he would have known how Peter described the events in the home of Cornelius as being the same as had happened 'to us at the beginning'. But Paul would still need to see how the Gentiles could ever be part of this, and God gave him the answer... by a revelation.

By revelation

Paul uses the word 'mystery'. This does not mean that it was particularly mysterious but that it was a hidden secret to be revealed only to those who have been initiated into the secret. In many ways it might have been better to translate the word 'a secret'. Paul makes some strong claims about this secret or 'mystery'. He claims that; *...the mystery of Christ, which in other ages was not made known to the sons of men, as it has now been revealed by the Spirit to His holy apostles and prophets:* Eph 3:4-5 NKJV. This is so important that it will bear repeating. The 'secret' that Paul is about to unfold had not been made known in 'other ages' as it was now being made known, by the Spirit, to Christ's apostles and prophets. Paul is about to reveal a secret that was not known, in its full scope, to Isaiah, Jeremiah or Ezekiel. However this 'secret' was now being made known to Christ's apostles and prophets. Something has happened here. A change has taken place. The full truth of many of those Old Testament prophets was not known even to those who gave the prophecies. This is a truth that Peter also states. Peter speaks of the predicted sufferings of Christ and the glories that would follow and then adds that the prophets themselves 'inquired and searched carefully' as they tried to understand the implications of their prophecies. Peter adds that it was revealed to those prophets that the things they were proclaiming were not for their own age but for another. (1 Pet 1:10-12)

What then is the 'secret' that was largely hidden from previous generations of God's saints? The answer is very plain, that the Gentiles should be *fellow heirs, of the same body, and partakers of His promise in Christ through the gospel, of which I became a minister according to the gift of the grace of God given to me by the effective working of His power. To me, who am less than the least of all the saints, this grace was given, that I should preach among the Gentiles the unsearchable riches of Christ, and to make all see what is the fellowship of the mystery, which from the beginning of the ages has been hidden in God who created all things through Jesus Christ;* Eph 3:5-9 NKJV. There it is, the secret is out! The Gentiles are to be included in the New Covenant! The new Israel is not just the remnant of the old Israel but has a hidden ingredient, a remnant from the Gentiles. It had been 'hidden' from 'the beginning of the ages' but now the secret is abroad.

The epistle to the Ephesians was probably a circular letter written to several churches in the same area of Asia Minor, modern day Turkey. The churches in this area were predominantly Gentile, non-Jewish, in their congregations. Paul wanted these people to understand the very great privilege that God had extended to them in the New Covenant and he spells out their previous disqualification very specifically; *at that time you were without Christ, being aliens from the commonwealth of Israel and strangers from the covenants of promise, having no hope and without God in the world.* Eph 2:12 NKJV. The Gentile nations had no covenant-rights in the way that God's ancient covenant people had had them. They had no share in the promises that God had made to the covenant people. This is one of the bleakest descriptions in the Scripture; without Christ, aliens, strangers, no promises, no hope, without God... *But now in Christ Jesus you who once were far off have been brought near by the blood of Christ. For He Himself is our peace, who has made both one, and has broken down the middle wall of separation, having abolished in His flesh the enmity, that is, the law of commandments contained in ordinances, so as to create in Himself one new man from the two, thus making peace,* Eph 2:13-15 NKJV.

"But now..." marks a watershed. Something has changed and it is what happened on the cross that has achieved the change.

One flock and one shepherd

In the work of the cross two things have become one. Not in Ezekiel's hands but through nail-pierced hands. From two 'old' things one 'new' thing has emerged. As a result of the work of the cross God has been able to start all over again with a 'new man' and in that new man Jew and Gentile meet without distinction as God's one, new, people. Paul makes reference to the cross breaking down a middle wall of separation. Many have seen this as a reference to the balustrade in Herod's temple that separated Jew and Gentile and had inscribed on it the ominous words "Whoever is captured will have himself to blame for his subsequent death". This separated the 'Court of Israel" from the 'Court of the Gentiles'. I want to unpack this idea to understand just what Paul means when he says Christ has broken down the middle wall of separation.

In a parallel passage in Colossians he says; *And you, being dead in your trespasses and the uncircumcision of your flesh, He has made alive together with Him, having forgiven you all trespasses, having wiped out the handwriting of requirements that was against us, which was contrary to us. And He has taken it out of the way, having nailed it to the cross.* Col 2:13-14 NKJV. Notice how he switches pronouns from 'you' to 'us'. In what way were 'you Gentiles' different to 'we Jews'? The difference was that 'handwriting of requirements'. In other words the written demands of God in Sinai's covenant Law. In Galatians Paul says that the Law was 'our' child-conductor to bring 'us' to Christ. Here, in Colossians, the law is 'the handwriting of requirements' against 'us'. To the Galatians Paul says 'we' Jews are no longer under a child-conductor now that faith has come. To the Colossians Paul says 'the handwriting of requirements that was against us' has been taken out of the way.

It was the written code that created the real barrier between Jew and Gentile. It marked off the Sinai Covenant people as distinct from the whole earth and was a constant source of irritation and hostility between the Gentile and the Jew; an insurmountable barrier between Jew and Gentile. But in the cross that barrier of the 'hand-written requirements' has come to its end and God has made peace between the two. *Now, says Paul, ...therefore, you are no longer strangers and foreigners, but fellow citizens with the saints and members of the household of God, having been built on the foundation of the apostles and prophets, Jesus Christ Himself being the chief cornerstone, in whom the whole building, being fitted together, grows into a holy temple in the Lord, in whom you also are being built together for a dwelling place of God in the Spirit.* Eph 2:19-22 NKJV. That is the effect of a New Covenant; a new man, a new Israel, a new family of God, a new temple. Christ's death has fulfilled all the righteous requirements of the law and now Jew and Gentile in Christ meet on common ground. Little wonder that Paul was so excited when God shared that secret.

In this chapter we traced the background and history of Paul. We noted his unique qualifications to be Christianity's "systematic theologian" but we also noted Paul's insistence that his understanding of the secret plan of God came by revelation and not native intelligence. We speculated on how Paul may have connected the separate parts of the mystery and his statement that other generations did not have the full revelation of what God was planning. Finally we saw that the issue that created the Old Covenant people, the Law, has been fulfilled in all its righteous requirements by Christ himself and that now Jew and Gentile are able to meet on new and common ground.

20: Branded for Life

Not everyone was as excited as Paul about his 'revelation'. For some, from a strong Jewish background, Paul had gone too far. The Nazarenes might be accepted as a sect within Judaism similar to the sects of the Pharisees or Sadducees, but they saw that opening the door to the Gentiles would close it to many of their fellow Jews. If the movement continued in this direction there could be no possibility of it staying within the larger family of Judaism. There was an alternative and that was to treat the Gentile converts as proselytes to Judaism. In that case as we have seen any candidates would need to submit to a conscious taking on of the yoke of the law; a water baptism, and offering in the Temple and... circumcision.

We've always done it this way

Circumcision was older than the Sinai Covenant, 430 years older. References to physical circumcision in the Sinai

Covenant are surprisingly few, in fact there is just one; *Speak to the children of Israel, saying: 'If a woman has conceived, and borne a male child, then she shall be unclean seven days; as in the days of her customary impurity she shall be unclean. And on the eighth day the flesh of his foreskin shall be circumcised...* Lev 12:2-3 NKJV. The Latin word 'circumcise' is an exact equivalent of the Greek word *peritome* and simply means 'to cut around'. The sign had been part of the covenant that God established with Abraham. Abraham, his male heirs, and the male members of his household were to carry in their body a secret brand that said they belonged to God. The removal of the foreskin was symbolic of the fact that God's purposes would not be fulfilled by human energies. It was a symbolic statement of trust that God must fulfil his own word in his own way. Much later Paul was to define true circumcision with the words; *For we are the circumcision, who worship God in the Spirit, rejoice in Christ Jesus, and have no confidence in the flesh,* Phil 3:3 NKJV. That can serve as a useful pointer to the significance of circumcision; it was a vote of 'no confidence' in the flesh.

On consideration circumcision was a strange sign for more than one reason. For the most part it was not a public sign but rather a secret one. It was a private sign between a man and God. Often we think of circumcision as the sign of the Sinai Covenant community although in fact it was not; the covenant 'sign' of the Sinai Covenant was the keeping of Sabbaths. (Ex 31:13) Circumcision was not a covenant community sign but a personal sign. It spoke of the kind of personal covenant that God had entered into with Abraham. It was, however, incorporated into the Sinai Covenant and fixed for the eighth day of a male child's life. As the child of a member of the covenant community Jesus himself was circumcised on the eighth day. He thus became, personally, a part of the covenant community. Modern Jews have a further ceremony in which the individual takes on the yoke of the law, called Bar Mitzvah, but this ceremony was instituted after the time of Christ. In ancient Israel the male child 'bore the yoke' from his eighth day. It was also a very permanent sign and, pretty much, irreversible so it branded the home-born Jew and proselyte forever. It burned the bridges behind them; there was no 'going back'.

Those who held that Gentile 'Nazarenes' should become full proselytes wielded strong influence, particularly in the areas of stronger traditional Judaism, for example in Jerusalem. We have come to know them as Judaizers and on a famine relief visitation to the Nazarenes in Jerusalem Paul discovered their determination to win their battle. Paul had taken a young Greek with him whose name was Titus. Reading between the lines in Galatians Chapter 2 we discover that there was a conspiracy to infiltrate the gatherings of the Christians and to insist upon the circumcision of Gentiles. The conspiracy was uncovered and the consensus of the church in Jerusalem was that Titus did not need to be circumcised. Round One to Paul. The church in Jerusalem refused to make circumcision a necessary part of being a member of the New Covenant community. James, Peter and John were happy to commend Paul to the work that God had clearly given him.

Love without pretending

Paul returned to Antioch in Syria and was later joined on a visit by Peter. In the beginning of his visit Peter was happy to mix with the Gentile converts and to share meals with them. He did not insist on them keeping Sinai food laws and all was well... until a party arrived from Jerusalem and ostensibly from James. It seems that Peter associated the Judaizing party with James and was anxious about how they would report things to the church in Jerusalem. An insidious process began. Peter began to withdraw from gathering with the Gentile converts and his example was followed by others from a Jewish background. Ultimately even Barnabas, who usually ran to champion the underdog, was drawn into what Paul called 'the hypocrisy'. Round Two to the Judaizers.

The defection of Barnabas was too much for Paul to bear and seeing clearly the implications of their behaviour he decided he must take a public stand. This is one of the great crisis moments of the early New Covenant community, a genuine watershed. From this point the whole history of the movement would be determined. Paul's protest was on the basis of 'the truth of the gospel'. This was not a matter of small or private importance and Peter was roundly rebuked by the man who would become known as the apostle of the Gentiles. If this movement had gone unchecked it would have resulted in two separate communities, two separate churches, two 'new men'. Paul saw the implications and tore into the thinking behind the hypocrisy.

He protested that Peter had been happy to live in a Gentile way until the visitors from Jerusalem arrived. Why then should Peter compel Gentiles to live as Jews? He then explained the implications of justification by faith, the teaching that God declares a man or woman to be right with him, not on the basis of their own life or achievement, but solely because they are relying on Christ alone for salvation. It was customary for Jews to divide the world, in their thinking, into two parts, the 'holy' nation and the Gentile 'sinners'. Paul takes up this theme. If Peter, as a member of the 'holy' nation needed to be justified by faith and not by his own achievements in keeping the law, it is plain that being declared right with God could never be on the basis of keeping the law. There are, according to Paul, no exceptions to this truth; *by the works of the law no flesh shall be justified.* Gal 2:16 NKJV.

This has other implications. If believing this truth has caused Peter to neglect the keeping of the law then this truth has directly led Peter into acts of sin. His faith in Christ's provision alone has taken him over the line into clear transgression of the law. Christ, and Peter's faith, in him has now become associated with transgression and sin. This would make Christ 'a minister of sin', unthinkable! Paul piled on the pressure; *For if I build again those things which I destroyed, I make myself a transgressor.* Gal 2:18 NKJV. To re-erect the need to keep the Sinai law, which Paul's and Peter's faith had pulled down, could only result in the re-establishing of the system that had inevitably branded them as transgressors.

And then the famous verses; *For I through the law died to the law that I might live to God. I have been crucified with Christ; it is no longer I who live, but Christ lives in me; and the life which I now live in the flesh I live by faith in the Son of God, who loved me and gave Himself for me. I do not set aside the grace of God; for if righteousness comes through the law, then Christ died in vain."* Gal 2:19-21 NKJV. The law had pursued Paul to the place where it executed its judgment upon him in the death sentence and now it no longer had authority over him. When was this death sentence executed on Paul? When he was united with Christ. Only the man who has been united with Christ in the death of the cross can give this testimony. We get the full sense of the words if we combine the old and the new King James versions; "I have been"- the New KJV, and still "am" - the Old KJV. This is the Greek Perfect Tense; beginning in the past and continuing through to the present. As a result of his union with Christ Paul now shares Christ's testimony, "I have been and still am co-crucified" and his current life is the expression of the Christ who 'lives in me'. This is neither jargon nor theory; this is Paul's personal experience of the New Covenant in action.

Wrestling with the truth

What was Peter's reaction to all this? We can gather evidence from a subsequent event. Some time later Peter addressed an inter-church conference in Jerusalem. The Judaizers had not given up their attempts and were now claiming boldly that; *"Unless you are circumcised according to the custom of Moses, you cannot be saved."* Acts 15:1 NKJV. Peter's uncertainties are long gone and we can see this from his contribution to the conference in which he reminded them of his visit to the home of Cornelius; *So God, who knows the heart, acknowledged them by giving them the Holy Spirit, just as He did to us, and made no distinction between us and them, purifying their hearts by faith. Now therefore, why do you test God by putting a yoke on the neck of the disciples which neither our fathers nor we were able to bear? But we believe that through the grace of the Lord Jesus Christ we shall be saved in the same manner as they.* Acts 15:8-11 NKJV. That is a wonderful summing up of Paul who was himself present at the same meeting! Perhaps it's just my imagination but I think I see a twinkle in Paul's eye! Round Three to Paul and Peter.

We might have thought that the matter was now completely resolved but it rumbled on for some decades and we find references to the issue in many of the New Testament's epistles.

The account of Paul's confrontation with Peter is part of a letter that was written to a group of churches in the Roman province of Galatia. It was probably written before the Jerusalem Conference and so shows us Paul's thinking in greater detail. Paul has to make it plain to these churches that entrance into what we are calling the New Covenant community was not through the gate of Judaism. Judaism had a great provenance stretching back to the time of Moses but Paul overleaps it and begins with Abraham himself. He makes some remarkable statements.

Calling the witnesses

In his letter to the churches of Galatia he brings his witnesses to the debate. The first witness is Paul himself and his experience. In spite of his adherence to the Law of Moses, in a way that outstripped his contemporaries, his own righteousness did not gain him entrance into this family. It was through a personal encounter with the risen Christ and complete reliance on his finished work of redemption. His second witness is the Galatian churches themselves. He asks by what route they came into the kingdom; *This only I want to learn from you: Did you receive the Spirit by the works of the law, or by the hearing of faith? Are you so foolish? Having begun in the Spirit, are you now being made perfect by the flesh?* Gal 3:2-3 NKJV. It is important to note how Paul appeals to their own experience here. He marks the beginning of their experience as the time they received the Spirit; this was their beginning, in the Spirit.

And finally he calls Abraham to the witness stand... He shows that Abraham's favour with God was not the result of a faithful keeping of the Law. In fact, as he points out later, the Law came 430 years after Abraham's crisis of faith in God. It is clear then that Abraham could not have been right with God on the basis of keeping the Sinai Law. Some of these thoughts are reproduced in his epistle to the Romans where he asks a telling question. He has shown in both letters that Abraham was 'justified by faith' and that 'God's righteousness was credited to Abraham's account as a result of Abraham's faith. Here is his question; *Does this blessedness then come upon the circumcised only, or upon the uncircumcised also? For we say that faith was accounted to Abraham for righteousness. How then was it accounted? While he was circumcised, or uncircumcised? Not while circumcised, but while uncircumcised.* Rom 4:9-10 NKJV. This is the knock-out blow. Abraham himself was not circumcised when God declared him to be 'justified'. If Abraham had not been circumcised how could the Judaizers insist on circumcision as a necessary precondition to being 'saved' or 'right with God'?

Circumcision then was not a precondition but a consequence of true faith and acceptance with God. *Abraham received the sign of circumcision, a seal of the righteousness of the faith which he had while still uncircumcised, that he might be the father of all those who believe, though they are uncircumcised, that righteousness might be imputed to them also,* Rom 4:11 NKJV. But if those promises were given to Abraham and his 'seed' how can the Gentiles qualify? The promise was given to Abraham and his 'seed' and the word 'seed', as we saw in Chapter 4, is singular pointing to one person. The one person, says Paul, is Christ himself who was 'the' descendant/seed of Abraham to whom the promise was made. The means of blessing for the Gentiles is from Abraham but through Abraham's 'seed'; *Christ has redeemed us from the curse of the law, having become a curse for us (for it is written, "Cursed is everyone who hangs on a tree"), that the blessing of Abraham might come upon the Gentiles in Christ Jesus, that we might receive the promise of the Spirit through faith.* Gal 3:13-14 NKJV. That is how the blessing will get to the Gentiles. The route is not Moses and the Sinai Covenant but is 'from' Abraham 'via' Christ and 'through' faith. The route to entrance into the New Covenant community completely bypasses Sinai and arrives safely at its destination direct.

Why the law then?

Let's revisit this key theme. If this is true what was the purpose of the Law? That's the obvious question but, as usual, Paul is ahead of his readers; *What purpose then does the law serve? It was added because of transgressions, till the Seed should come to whom the promise was made;* Gal 3:19 NKJV. The purpose of the law was not to make the achieving of righteousness possible but was to identify the nature and degree of sin. And it had always been a temporary expedient. It had been 'added' and only 'until the Seed should come'. It served, as we have seen as a kind of personal policeman to escort the reluctant pupil into the presence of his tutor. The Law fulfilled this role and once it has brought the Sinai Covenant child to Christ the Law is redundant.

The Law, says Paul, belongs to the childhood of God's people. The Judaizers who said that a genuine beginning and genuine progress in faith could only come as a result of becoming full proselytes and submitting to circumcision were completely wrong. There is now no longer any need for a preliminary period of 'childhood', now both Jew and Gentile begin as full-grown sons, and the proof is that God's Spirit who has taken up residence in the heart has recognised its true family and cries; Abba, Father. Abba is the Aramaic word for 'father' and is followed by the Greek word for 'father.' Both Jew and Gentile instinctively lift their hearts to recognise their true spiritual genealogy. There is now, no longer, any distinction in the New Covenant community; *For you are all sons of God through faith in Christ Jesus. For as many of you as were baptized into Christ have put on Christ. There is neither Jew nor Greek, there is neither slave nor free, there is neither male nor female; for you are all one in Christ Jesus. And if you are Christ's, then you are Abraham's seed, and heirs according to the promise.* Gal 3:26-29 NKJV.

In some of his later epistles Paul takes up the idea of circumcision again. Writing to the Colossian believers he describes true New Covenant community people; *In Him you were also circumcised with the circumcision made without hands, by putting off the body of the sins of the flesh, by the circumcision of Christ, buried with Him in baptism, in which you also were raised with Him through faith in the working of God, who raised Him from the dead* Col 2:11-13 NKJV. He is speaking of Christ's death as a circumcision and says all true believers share this brand-mark of people in personal relationship with God, 'circumcision made without hands'.

Men and women of the day were used to distinguishing between 'the circumcised' meaning those who continued allegiance to the Sinai Covenant and the 'uncircumcised' meaning those who had no such allegiance. In a striking contrast between the physical and the spiritual he redefines the covenant community in his epistle to the Philippians. Paul uses a play on words which is shocking even today; *Beware of dogs, beware of evil workers, beware of the mutilation! For we are the circumcision, who worship God in the Spirit, rejoice in Christ Jesus, and have no confidence in the flesh,* Phil 3:2-3. As we said earlier, circumcision is the Greek word *peritome* cutting around. Mutilation is the Greek word *katatome* it means a complete removal, an amputation. The lines are clearly drawn now; there can be neither confusion nor compromise. The true 'covenant community' are not those with a physical brand in their flesh, but those whose lives reveal plainly whose they are and who they serve. They are the true servants of God who serve in his temple. Their boast is in the achievements of Christ himself. They have no confidence in the flesh.

In this chapter we followed the events that threatened the nature of the early New Covenant community; was this just another branch of Judaism or something quite different? If it was part of Judaism then entrance into Judaism must include circumcision but if not... We traced Paul's confrontation with Peter and its follow-up in Jerusalem and in Peter's letters. We saw how Paul redefined 'circumcision' in his letter to the Philippians as 'no confidence in the flesh' and claimed that it was the New Covenant people and not the Old Covenant people who fulfilled the requirements to be regarded as God's people.

21: Something Better for us

As a Bible character Melchizedek has a somewhat erratic career. He makes his first appearance in three verses in the story of Abraham, and then disappears for over a thousand years before reappearing in a single verse in one of David's psalms. He then disappears for another thousand years before taking centre stage through four chapters of the book of Hebrews. Why does this mysterious character suddenly become prominent in the book of Hebrews? To discover the answer we need to think about the context of Hebrews. Strictly speaking the epistle to the Hebrews is anonymous. Different Bible students have their strong opinions but the only definite answer is 'we don't know'. The recipients of the letter are much easier to identify. They are Jewish Christians who are on the verge of defecting back into Judaism.

Nostalgia v Revelation

We have seen that in spite of the confrontations, and epistles and even an inter-church conference the Judaizers continued on their mission of trying to make the New Covenant a sub-division of the Old Covenant. There was one weapon that threatened to be the most powerful of all... nostalgia. The sights and sounds and smells of Herod's temple must have been truly intoxicating. The magnificent building, its gilded roof glistening in the sun, the priests and the High Priest in his beautiful vestments, the singing of the choirs, the blowing of ram's horns and silver trumpets. The milling crowds, the scents of scorched flesh and incense, the sense of solemn awe that pervaded the services. How is a house meeting going to compete with this?

The 'pull' of the Temple had a strong attraction to all who had experienced it. It always did have. In the days when the nation split into two nations Jeroboam, king of the house of Israel, knew that the power of the Temple and its worship would be irresistible. He tried to counter it by creating his own holy sites and sacrifices and priesthood. It was his attempt to provide a stronger counter-attraction that led him and his people inevitably into idolatry and disaster. (1 Kings 12:25-27) Throughout the centuries Christendom has continually developed elaborate rituals and magnificent buildings, often loosely based on the patterns of priesthood and the splendour of the Temple. This was never God's intention and always blurs the vision of the saints.

In the days when the book of Hebrews was written there was a clear perception in the mind of the author that many believers with a Jewish background stood again at a point of decision. Would they go on or would they turn back? To make sure there was no possible misunderstanding the writer brings a strong word from the prophecy of Habbakuk; *Now the just shall live by faith; But if anyone draws back, My soul has no pleasure in him." But we are not of those who draw back to perdition, but of those who believe to the saving of the soul.* Heb 10:38-39 NKJV. He speaks of the ways that God had spoken in the past and warns them of the danger of neglecting the word of God that has come not through the intermediaries of angels and Moses but from Christ himself. And he constantly repeats the refrain 'it is better'. Christ is better than the angels, better than the prophets, better than Aaron and his priesthood, better than Moses and his service of God. He declares that Christ has instituted a better covenant, which has a better hope and is built on better promises. Christ's sacrifice is better. He is a better mediator. At one point he trawls through great sections of the Old Testament drawing attention to kings and leaders and heroes of faith and ends with the statement; *And all these, having obtained a good testimony through faith, did not receive the promise, God having provided something better for us, that they should not be made perfect apart from us.* Heb 11:39-40 NKJV. It is simply 'the better covenant'.

The writer's way is to define and describe by way of contrast. Jeremiah had begun his introduction of the New Covenant by contrasting it with the Sinai Covenant and the writer to the Hebrews follows that pattern. The New Covenant is not 'in addition to' but 'different to' and 'a replacement for' the Old Covenant. It is not complementary but a stand-alone covenant that is perfect in its provision.

The Priest-King

This is where Melchizedek comes into the story. The author of Hebrews shows that the New Covenant is different 'in kind' to the Old Covenant and part of the way he does this is by contrasting the Levitical Priesthood, the kind of priesthood that Aaron and his sons exercised, with a Melchizedek kind of priesthood. In the history of the nation there had been a clear division of labour between the kings and the priests. The monarchy was provided by the 'house of David' and was descended from Judah, one of Jacob/Israel's sons. The priesthood, on the other hand, was provided by the 'house of Levi', and particularly through the family of Aaron. The priesthood and the crown were thus carefully separated. In Israel's Biblical history there were no 'priest-kings'. But in Israel's pre-history there was such a priest-king, a man who held in himself the twin function of priest and king, but only one such man, and his name was Melchizedek; *Then*

Melchizedek king of Salem brought out bread and wine; he was the priest of God Most High. Gen 14:18 NKJV. Melchizedek appears in the story of Abraham without introduction. Like a meteorite he flashes across the scene and is gone almost before we have time to notice him, but he provides another of those shadows and patterns; another colour for our palette. Melchizedek is a priest-king.

Occasionally prophets bringing the word of God were given messages that must have been quite incomprehensible to them. During the rebuilding of the Temple after the Babylonian return Zechariah and Haggai encouraged the temple builders with their prophecies. On one occasion Zechariah brought a perplexing message; *Yes, He shall build the temple of the LORD. He shall bear the glory, And shall sit and rule on His throne; So He shall be a priest on His throne, And the counsel of peace shall be between them both.* Zech 6:13 NKJV. This prophecy was in direct contradiction to all that God had revealed about kings and priests. Kings had thrones, priests 'stood' to serve God. No doubt Zechariah was one of those prophets referred to by Peter who 'enquired and searched diligently' as to the meaning of his prophecy and was told that his words belonged to a later time.

In the Tabernacle of old and in the Temples that followed there were no seats for the priests. There was only one seat that is usually translated as 'the mercy seat' in our different Bible versions; from that throne God reigned over his people. Later, kings would have thrones, but priests... never. During his explanations to those being tempted to be drawn back into Judaism and the Old Covenant the writer refocuses his readers' attention on his main point; *Now this is the main point of the things we are saying: We have such a High Priest, who is seated at the right hand of the throne of the Majesty in the heavens,* Heb 8:1 NKJV. A priest is found sitting on a throne; this cannot possibly be a Levitical priest. It is an entirely different kind of priest, a priest like Melchizedek.

He also makes the point that Levitical priests stood to their work and that it had to be repeated day after day. In the symbolism of the shadow and pattern, there was no rest for the priests, not even on the Sabbath. Christ however is a different kind of priest; *And every priest stands ministering daily and offering repeatedly the same sacrifices, which can never take away sins. But this Man, after He had offered one sacrifice for sins forever, sat down at the right hand of God, from that time waiting till His enemies are made His footstool.* Heb 10:11-13 NKJV. There is the stark difference; the Old Covenant had standing priests, the New Covenant has a sitting priest.

He also makes the point that the blood of animal sacrifices could never, in its own power, take away sins. Sins were remitted, released, in the Old Covenant but the basis of that remission was never the value of the animal sacrifice but was based on the value of the sacrifice of Christ; *Therefore it was necessary that the copies of the things in the heavens should be purified with these, but the heavenly things themselves with better sacrifices than these.* Heb 9:23 NKJV. Symbolically their blood cleansed the earthly sanctuaries but they were only shadows and patterns of the coming Lamb whose 'once for ever' sacrifice has always been and will always be the legal basis on which God remits sin. This is the same truth that Paul declares in his epistle to the saints in Rome; *...Christ Jesus, whom God set forth as a propitiation by His blood, through faith, to demonstrate His righteousness, because in His forbearance God had passed over the sins that were previously committed,* Rom 3:24-25 NKJV.

All change

Why is the writer going to such lengths to show that Christ's kind of priesthood is better than the Levitical priesthood? Christ's priesthood is not an alternative to Aaron's; it is a replacement. *For the priesthood being changed, of necessity there is also a change of the law.* Heb 7:12 NKJV. The word translated 'changed' here is only used in the letter to the Hebrews but the other instances are significant in understanding its true sense. The writer at one point speaks of Enoch and says that he was 'translated' from earth to heaven. (Heb 11:5). He 'exchanged' earth for heaven. Enoch's two locations were mutually exclusive; he could not be in both at the same time. His place of residence was 'changed'. In the other instance the reference is to the 'removal' of one state so that it can be 'replaced' by another. (Heb 12:27) This key verse is one we really need to allow to shape our thinking. The New Covenant is not an additional covenant; it is a replacement. *then He said, "Behold, I have come to do Your will, O God." He takes away the first that He may establish the second.* Heb 10:9 NKJV. The Messenger of the Covenant did not come to put a New Covenant patch on an Old Covenant piece of clothing. Nor did he come to put New Covenant wine into Old Covenant wine-skins; that could only result in the loss of both wine and wineskin. He had come to consciously 'take away' the first, Old Covenant, so that he would be able to establish the second, New Covenant.

But there is a second serious consequence to this that we have already noted. *For the priesthood being changed, of necessity there is also a change of the law.* Heb 7:12 NKJV. We cannot change the priesthood and leave the basis of the law unchanged. There is an absolute 'necessity' that the law must be changed also. Not merely the ceremonial law but the whole basis and pattern of the law. The Sinai law, as we saw earlier, was inseparable from the priesthood. The Law on its own would have instantly brought the covenant to an end with the first transgression. The covenant parties had their individual responsibilities under the covenant. God must keep his promises and his people must keep theirs. These were the conditions of the covenant and if the conditions are not kept the covenant is in breach. It was the provision of the priesthood with its sacrifices that provided a continuing maintenance of the covenant by making it possible for God to continue to reside in the midst of a sinful people. Without the Levitical priesthood the Sinai Covenant is dead in the water. It is utterly unworkable.

The Levitical priesthood's 'term of office' was terminated by Christ's death on the cross. For some years the Levitical priests would continue to go through the motions but their priesthood no longer had any efficacy. The reality of Christ's death made the Old Testament shadows of his death superfluous. When there is no clear sight of the reality shadows and patterns can serve a valuable purpose but when the true has come into view then the shadows may only serve to obscure. When the shadow is no longer a help it becomes an obstacle to clear sight.

Now this is going to have other consequences because it was that Sinai Covenant that brought the covenant people of Israel into being as a spiritual entity. Israel did not simply evolve from the descendants of Jacob; Israel was a unique *bara*-creation. Isaiah 43:15 NKJV. The covenant was not based on sentiment or on nostalgia. It was based on a legal understanding agreed by both parties; *And Moses took the blood, sprinkled it on the people, and said, "This is the blood of the covenant which the LORD has made with you according to all these words."* Ex 24:8 NKJV. The 'words' referred to are the words that Moses had written in the Book of the Covenant. This is what we said earlier, in Chapter 2, when we described the Sinai Covenant as being 'Book-based' or 'bible-based'. Even though the legal documents in stone and parchment had been lost God had maintained his faithfulness to his covenant people, but now the agreement had ended, and both the terms and conditions are all terminated.

Where does this leave the Old Covenant community? Its promises originating in Abraham are transferred into the New Covenant. Old Israel is not rejected. The New Covenant is specifically addressed to the 'house of Israel' and the 'house of Judah'; they are not excluded. But the terms of the New Covenant constitute a New Israel in which believing Jews and believing Gentile are 'at peace' in one new man.

Melchizedek had functioned as a mediator between God and Abraham. Moses had functioned as a mediator between God and the nation of Israel. Continuing its theme of contrast and things 'better', the epistle tells us, that Christ has fulfilled the shadows and patterns of the Sinai administration; *But now He has obtained a more excellent ministry, inasmuch as He is also Mediator of a better covenant, which was established on better promises.* Heb 8:6 NKJV. What are the better promises? They are the promises found in the prophecies of Jeremiah and Ezekiel. Promises of God's law written in hearts and minds. Promises that God would 'cause' his people to walk in his ways. Promises of a new inner centre, a new heart and a new spirit. Promises that God's own Spirit would come to indwell.

Access

With breathtaking boldness the writer again contrasts the Levitical priesthood and Christ's High Priesthood with a telling insight. In the old, Sinai, Levitical, covenant God established ceremonies that were in themselves shadows and patterns. The great embroidered curtain that separated the Holy Place where the priests served and the Holy of Holies where God dwelt in *shekinah* glory was also a shadow and pattern. It made the point that during the time of the Levitical covenant the way into the immediate presence of God was prohibited. The Spirit who inspired Moses and gave the pattern for the Tabernacle was pointing to a significant fact of spiritual life; *the Holy Spirit indicating this, that the way into the Holiest of All was not yet made manifest while the first tabernacle was still standing. It was symbolic for the present time in which both gifts and sacrifices are offered which cannot make him who performed the service perfect in regard to the conscience— concerned only with foods and drinks, various washings, and fleshly ordinances imposed until the time of reformation.* Heb 9:8-10 NKJV. Although God continued in grace with his people their ceremonies constantly made the point that sinful man was still separated from a holy God. The Levitical High Priest entered, briefly, once in each year, but man could not 'dwell' in the presence of God. The veil with its elaborate embroidery of the angel guardians of God's presence barred the way, just as the angel guardians themselves had barred the way of return into Eden. (Gen 3:24)

No doubt the Levitical High Priest approached that veil on the Day of Atonement with considerable trepidation. Would the atoning sacrifice be accepted? If not he could never survive the presence of God even for a brief moment. Now the writer describes Christ as High Priest and sees him coming not with the blood of sacrificial beasts but with his own blood and gaining access to the Most Holy Place. He explains that the blood of Christ, and this is the Bible's way of saying 'Christ's sacrificial death' was the outward expression of an offering in the Spirit as he offered himself, without spot, to God; *...how much more shall the blood of Christ, who through the eternal Spirit offered Himself without spot to God, cleanse your* *conscience from dead works to serve the living God* Heb 9:14-15 NKJV. Christ did die physically at a specific place in time but it was not the outward suffering that achieved atonement but the offering of himself. The real passion of the cross was invisible to human sight.

As a consequence... *Christ has not entered the holy places made with hands, which are copies of the true, but into heaven itself, now to appear in the presence of God for us;* Heb 9:24 NKJV. The human race now has its own representative who has entered into heaven itself to 'appear in the presence of God for us'. He is our sufficient sacrifice, or to mix the language of the law court with that of the temple; *we have an Advocate with the Father, Jesus Christ the righteous. And He Himself is the propitiation for our sins, and not for ours only but also for the whole world.* 1 John 2:1-2 NKJV. And this entering into the Most Holy Place is not a gesture to prove a point but opens up the way for others to follow him. A race of utterly disqualified men and women may now 'boldly go where no man has gone before'; *Therefore, brethren, having boldness to enter the Holiest by the blood of Jesus, by a new and living way which He consecrated for us, through the veil, that is, His flesh, and having a High Priest over the house of God, let us draw near with a true heart in full assurance of faith, having our hearts sprinkled from an evil conscience and our bodies washed with pure water.* Heb 10:19-22 NKJV.

This is not 'heaven when we die' but a present reality in the Spirit in which we can now draw near to God. The Old Covenant could never achieve this; *for the law made nothing perfect; on the other hand, there is the bringing in of a better hope, through which we draw near to God.* Heb 7:19 NKJV. There is now a new and living way by which men and women can draw near to God. In the language of Hebrews it is 'through the veil, that is, his flesh'. This is another vital truth. It is not as though Christ's death has taken the veil away, although several well known hymns suggest he has. The veil is not removed, it is torn, and entrance into the presence of God is only through that tear. The 'barrier' is not removed, but there is a tear in it that gives all who will come, through that tear only, access to God. This is highly figurative language but the writer is saying what Paul says more plainly in the epistle to the Romans; *Therefore, having been justified by faith, we have peace with God through our Lord Jesus Christ, through whom also we have access by faith into this grace in which we stand, and rejoice in hope of the glory of God.* Rom 5:1-2 NKJV. Our access is 'through Christ' and through the 'torn veil', the work that he accomplished at Calvary.

In this chapter we read of Melchizedek and saw why he can be used as a symbol of a different kind of priesthood; a king-priest. We saw why the author of the letter to the Hebrews declares so defiantly that the New Covenant is better than the Old Covenant. We saw that in Old Covenant times the way into God's presence was symbolically barred but that in the New Covenant there is a tear in the barrier through which all may enter. We saw the difference between Old Covenant priests who constantly 'stood' and never finished their work, with the New Covenant High Priest who offered one single sacrifice and has now sat down.

22: A Different Dynamic

We have seen the way in which the New Covenant, new birth, entrance into the kingdom of God, and the coming of the Spirit are different expressions used to describe what is essentially the same thing; the process whereby a man or woman becomes 'joined in Spirit' with Christ himself to create a new man which can be described as 'I in you and you in me'. It is time to look at the way the Scriptures explain the means whereby this miracle of the Spirit takes place. To do so we shall have to revisit some of those ancient prophecies and see how they are interpreted in the New Testament.

Curing the incurable

We are indebted to Jeremiah for this first use of the term 'New Covenant'. The book of Jeremiah is a series of prophecies given over quite a period of time but we can identify common themes and threads. Our starting point for this book has been;

Behold, the days are coming, says the LORD, when I will make a New Covenant with the house of Israel and with the house of Judah— not according to the covenant that I made with their fathers in the day that I took them by the hand to lead them out of the land of Egypt, My covenant which they broke, though I was a husband to them, says the LORD. But this is the covenant that I will make with the house of Israel after those days, says the LORD: I will put My law in their minds, and write it on their hearts; and I will be their God, and they shall be My people. Jer 31:31-33 NKJV. There is much more than this but this will remind us of our starting point. We can make two broad points about these three verses. They make it clear that the New Covenant is different to the Old Covenant, and secondly they contain God's promise to internalise his mind and will in those who entered into that New Covenant.

The way that Jeremiah describes it is in terms of 'heart and mind'. We will not try to define these terms precisely at this point but just make the comment that these terms have to do with the 'innermost' aspect of humanity. To get to the 'heart' of the matter is to get to the very centre of the issue. This predicted New Covenant is going to get to the heart of the matter. God is going to put his revealed will into the inner man. He will write it plainly in the inner consciousness of men and women and the consequence of this will be that God will be the God of this New Covenant people, and this New Covenant people will belong exclusively to God.

This is not the first time that Jeremiah speaks of things written on the heart and his early use will give us some pointers as to what he is saying. For this we need to turn to one of the most used Old Testament texts in older evangelical preaching; *The heart is deceitful above all things, And desperately wicked; Who can know it?* Jer 17:9 NKJV. Generations of Sunday School children have committed this verse to 'heart', but what does it mean? The original Hebrew declares, "the heart is crooked above all things and incurable, who can know it?" The word crooked is almost the word 'Jacob' in Hebrew. The phrase points to a depth of crookedness in the heart that is far beyond human comprehension and which is incurable. What is this disease and how do you treat something that is incurable?

Indelible sin

At the beginning of this same chapter Jeremiah describes the behaviour of the 'house of Judah'. At this point the 'house of Israel' had been taken into captivity by Assyria and the 'house of Judah' was about to suffer the same fate in Babylon. Jeremiah describes the heart condition of the southern kingdom and declares; *The sin of Judah is written with a pen of iron; With the point of a diamond it is engraved On the tablet of their heart,* Jer 17:1 NKJV. The pen of iron, of course, is a chisel. Judah's sin was carved indelibly into its innermost being. Judah's sin was not something that could be treated cosmetically with a coat of paint. Their sin had become permanently etched into their inner man. We can see why later Jeremiah declares that their condition is incurable. The law of God had been carved into tablets of stone on Sinai; his will permanently expressed. Now Jeremiah says the nation's disposition is carved into their hearts; permanently expressed. So how shall we diagnose Judah's condition and identify the disease?

The answer is in the following verses; *The sin of Judah is written with a pen of iron; With the point of a diamond it is engraved On the tablet of their heart, And on the horns of your altars, While their children remember Their altars and their wooden images By the green trees on the high hills.* Jer 17:1-2 NKJV. The words describe a proneness to idolatry that was relentless. Their sin is spiritual promiscuity; they constantly seek for other gods, they are insatiable. They have become addicted to false gods and false religion and at the heart of all idolatry is a refusal to surrender to the true God. The Bible is a down-to-earth book in many ways and Jeremiah's language is certainly down to earth and downright earthy at times. He had described symptoms of this disease earlier; *A wild donkey used to the wilderness, That sniffs at the wind in her desire; In her time of mating, who can turn her away? All those who seek her will not weary themselves; In her month they will find her.* Jer 2:24 NKJV. The nation was like a female donkey 'in heat'; there was no stopping her. Now Jeremiah says the condition is etched upon the nation's heart and it is incurable.

It is against this background of a nation's nature that Jeremiah gives the amazing promise of a New Covenant. A New Covenant in which God will etch his will into the hearts and minds of a people who will, thereby, become God's people and he, their God. It is breathtaking in its audacity and its implications. This is nothing less than the promise of a new nature. Is it possible that the lust for other gods could be replaced by a lust for the true God? The word 'lust', by the way, is used of strong passions in the Scriptures, passions both good and bad.

When Paul wrote of certain Old Testament accounts he said that the things that had occurred were written for our admonition, a cautionary reminder. (1 Cor 10:11) The events were true in themselves but they were recorded for a continuing purpose. The description of the house of Judah is not recorded because they were unique in their spiritual promiscuity but because they serve as a template for us all. The house of Judah is not exceptional; it is a description of the heart of every man and woman who is not as yet enjoying the blessings of the New Covenant.

Prone to wander?

In the 18th century an unhappy preacher, Robert Robinson, wrote a hymn that begins 'Come thou fount of every blessing' and has a stanza that says;

> O to grace how great a debtor
> Daily I'm constrained to be!
> Let Thy goodness, like a fetter,
> Bind my wandering heart to Thee.
> Prone to wander, Lord, I feel it,
> Prone to leave the God I love;
> Here's my heart, O take and seal it,
> Seal it for Thy courts above.

The hymn has some fine sentiments but some sub-Christian elements too. In his honesty he describes his heart in terms that Jeremiah would happily have used to describe the house of Judah, but for the hymn-writer the joys of the New Covenant must await a heavenly fulfilment. When I call these elements 'sub-Christian' I am not saying that Robinson was 'sub-Christian' but only that his experience or expectation was 'sub-Christian'. Wandering heart and proneness to turn our back on God are not to be regarded as the norm of Christian experience. The hymn misses the great before and after statements of the New Testament. It has lost the assurance of the 'but now' with which Peter speaks; *who Himself bore our sins in His own body on the tree, that we, having died to sins, might live for righteousness—by whose stripes you were healed. For you were like sheep going astray, but have now returned to the Shepherd and Overseer of your souls.* 1Pet 2:23-3:1 NKJV. The 'but now' points to the watershed in genuine Christian experience. In Robinson's hymn the healing of spiritual promiscuity is conspicuously missing.

If Jeremiah is bold, Ezekiel is more so. Ezekiel does not use the term 'New Covenant' but it is plain that he has the same promises in mind when he issued his prophecies in Babylon itself. And Ezekiel does not use the language of God carving his own will into the hearts of men and women. Ezekiel's language is even more radical. He has the same themes of restoration but his expression is even more breathtaking; *Then I will sprinkle clean water on you, and you shall be clean; I will cleanse you from all your filthiness and from all your idols. I will give you a new heart and put a new spirit within you; I will take the heart of stone out of your flesh and give you a heart of flesh. I will put My Spirit within you and cause you to walk in My statutes, and you will keep My judgments and do them. Then you shall dwell in the land that I gave to your fathers; you shall be My people, and I will be your God.* Ezek 36:25-28 NKJV. He is addressing the same condition of spiritual promiscuity and he comes to the same point as Jeremiah in declaring that 'you shall be my people, and I will be your God'. Ezekiel, however, uses the language of replacement, and very specifically too. The old heart will be removed and a new heart put in its place.

Ezekiel declares that God's purpose is to both cleanse and to renew. The centre of his prophecy is that God will give them a 'new heart and a new spirit'. Jeremiah's incurable condition has a remedy, a transplant. Of course, this was long before the possibility of physical heart transplants but the language is very precise. The old 'stone heart', the one on which Jeremiah said the nation's nature was written, is to be removed and replaced by a 'heart of flesh'. Here the ideas of intractable stone and responsive flesh are contrasted. The prophecy is remarkable for its clarity of the process by which God would achieve his purposes. Not only would a new heart be given but the old heart would be taken away. He would give a new heart and put a new spirit at the innermost point, but more... His own Spirit would take up residence in the renewed nature. The replacement of the old 'heart and spirit' with a new 'heart and spirit' is a wonderful promise but in itself there is not necessarily a greater security in it. If other things were not added even a cleansed temple might well revert to its old state, as we have seen earlier. The physical temple of Christ's day was cleansed twice, once at the beginning and once at the end of his earthly ministry. In the space of three years the 'cleansed' temple had reverted to its original state of defilement. Reformation alone has no power to maintain itself. If the replacement were the end of the matter the human race might well find itself in that state which is sometimes described as 'rearranging the deck-chairs on the Titanic'. But the promise is not only of taking away, and replacing but of God himself taking up residence in the cleansed temple.

God on the inside

This promise of "I will put my Spirit within you" is surely a pre-echo of the promise of Christ; *the Spirit of truth, whom the world cannot receive, because it neither sees Him nor knows Him; but you know Him, for He dwells with you and will be in you.* John 14:17 NKJV. We are back to the essential criteria of the New Covenant, "you in me, and I in you". If you have got your breath back from the implications of this we will move on to the next clause.

Perhaps the next clause is the most challenging of all; *I will put My Spirit within you and cause you to walk in My statutes, and you will keep My judgments and do them.* Ezek 36:27-28 NKJV. To get the sense of the greatness of this promise we can remind ourselves of something that Moses declared when the Old Covenant people were poised to enter the promised land; *For I know that after my death you will become utterly corrupt, and turn aside from the way which I have commanded you. And evil will befall you in the latter days, because you will do evil in the sight of the LORD, to provoke Him to anger through the work of your hands.* Deut 31:29 NKJV. Moses predicted the ultimate failure of his Sinai Covenant. But here in Ezekiel is a prediction and a promise that God will 'cause them to walk in his statutes' and 'keep my judgments and do them'. The purpose, as we see here, of the indwelling Spirit is to 'cause' them to live in accordance with the will of God. To 'cause them'? How can this be so unless God changes man into an automaton with no ultimate power of choice?

Perhaps if we explain in terms of contrast? Adam's first act of rebellion had more than one dimension. It not only affected him and caused him to forfeit his destiny, it also had an impact on the whole human race; *...by the one man's offense many died...* Rom 5:15 NKJV. That is not referring just to physical death. Adam himself did not immediately die physically but, in fulfilment of the terms of that covenant, he did die in the day that he ate the forbidden fruit. The death that all human beings share is not merely physical but is also spiritual. Paul introduces this profound topic by saying; *Therefore, just as through one man sin entered the world, and death through sin, and thus death spread to all men, because all sinned—* Rom 5:12 NKJV. Something entered the world as a result of one man's action and Paul calls this Sin. He is not thinking now in terms of a personal failure or an individual transgression but of a spiritual dynamic called Sin and Death that entered the human race. Something happened to the race in Adam and the race continues under that sentence of spiritual death for all who are still connected to him in spirit. In this sense 'Sin and Death' are inseparable.

Elsewhere Paul describes this spiritual dynamic as a spirit; *And you He made alive, who were dead in trespasses and sins, in which you once walked according to the course of this world, according to the prince of the power of the air, the spirit who now works in the sons of disobedience, among whom also we all once conducted ourselves in the lusts of our flesh, fulfilling the desires of the flesh and of the mind, and were by nature children of wrath, just as the others.* Eph 1:23-2:3 NKJV. That's quite a complex statement but we can simplify it by explaining Paul's purpose. He is making the point that Christ has given them life where their natural state was to be 'dead in trespasses and sins'. In that state these 'dead men' were still 'walking', so we know we are not reading about physical death! 'Walking' is a Bible idiom for a pattern of life. Those to whom he writes had, in the past, walked in a pattern of life that was aligned to 'this world' and was aligned to someone that he calls "the prince of the power of the air, the spirit who now works in the sons of disobedience". This is God's enemy and ours, the being that the Bible calls Satan or the devil.

Either/Or

There have been forces at work in our lives for which there is no real explanation other than this one given by Paul. Jesus once described this enemy of the human race very simply; *The thief does not come except to steal, and to kill, and to destroy. I have come that they may have life, and that they may have it more abundantly.* John 10:10 NKJV. His nature is characterised in this brief description. This spirit, the spirit of disobedience, has continued to work on and in the human race to create a disposition which reveals that, in our innermost centre, we are the children of another spirit and our behaviour has shown it. Paul says the whole race has been like this. It is another way of saying what Jeremiah said when he spoke of an incurable and crooked heart. But this passage holds one of those 'before and after' words, this time it is the phrases "you once walked" and "once conducted yourselves". He is writing to people that 'no longer walk' in alignment with this spirit, and to people who are no longer conducting themselves in alignment with that spirit. Although others may still walk that way those to whom Paul writes have changed their pattern of life.

So we have a contrast between two kinds of human beings, those who once behaved like this and those who still do. In their own way all the race is 'walking in the spirit', but not all the race is walking in the same spirit. The pattern of life of those who walk according to the wrong spirit will, in the words of Robert Robinson, have a wandering heart, and a proneness to turn their back on God. The dynamic of that wrong spirit will, by default, always head in the wrong direction. That does not mean that we are automatons to that spirit either. God always gives grace to obey so if we do not obey it is because we are not relying upon him but following our own instincts. It is not impossible for a man or woman, who by nature is walking in alignment with a wrong spirit, to perform a righteous act. Adolf Hitler was famously kind to his dog, but that did not indicate a change in his nature. When the pressure is on the human being will instinctively revert to type. The one righteous act does not make him a righteous man.

So in the promise of the New Covenant we have the promise not only of a renewed human spirit but the indwelling presence of God's own Spirit. If we understand the nature of God's Spirit we will understand that there can be no mutual co-existence between the Holy Spirit and the spirit of disobedience. It will inevitably be 'either/or'. For the man or woman who has genuinely entered into a New Covenant there exists a new inner spiritual dynamic; *the law of the Spirit of life in Christ Jesus has made me free from the law of sin and death.* Rom 8:2. NKJV. We ourselves will still need to choose, but the new default position, the new instinct, is that expressed in testimony by Christ in the moment of incarnation; *Therefore, when He came into the world, He said: "Sacrifice and offering You did not desire, But a body You have prepared for Me. In burnt offerings and sacrifices for sin You had no pleasure. Then I said, "Behold, I have come— In the volume of the book it is written of Me— To do Your will, O God.' "* Heb 10:5-7 NKJV.

In this chapter we reminded ourselves of the old verse that says 'the heart is deceitful above all things and desperately

225

wicked' and saw how Jeremiah contrasts what may be written on the hearts of men and women. We saw that Ezekiel speaks of the old heart of stone being removed and replaced by a new sensitised heart. We challenged the idea that we are 'prone to wander' when God brings us into his New Covenant and showed how the dynamic bias of the human heart is transformed in the New Covenant. We saw that 'Walking' is a Bible idiom for a pattern of life. Those to whom Paul writes had, in the past, walked in a pattern of life that was aligned to 'this world' and was aligned to someone that he calls; "the prince of the power of the air, the spirit who now works in the sons of disobedience". We saw that all men 'walk in the spirit' but that our whole race is not walking in the same spirit. Some who once walked in a 'disobedient spirit' are now walking in the Holy Spirit.

23: If that is true so is this

It did seem such a strange way of expressing something. They were gathered in an annual celebration designed to look backwards to the key event of their history and yet he seemed to have his gaze in the opposite direction, not backwards but forwards. I am referring to Christ's comment in the upper room. We have seen previously how key this time was and the enormous percentage of time, in the gospels, that is given to these few hours. His words were; *"With fervent desire I have desired to eat this Passover with you before I suffer; for I say to you, I will no longer eat of it until it is fulfilled in the kingdom of God."* Luke 22:15-16 NKJV. There are three elements in this sentence. There is the celebration of the Passover, the annual remembrance of the first step of God's deliverance and the first step towards the making of a covenant between the nation and God at Sinai. Then there is the clear prediction of his suffering. Then there is a statement that the

Passover will be fulfilled in the kingdom of God. How can we understand the Passover as needing a 'fulfilment'?

The Last Supper or the First?

As far as we know from the Scripture record the Passover Lamb is the only sacrifice that Jesus offered personally. Jewish patterns have changed over the centuries but we can create a legitimate scenario for the celebration in the upper room. The very first Passover meal had taken place with the guests all standing in readiness for the Exodus, but from the time that the nation inherited the land the pattern was to sit, or rather recline, to indicate that they had entered into God's rest. The cup or chalice was shared several times in the feast and Luke's record mentions two of these. According to the Jewish ritual the 'third cup' was shared at the end of the meal and it seems that this is the point at which Christ transposed the backwards look of Passover into the forward look of the Communion meal. It seems as though the last or fourth 'cup' was being postponed until the kingdom of God fully arrived.

The 'kingdom of God' is a phrase that can be understood at different levels. In a sense where the king is, there is the kingdom. It is not a physical realm but the comprehensive rule of the king. Consequently, in Christ 'the once and future king', the kingdom of God is both present and future. He lived his life within the kingdom but for others entrance into that kingdom must be by a birth that is 'by water and by Spirit'. As the Spirit had not yet been given at the first sharing of the Communion meal, entrance into that kingdom was still in the future when the meal was first celebrated.

The Luke account goes on to quote the words of the institution of the Communion and includes the phrase; *"This cup is the New Covenant in My blood, which is shed for you."* Luke 22:20 NKJV. We begin to see the same alignment of phrases; the kingdom of God and the New Covenant in this passage. These concepts are really inseparable. This is the significance of the reference to the need for the 'Passover' to be fulfilled. The Passover was not merely an historical event it was another of those shadows and patterns. The original Passover gave an outline in two dimensions that must now be fulfilled in three dimensions with full colour in spiritual reality. This idea became a settled concept in the early church. When Paul instructs the church in Corinth to put their house in order his proof text is this concept; *Therefore purge out the old leaven, that you may be a new lump, since you truly are unleavened. For indeed Christ, our Passover, was sacrificed for us.* 1 Cor 5:7 NKJV. With that clear identification of Christ as the fulfilment of the Passover shadow we can expand the type.

The original Passover was the first event in the process that led to Israel's redemption and their acceptance as God's covenant nation. A sentence of death hung over all the first-born sons in Egypt and only those who shared in the Passover meal were spared. The sign that the inhabitants of a home were sharing the Passover meal, the lamb's blood, was daubed on the lintels and doorposts. God 'saw the blood' and 'passed-over', hence the name of the annual celebration. It is important to draw attention to the meaning of the outward sign. (In future celebrations of the Passover they never daubed the doorposts and lintels again but they did eat the lamb year by year.) It meant that those within that home had sacrificed their lamb and were even now eating its flesh. They ate with their shoes on their feet, their staff in their hands, their packs on their back and with their robes tucked into their belts; they were ready to march. Most of the details of the Exodus Passover are concerned with the manner of 'eating' rather than of 'splashing' blood on the entrance.

The story is too well known to need a retelling here. Ultimately they came to the Red Sea and crossed safely on dry ground. Their enemies, attempting to follow them, came under judgment. They were not spared. The event is described, as we have seen, as a baptism by Paul in his first letter to the Corinthians. They were baptised into, or united by baptism into, Moses. They were one people but not yet in the fullest sense 'God's people', that must await the making of the Sinai Covenant; *"You have seen what I did to the Egyptians, and how I bore you on eagles' wings and brought you to Myself. Now therefore, if you will indeed obey My voice and keep My covenant, then you shall be a special treasure to Me above all people; for all the earth is Mine. And you shall be to Me a kingdom of priests and a holy nation.' These are the words which you shall speak to the children of Israel."* Ex 19:4-6 NKJV. These are the opening words of the covenant-making event. They do deserve a pause and an observation even though we are treading on familiar ground.

"You shall be, to me, a kingdom of priests". This people were about to become 'God's kingdom'. A kingdom made up not of warriors but of those who served God as his personal servants. The nation was designed to be, in essence and type, the living embodiment of the kingdom of God. The first/old covenant created a physical kingdom of God; the second/New Covenant would create a spiritual kingdom of God. The kingdom and the covenant are synchronised concepts. In its earthly expression the 'kingdom of God' is most closely seen in the pattern of the priests and their service of God. The Tabernacle was God's kingdom in microcosm, entrance to the Holy Place was only permitted to those who had undergone a ritual bathing and received ritual sprinklings of blood and sprinkling of anointing oil; the priests themselves. This was like a kingdom within a kingdom and accessible, in ancient times, only to Aaron and those who shared his bloodline.

Going, going... gone!

It was glorious. So says Paul in his second letter to the Corinthians, but it was a fading glory. Typified in the fading glory seen in the face of the mediator of the Old Covenant, it changed from glory to glory in a descending spiral. We must never denigrate the Sinai Covenant. It *was* glorious. But it was not, says Paul, like the glory of the New Covenant. (2 Cor 3:7-11) It was, in that sense, just a promise of greater things; the earthly natural Passover was but a prelude to the heavenly and spiritual reality. It was not an end in itself but a pattern of a greater Passover leading to a better covenant. This better or new covenant also 'changes from glory to glory' but in an ascending spiral!

The pattern of the Exodus and the Sinai covenant is frequently just under the surface in the New Testament writings. The language with which they describe the New Covenant is taken from the events of the Passover and Exodus and the Conquest of the Land. A good example of this is found in the epistle to the Colossians. Colossians is a very helpful letter and can serve a very valuable purpose other than that for which it was first written. It was written to a gathering of 'saints' in the city of Colossae who were coming under pressure from a philosophical view that was happy to regard 'Christ' as a relevant ingredient in salvation but which did not see Christ as 'all and in all' as Paul described him. Its valuable purpose for today is the same as an answer to all who would regard Christ as 'making a valuable contribution' but who do not regard him as the Only Way, the Only Truth and the Only Life. However, we can use it for a second purpose, it will enable us to get an idea of what the early Christians meant by 'receiving Christ'.

Paul encourages the community at Colossae to continue in the way in which they began their pilgrimage with the words; *As you therefore have received Christ Jesus the Lord, so walk in Him, rooted and built up in Him and established in the faith, as you have been taught, abounding in it with thanksgiving.* Col 2:6-7 NKJV. It is plain that Paul regarded these 'saints' as having authentically 'received Christ Jesus the Lord'. The thing that makes the letter so valuable is that Paul had never met any of them. His conviction that they had truly 'received Christ Jesus the Lord' was based on eye-witness evidence from a colleague who we know as Epaphras.

The little we know of Epaphras makes us wish we knew more, much more. He had been a faithful messenger of the gospel to the people in Colossae and had seen this group of men and women being transformed. Epaphras continued to support them with his love and fervent prayer. It has been said that 'it was Epaphras kneeling which kept the church in Colossae standing'. We can do a little detective work in the epistle to the Colossians to discover just what it was that Epaphras wrote to Paul that caused Paul to conclude that these people had 'received Christ Jesus the Lord'. We don't know all that Paul heard but there is enough evidence to show clearly how Paul understood the phrase.

Receiving Christ

Studying the epistle to the Colossians will also serve this purpose. It will help us to distinguish between subjective experience and objective reality. Some aspects of being in the New Covenant community can be felt and touched. The Bible would use the word 'tasted'; this word means much more than 'sampled'. When the Scriptures speak of Christ 'tasting death for every man', they do not mean that he 'sampled' death but that he 'experienced' it consciously. There are some aspects of genuine Christianity that can be 'tasted' or experienced consciously or subjectively but there are other truths which are just as true but which must be received by objective 'revelation'. We shall see the implications of this as we examine the invisible pattern upon which Paul bases his epistle.

Epaphras had witnessed and reported to Paul key aspects of the Colossian's experience and Paul bases his letter on his conviction that these key aspects show that they have 'received Christ'. Epaphras had reported their 'faith in Christ Jesus', as Paul writes... *We give thanks to the God and Father of our Lord Jesus Christ, praying always for you, since we heard of your faith in Christ Jesus...* Col 1:3-4 NKJV. Many regard John 3:16 as the golden verse of the Bible with its statement that... *God so loved the world that He gave His only begotten Son, that whoever believes in Him should not perish but have everlasting life.* But many who quote it do not realise that we need to go back at least 2 verses to get a Biblical definition of 'believing'; *And as Moses lifted up the serpent in the wilderness, even so must the Son of Man be lifted up, that whoever believes in Him should not perish but have eternal life* John 3:14-16 NKJV. Faith is not mental assent to a series of doctrinal propositions but a personal, life or death, reliance on God's only remedy for our condition. I have an old family Bible with a colour plate by Harold Copping that illustrates the event. A distraught mother is cradling her teenage son in her arms and the father desperately tries to get him to open his eyes to look at the bronze snake on its pole. All he has to do is 'Look and live', but he must look away from his own condition and the snakes still crawling around his body and fix his gaze on God's provision. When Epaphras reported that they had 'faith in Christ Jesus' he means this kind of absolute reliance, not upon an idea, but in the person of Christ himself. This faith is a personal encounter between the Colossians and the living Christ.

Epaphras has also reported on their 'love for all the saints'. (Col 1:4) and further that the love they have expressed is 'love in the Spirit' (Col 1:8) John later wrote...*We know that we have passed from death to life, because we love the brethren. He who does not love his brother abides in death.* 1 John 3:14 NKJV. This 'love' for the brethren is one of the true 'initial evidences' of the Spirit's coming. There is a wonderful and famous testimony that will illustrate my point;

"In the evening I went very unwillingly to a society in Aldersgate Street, where one was reading Luther's preface to the Epistle to the Romans. About a quarter before nine, while he was describing the change which God works in the heart through faith in Christ, I felt my heart strangely warmed. I felt I did trust in Christ, Christ alone, for salvation; and an assurance was given me that He had taken away my sins, even mine, and saved me from the law of sin and death. I began to pray with all my might for those who had in a more especial manner despitefully used me and persecuted me. I then testified openly to all there what I now first felt in my heart."

These are the words from John Wesley's journal dated Wednesday 24th May, 1738. The last sentences are seldom quoted but Wesley's instinct to 'pray with all my might' for his persecutors is a sure expression of the love of God poured out in a man's heart by the Holy Spirit.

This conscious love is not to be confused with emotion or sentimentality. It is not human love on a grand scale but a love of a completely different order. In his epistle to the Romans Paul declares that the reason he is not embarrassed, or as the NKJV translates it 'disappointed' is... *because the love of God has been poured out in our hearts by the Holy Spirit who was given to us.* Rom 5:5 NKJV. For Paul the love of God poured out 'within' the heart is a clear evidence of a supernatural event. He continues, in Romans, to illustrate the nature of the 'love of God' and distinguishes it from the highest forms of human love. It was God's love, in the power of the Spirit, that Epaphras had seen in the Colossian believers and Paul had drawn his own conclusions.

Epaphras had also clearly reported that the Colossians were showing the evidence of new life in fruit and as Paul recounts it... *and is bringing forth fruit, as it is also among you since the day you heard and knew the grace of God in truth;* Col 1:6 NKJV. Perhaps this is the sum of it all. They had 'heard and knew the grace of God in reality'. The word translated 'truth' can often be translated 'reality' in the New Testament. They had heard and knew God's grace authentically. This was no play-acting or a mere cosmetic change. This was the real thing!

Experience and revelation

These subjective, personally experienced, truths might have been the testimony of any of the saints at Colossae. They might not have used these words but if asked they would have been able to say 'I know'. "I know that I have put all my trust in the person of Jesus Christ himself. I know that he has poured out the Spirit of God's own love in my heart. I know that I have genuinely received the grace of God." I had an old preacher friend who used to say; "When people say 'I believe' they mean they are trying to believe. When they really believe they say 'I know'". These are elements of the New Covenant in action, and there are no doubt others, but these were all the evidence that Paul needed. He had no hesitation in discerning that these people had 'received Christ', and his counsel was simply to continue as they had begun. These are the tangible, taste-able, evidences of the New Covenant but there are other elements that are just as true although the saints may not have tasted or experienced them. We will turn to these and see the underlying pattern of Paul's thinking. Although he never mentions the words he is thinking about the Exodus, Sinai and the Promised Land.

The truth that we experience and to which we can testify is only the tip of the iceberg; there's more, much more. This is why Paul frequently prays that the saints will receive 'revelation' or as here in Colossians... *For this reason we also, since the day we heard it, do not cease to pray for you, and to ask that you may be filled with the knowledge of His will in all wisdom and spiritual understanding;* Col 1:9 NKJV. Revelation is God's work. Only he can lift the veil and reveal truth. We may have the words of Scripture and be assisted by able and God-gifted teachers but this is God's prerogative and he alone can do it. Personal faith is, in truth, simply the right response to revelation.

We cannot create revelation but when we receive that inner sense of the truth and know that its origin is God himself, we are required to respond to it. To 'reckon' it so, but only when God has made it plain. It is safe to... *reckon yourselves to be dead indeed to sin, but alive to God in Christ Jesus our Lord.* Rom 6:11. But only if we... *know that as many of us as were baptized into Christ Jesus were baptized into His death?* Rom 6:3 and that... *knowing this, that our old man was crucified with Him, that the body of sin might be done away with, that we should no longer be slaves of sin.* Rom 6:6-7 NKJV. If we are without this inner knowledge and conviction that has come through revelation but then try to 'reckon' a thing true we stand in danger of behaving presumptuously and are likely to suffer major problems in our future pilgrimage.

So Paul prays for 'revelation' and 'spiritual understanding' to enable the Colossians to... *walk worthy of the Lord, fully pleasing Him, being fruitful in every good work and increasing in the knowledge of God;* Col 1:10 NKJV. It was part of Ezekiel's description of the New Covenant that those who had received a new heart and spirit would experience more; the promise continues...*I will put My Spirit within you and cause you to walk in My statutes, and you will keep My judgments and do them.* Ezek 36:27 NKJV. Paul believed that those who have 'received Christ Jesus the Lord' are able to receive truth from God that will enable them to live their lives in a way that always pleases him, and he does not hesitate to pray for it to be so. Do we? He also believed and prayed that this walking in a way that was 'fully pleasing' to God would cause a continuing increase in the true knowledge of God. And he was praying these things for people that we would normally describe as new converts. Where did he gain such faith? From an understanding of the comprehensively 'better covenant'. *No more shall every man teach his neighbor, and every man his brother, saying, "Know the LORD,' for they all shall know Me, from the least of them to the greatest of them, says the LORD. For I will forgive their iniquity, and their sin I will remember no more."* Jer 31:34 NKJV.

He continues to tell the Colossians what he is praying for and for what he is already giving thanks and it is in this thanksgiving that we see his underlying patterns of thought so clearly; *giving thanks to the Father who has qualified us to be partakers of the inheritance of the saints in the light. He has delivered us from the power of darkness and conveyed us into the kingdom of the Son of His love, in whom we have redemption through His blood, the forgiveness of sins.* Col 1:12-14 NKJV. In these three verses he speaks of inheritance, exodus and deliverance. Perhaps if we reverse Paul's order we shall see the pattern emerging. Redemption through blood, was foreshadowed in the Passover. Deliverance from the power of darkness into another kingdom was foreshadowed in the Exodus and Sinai. The inheritance is a foreshadowing of the Promised Land and its possession. But these are not future pictures that Paul is painting. They are all things that have already been accomplished. His readers may not have personally 'tasted' or 'experienced' these truths but, if they have *received Christ Jesus as Lord*, they are just as true as if they had.

Paul is extrapolating. If this is true then so is this. If it is true that you have placed full reliance upon God's provision for salvation in the person of Jesus Christ, if it is true that the Holy Spirit has poured out in your hearts the love of God, if it is true that you heard and knew the grace of God in reality, if it is true that you received Christ Jesus the Lord... then these things are also true. These are not subjective experiences but are, nevertheless, objective realities. Those who have 'received Christ Jesus the Lord' had become part of God's people and their personal history includes a fulfilled Passover, a fulfilled Exodus, a fulfilled Sinai and a fulfilled Inheritance. If we lived in the consciousness of these great spiritual facts how would we walk? Little wonder then that Paul's frequent prayer is for revelation (Eph 1:15-20).

In this chapter we used Paul's letter to the Colossians to identify subjective experience and objective reality. The Colossians had 'tasted' reality in their experience and Epaphras has borne testimony for them in his report to Paul. Paul knows that if their subjective experiences are in place then there are objective realities in place too. They may not be 'tasted' but they are none-the-less true for that. We saw that Paul was working to an underlying pattern; that of the Old Covenant's beginning. The saints in Colossae have already been translated from the power of darkness into the kingdom of God's Son; just like those in the Old Covenant. They have already begun to share in their inheritance in Christ; just like those who lived in the Old Covenant.

24: Spontaneous Moral Originality

I am told, by those who ought to know, that I had to learn
to walk three times. Most folks manage to do this just once but
my slow learning was caused by recurring bouts of tonsillitis
which laid this toddler low. Most of us take walking for
granted, until something goes wrong. Some years ago I tore the
cruciate ligament in my knee and the knee locked in severe
pain. I suppose in all the years that preceded it I had never
given 30 seconds thought to my knee geometry. When things
are working well we hardly notice them. In the initial learning
process our attention to what we are doing can become intense
but once we have mastered the technique, it just flows.

Step by step

Walking is a word you would not usually spend time trying
to define. After all, everyone knows what walking is. I am told
that anatomists would argue it is a highly complicated process

involving more than 200 muscles, but to the user, once initiated, it is a simple process. First you decide where you want to be, and then you lift one foot and reposition it closer to your destination. Once you have completed this first 'step', you just do it again with the other foot. As a child you learn that to take two steps at once is likely to meet with a crash. It is a skill that doesn't give much room for sophisticated variety. The simpler we keep it the less likely we are to fall on our faces. Perhaps that is why the Scriptures constantly use the idea of 'walking' for the way in which we continue what we have begun in 'receiving Christ'; *As you therefore have received Christ Jesus the Lord, so walk in Him,* Col 2:6 NKJV. Some modern translations prefer to translate the word as 'live' but this confuses the picture as the Scriptures clearly distinguish between 'living' and 'walking'; *If we live in the Spirit, let us also walk in the Spirit.* Gal 5:25 NKJV.

The idea of 'walking' as a picture of the steady step by step pattern of daily life is a favourite of Paul. He uses the idea almost 40 times in his writings. Usually the word he uses is the simple word for 'walking around' but occasionally he uses another word which has the sense of a more deliberate action; the idea there is of taking clear, specific steps; the sense of deliberate choice towards a destination. He uses this word to describe Abraham's deliberate 'steps of faith' and again in the verse quoted earlier, 'walking in the Spirit' is not a gentle ramble but the making of deliberate choices that shows itself in the taking of definite steps.

Paul encourages his readers in Colossae to keep to the pattern in which they began. The verse could be translated simply as "having received Christ Jesus the Lord, walk in Him". That makes a simple point even simpler. We cannot continue until we have begun. We cannot 'walk in the Spirit' unless we have 'received Christ Jesus the Lord'. This may explain the struggles that many young converts have and the different methodologies that we have devised to make their way easier. The point is, it is not possible to live in a New Covenant way unless we have been brought into that covenant. No amount of praying, bible reading, fellowship-ing, or discipling can alter that simple fact. It is the same basic truth that Jesus declared to Nicodemus; *That which is born of the flesh is flesh, and that which is born of the Spirit is spirit.* John 3:6 NKJV. The Old Covenant was designed for the Old Man and the New Covenant is designed for the New Man. The New Covenant functions in an entirely different way to the Old. The Old was good when it was used for its proper purpose; *But we know that the law is good if one uses it lawfully, knowing this: that the law is not made for a righteous person, but for the lawless and insubordinate, for the ungodly and for sinners, for the unholy and profane, for murderers of fathers and murderers of mothers, for manslayers...* 1 Tim 1:8-9 NKJV. The list continues but we have enough here to make an observation. The law was not designed to address individual transgressions but to expose the nature behind those transgressions.

Does one dance make me a dancer? Does one sin make me a sinner? The law, as Paul explains here, was intended to show the 'exceeding sinfulness of sin' and in that role it still has a limited purpose, but the law was not made for a 'righteous person'. There is a construction in Biblical Greek that draws attention to the character rather than the act. We will try to keep this simple but it is created by putting a definite article 'the' in front of a present participle of a verb, e.g. 'believing'. To translate it literally would give 'the believing...' and we would add the word 'person' to complete the sense. So we have 'the believing one' or more appropriately in English, 'the believer'. A believer is not someone who believed once on a particular date in a revival crusade. A believer is a person whose life style is characterised by the fact that he is a 'believing one'. He may suffer deep trials but his underlying characteristic is that he is a believer. The effects of the New Covenant in giving a new heart and spirit and God's own spirit coming within to take up residence is that the essential nature of the person is changed; the old heart of stone is removed and a new heart of flesh replaces it. The characteristic of this person is that he is no longer a 'sinner' but a 'saint'. He may act uncharacteristically in an act of sin, but this is against his nature and does not mean his character has changed.

Sinless perfection?

This brings us face to face with two very awkward passages of scripture in John's first letter. They produce a profound sense of unease in many Christians who read them. They are so absolute in the way they express a truth that many have just given up trying to include them in their theology. The first says; *Whoever abides in Him does not sin. Whoever sins has neither seen Him nor known Him.* 1 John 3:6 NKJV. And the second is much the same; *We know that whoever is born of God does not sin; but he who has been born of God keeps himself, and the wicked one does not touch him.* 1 John 5:18 NKJV. If we put both together we find that someone who is 'born of God' and who 'abides in Him' does not sin. These verses certainly need to be unpacked carefully if we are not to damage the contents. So please bear with me if we proceed slowly.

It is a well-established pattern of interpretation of written documents that we take our initial understanding from things said first and then adjust our understanding later in the light of later information. This simply means that we need to go further back in John's first letter to be ready to understand the later statements. Throughout John's first letter we get instances of that 'definite article followed by a present participle' effect. We said that this is the equivalent, in English, of putting the letters '-er' onto the stem of the verb to create words like 'believer' or 'baptiser'. This construction is drawing our attention to the character rather than a single instance. Many have baptised others but in the Scriptures only John and Christ himself are referred to as 'baptisers'. The word that John uses in these verses is the Greek verb *'poieO'* which is a general purpose word meaning to make or to do. It is translated by various words in our modern translations; make, do, practise, commit and others. In these verses it is used with that 'article' plus 'present participle'; he is speaking of characteristic action not single events.

In the first instance he speaks of those who 'characteristically' do the will of God; *And the world is passing away, and the lust of it; but he who does the will of God abides forever.* 1 John 2:17 NKJV. Or as we might paraphrase it "he who is characteristically doing the will of God". In the second instance he speaks of those who 'characteristically' practise righteousness; *If you know that He is righteous, you know that everyone who practices righteousness is born of Him.* 1 John 2:29 NKJV. Remember that Paul has informed Timothy that the law was not designed for a righteous man. Here John says that anyone 'born of God' is characterised by his righteous behaviour. In the third instance he speaks of some who 'characteristically' commit sin, those we might call 'sinners'; *Whoever commits sin also commits lawlessness, and sin is lawlessness.* 1 John 3:4 NKJV. In the fourth instance he says that we are not to be deceived but that anyone who 'characteristically' behaves in a righteous way is righteous; *Little children, let no one deceive you. He who practices righteousness is righteous, just as He is righteous.* 1 John 3:7 NKJV. He follows this by stating the opposite truth that anyone who 'characteristically' sins, literally 'the sinning one', is 'of the devil'; *He who sins is of the devil, for the devil has sinned from the beginning.* 1 John 3:7-8 NKJV. In the sixth instance he declares that the 'characteristic' behaviour of a person shows whose children they are; *In this the children of God and the children of the devil are manifest: Whoever does not practice righteousness is not of God, nor is he who does not love his brother.* 1 John 3:10 NKJV.

It is in this context of the continual repetition of the one idea that John's statements of "Whoever abides in Him does not sin. Whoever sins has neither seen Him nor known Him." and "We know that whoever is born of God does not sin;" must be understood. John is not proclaiming a sinless perfection in which sin has become impossible to one who is 'born of God'. He is simply declaring that the characteristic pattern of behaviour of the regenerate is that they are, in the language of Ezekiel, being caused to walk in God's statutes and keeping his judgments and doing them. Ezek 36:27 ...as a result of God's indwelling Spirit.

The anointing

There is another theme in John's first letter that is equally important; it is the theme of truth. But truth for John is not so much factual accuracy but rather a right way of living; *My little children, let us not love in word or in tongue, but in deed and in truth. And by this we know that we are of the truth, and shall assure our hearts before Him.* 1 John 3:18-19 NKJV. In our Christian experience we may well meet with factual inaccuracy or doctrinal error at work and John is mindful of this but his references to the Spirit ensuring truth is not to be limited to wrong ideas, it must include wrong living. He says that they have 'an anointing' and that they know or recognise 'all things'. (1 John 2:20) but he turns them for their instruction not to written codes of law but to an inward working of God's spirit who will teach them how to live; *Therefore let that abide in you which you heard from the beginning. If what you heard from the beginning abides in you, you also will abide in the Son and in the Father. And this is the promise that He has promised us—eternal life. These things I have written to you concerning those who try to deceive you. But the anointing which you have received from Him abides in you, and you do not need that anyone teach you; but as the same anointing teaches you concerning all things, and is true, and is not a lie, and just as it has taught you, you will abide in Him.* 1 John 2:24-27 NKJV. It is another of John's absolute statements that leaves modern minds, which are used to a more gentle consensus, reeling.

The ancient anointings were all external events but here John takes the imagery and internalises it; *the anointing... abides in you.* The persistence of the Scripture in insisting that in this new era truth is written within, on the heart, is conspicuous. It is no longer an outward expression written on tablets of stone that will be the guide to righteousness but an indwelling Spirit whose continuing presence forms the likeness of Christ in the heart. He will cause them to walk in his statutes and to keep his judgments and do them.

The righteous requirements of the law are thus satisfied in the righteous lives of God's New Covenant people but the 'handwriting' of that law is taken away. In one sense this New Covenant people does not 'keep' the Ten Commandments, it fulfils the greater law that was behind the Sinai expression. The Sinai law was given specifically to the Sinai Covenant people of God and several of its points were only possible when 'church' and 'state' were one and the same thing. The honouring of parents held the promise of a long life in Eretz Israel, the Promised Land. The Sabbath could only be kept precisely in a territory that was itself committed to the keeping of the Sabbath. Sabbath keeping outside the Land would always be a compromise. The 10 Commandments themselves were addressed specifically to a people with a specific history; *And God spoke all these words, saying: "I am the LORD your God, who brought you out of the land of Egypt, out of the house of bondage. "You shall have no other gods before Me.* Ex 20:1-3 NKJV. As we have seen earlier in Chapter 2, the Sinai Law was a unique application of universal law to a specific people in a specific context, but the universal law itself still holds true and has its witness as 'the work of the law written in the hearts' of men and women who have no link to the Sinai Covenant.

Behind the Sinai Covenant Law was a very simple but profound idea. *And thou shalt love the Lord thy God with all thy heart, and with all thy soul, and with all thy mind, and with all thy strength: this is the first commandment. And the second is like, namely this, Thou shalt love thy neighbour as thyself. There is none other commandment greater than these.* Mark 12:30-31 NKJV. It was expanded into Ten Commands and numerous judgments but in essence it is very simple. In his epistle to the Galatians Paul reduces the man-wards aspect of the law to a single word; *For all the law is fulfilled in one word, even in this: You shall love your neighbor as yourself.* Gal 5:14 NKJV. In fact, in the original language, 'you shall love' *is* one word!

The sons are free

While on earth Christ showed that the prohibitions of the Sinai Law were much more comprehensive than had been thought and that intention was no less a transgression than the outward performance. It is still true. The specific details of the Ten Commandments were something like the way in which a beam of light entering a triangular prism is split into its different parts, but the original beam is seen in the simple but comprehensive statement "thou shalt love"... God above all and your neighbour as yourself; *On these two commandments hang all the Law and the Prophets.* Matt 22:40 NKJV.

We saw earlier that the moment of Christ's public acknowledgement as the Son of God marked a turning point in his life. Up until this time, so far as the record tells us, he was content to live his life within the circle of his family. Luke's gospel tells us that in his early teenage years his heart stirred to be about his Father's work but it also tells us that under his family's rebuke he returned to Nazareth and was 'subject' to Mary and Joseph. This is a wonderful glimpse into those hidden years. The general supposition is that at some time during the eighteen years between his visit to the temple and his arrival at John's baptism Joseph died and Jesus took on the headship of the family. That would certainly have been the pattern and there is no need to challenge it, but it seems that his 'subjection' to Mary may have continued. We might deduce this from the details of the miracle at the wedding in Cana. It seems that Mary was accustomed to 'instructing him' and at least (as do many fine women!) pointing him in the right direction. Perhaps his answer surprised her; *Jesus said to her, "Woman, what does your concern have to do with Me? My hour has not yet come."* John 2:4 NKJV. The word 'woman' is not quite so stark as it might sound in English but the point is the same, he was consciously distancing himself from Mary, and from a previous pattern of behaviour.

From the moment that he heard the Father's voice at Jordan he never again submitted himself to Mary. He loved her, respected her, made provision for her at his death, but never again would he subject himself to this old order. The words from heaven had declared him to be a son and from this time he lived as one. Sons are free; *Jesus said to him, "Then the sons are free."* Matt 17:26 NKJV. A son lives in fellowship and harmony with his father and does not pattern his life on written rules and regulations. An older and much loved writer, Oswald Chambers, has a wonderful phrase for the pattern of life that Christ lived; he called it 'spontaneous moral originality'. Christ was not acting out a script nor conforming to an outward law, but his every act pleased his father.

Matthew's account of the scene is interrupted by the positioning of a chapter break and the flow is easily missed; *And suddenly a voice came from heaven, saying, "This is My beloved Son, in whom I am well pleased." Then Jesus was led up by the Spirit into the wilderness to be tempted by the devil.* Matt 3:17-4:1 NKJV. The moment of the acknowledgment of sonship was the moment that he became Spirit-led in the sense of living independently from the Law and its cultural patterns. From this time onwards he is no longer subject to Mary or to the outward rules of his race, his behaviour sometimes appears erratic and bizarre. It is impossible to guess what he will do next. He is living his life with a 'spontaneous moral originality'. He fulfilled all righteousness but he did not do so by patterning his life on a series of commandments. He was living the life of a son with a father; *And the Word became flesh, and dwelt among us (and we have contemplated his glory, a glory as of an only-begotten with a father), full of grace and truth;* John 1:14 Darby's Translation.

According to Paul this pattern of life is what characterises the life of a 'son of God'; *For as many as are led by the Spirit of God, these are sons of God.* Rom 8:14 NKJV. This is a definition of sonship that we hear little of in contemporary Christianity but it is one of the ways we may recognise those who 'have the Spirit of Christ'. This is the explanation of the apparently unpredictable behaviour of Paul in the Acts of the Apostles. He is not living his life according to a set of rules; not Sinai rules, not 'Christian' rules, not even 'evangelical' rules; he is living a life of spontaneous moral originality. "But won't this just result in every man doing what is right in his own eyes?" Not if the safeguards are all in place, and it is to these that we must turn next.

In this chapter we considered the questions of 'sinless perfection' and the 'anointing'. We also introduced Oswald Chambers' phrase 'Spontaneous Moral Originality' and saw that Christ did not live his life according to a script but in daily dependence on the leading of the Spirit. We saw that Paul said that this way of life is what identifies 'the sons of God'. We saw too that all of the Old Covenant commandments can be condensed into a single idea... 'you shall love'.

25: My right to myself

However, although the New Covenant man or woman is free from the law in terms of a list of written instructions he is not 'free'. He has been redeemed. His ownership has changed and he is not his own. He is not 'free' to go his own way or to please himself but 'free' to go God's way and to please Him; *For the love of Christ compels us, because we judge thus: that if One died for all, then all died; and He died for all, that those who live should live no longer for themselves, but for Him who died for them and rose again.* 2Cor 5:14-15 NKJV. If we compress the sentence temporarily we may see the point more clearly... *'we judge thus;'... 'He died for all... that those who live should no longer live for themselves'.* This was one of the great purposes of the cross. It was not only that we should escape hell but that lives should become re-orientated. The cross, in the Biblical revelation, is not only the physical torture stake that stood outside a city wall; it is a deep principle that has been applied at different levels. Christ's cross was once and for all, never needing and never possible of repetition, but my cross is a very different matter. That cross, and not Christ's, I must take up daily.

A route-map for sin

Eve sinned first, but it was Adam's sin that had such a devastating effect upon his race and the whole creation. Why should that be? Primarily, it would seem, because Adam was the federal head of the human race and its root. It was, says Paul, "by one man that sin entered". Eve's sin did not change Adam but Adam's sin changed Eve. In his first letter to Timothy Paul distinguishes the nature of Eve's transgression from that of Adam and agrees with Eve herself in her claim that she was deceived; *And Adam was not deceived, but the woman being deceived, fell into transgression.* 1 Tim 2:14 NKJV. Adam, on the other hand, sinned with his eyes wide open. Paul refers to another characteristic of Eve in his second letter to the Corinthians; *For I am jealous for you with godly jealousy. For I have betrothed you to one husband, that I may present you as a chaste virgin to Christ. But I fear, lest somehow, as the serpent deceived Eve by his craftiness, so your minds may be corrupted from the simplicity that is in Christ.* 2 Cor 11:2-3 NKJV. Eve was 'simple' not in a derogatory sense, she was innocent. Innocent but not yet holy; holiness is much more than innocence. Simplicity is a forgotten Christian virtue. It is frequently used in the New Testament and is sometimes translated as 'single'. Often it is sophistication and a street-wise mind-set that is the greater danger.

Eve may be very valuable to us. The record of her transgression is told with some detail and provides us with an almost unique insight into the way in which someone who is 'innocent' and not tainted with Adam's sin may still come under temptation. She is only 'almost unique' because we have another record of someone who was truly holy, who was not tainted with Adam's congenital sin and yet who still came under temptation, Christ himself. It is possible, according to these examples, for a human being who has no indwelling sin to come under strong temptation to sin.

Regeneration is the means whereby God takes us from being 'in Adam' and makes us 'in Christ'. God's provision for our tragedy is fully comprehensive. He provides a remedy for what we became in Adam and brings the reign of that 'Old Man' to an end; *knowing this, that our old man was crucified with Him, that the body of sin might be done away with, that we should no longer be slaves of sin.* Rom 6:6 NKJV. His Calvary-baptism united him fully with what the human race had become and he took it down into death with him; *For He made Him who knew no sin to be sin for us, that we might become the righteousness of God in Him.* 2 Cor 5:21 NKJV. The grip of Adamic sin was broken at Calvary and is broken in each one who is joined to Christ in Spirit-baptism. He was baptised into our death so that we might be baptised into his. Adam's 'reign of death', as Charles Wesley called it, is over for those who are in Christ.

The ancient legacy is dealt with and so also is our own contribution in the form of our own transgressions; both Sin and sins find their answer in the work that was accomplished at Calvary. Our own sins are remitted and in the conscious receiving of God's mercy we, unlike Israel of old, can be conscious of sins forgiven. But that is by no means the final score. Christ's death brought to an end the inevitable consequences of Adam's transgression on the whole human race. So Adam is dealt with, and so is my debt, where does that leave us? Eve had no 'Old Man' and no debt and yet she was tempted and fell. Christ had no 'Old Man' and no debt and was *in all points tempted as we are, yet without sin.* Heb 4:15 NKJV. Is the New Covenant man or woman immune to the temptation to sin? There is a balance to be struck here which is perfectly achieved by Paul; *Therefore let him who thinks he stands take heed lest he fall. No temptation has overtaken you except such as is common to man; but God is faithful, who will not allow you to be tempted beyond what you are able, but with the temptation will also make the way of escape, that you may be able to bear it.* 1 Cor 10:12-13 NKJV. Traditionally it has been difficult for Christian teaching to maintain that balance. The danger lies in straying into the one extreme or the other. There are two opposite dangers of proclaiming either a false triumphalism in which a man thinks he is no longer vulnerable or concluding that we are doomed to failure with every step.

For Eve and for Christ the temptation to sin did not arise from inside but from outside. Nevertheless the temptation encountered something within which had the ability to respond and to receive the temptation. In his letter James uses the illustration of 'conception'. *Let no one say when he is tempted, "I am tempted by God"; for God cannot be tempted by evil, nor does He Himself tempt anyone. But each one is tempted when he is drawn away by his own desires and enticed. Then, when desire has conceived, it gives birth to sin; and sin, when it is full-grown, brings forth death.* James 1:13–15 NKJV. Both Eve and Christ were capable of this kind of spiritual conception; they had the power to receive the 'seed' of a temptation and to bring it to birth as a sin. Eve failed in that she received the temptation and conceived. Christ refused the temptation and did not 'conceive'. For the man or woman who has genuinely been brought into the good of the New Covenant there is a close parallel; we may yet receive or reject the temptation. If we receive the temptation a conception will take place that, unless God intervenes, will result in the birth of a sin.

How can we maintain our purity and faithfulness to God in the face of such a fierce and relentless seducer? Now that our ancient past in Adam and the more recent past of our own transgressions are remedied is it inevitable that we shall fall again? And if we do fall does it undo all that God has accomplished? It will be our task in this chapter to try to answer those questions.

My cross

I am reluctant to use the language of Freudian psychology and to speak of 'the self' or the 'ego' so we may leave some phrases undefined other than by describing their actions. Christ's cross was unique; it is never to be repeated. Unfortunately Freudian concepts have crept into much modern evangelical theology so that we now frequently hear the language of 'the self' and 'the ego', sometimes even in Bible translations. The phrase 'the cross' as applied to Christ's cross is a short-hand term intended to include his suffering and death as substitute for the sins of the whole world. It includes the real price of our redemption in his separation from the Father as he *Himself bore our sins in His own body on the tree*, 1 Pet 2:24 NKJV. It speaks of his baptism and complete union with all that man had become, and his drinking of the cup of God's righteous anger against sin. It is the once and sufficient sacrifice for the sins of the whole world. To endeavour to reproduce that 'death of the cross', or to add to it, by religious ritual or personal experience is blasphemy. It is his and his alone.

And yet while on earth he spoke of the cross in another sense, not as the place of sin-bearing and propitiation but of a means whereby God's perfect will could triumph over every other will, even mine. By 'will' I simply mean the power of choice that is part of our human experience; the whole man focused in a choice. It is in the power of free choice that God's image and likeness is seen. Human beings are moral agents and are enabled and required to make their choices for which they will be held accountable. This leads us to the nature of Eve's transgression and to Christ's temptation. What we have in both of these accounts and in our own daily experience is the prospect of a clash of wills. At its heart, sin is a clash of wills in which my will, my power of choice, wins. Its outward forms are varied but its inner reality is the same every time. Sin is the consequence of a man or a woman saying 'Not thy will but my will be done'. Faith is right response to revelation; *So then faith comes by hearing, and hearing by the word of God.* Rom 10:17 NKJV. Sin, on the other hand, is wrong response to revelation; *Therefore, to him who knows to do good and does not do it, to him it is sin.* James 4:17 NKJV.

Eve and Christ are both the recipients of a 'revelation'. They both know what God has said and they are both faced with the choice to agree with the will of God or with the will of another. When this clash comes, and it may occur a thousand times in a day, the outcome will be 'thy will' or 'another's will'; faith or sin. Part of the provision of the New Covenant is that the man or woman who has entered that covenant knows what the will of God is. Concerning the old stone-inscribed law

Moses said; *The secret things belong to the LORD our God, but those things which are revealed belong to us and to our children forever, that we may do all the words of this law.* Deut 29:29 NKJV. They knew, it was written in stone, how they should behave. Many secrets remain in God's own knowing but the people of the Old Covenant could never claim that they did not know the will of God. The parallel is maintained in the New Covenant. We will never be able to claim ignorance if the law of God is written in our hearts. It was not ignorance of the will of God that caused Israel to sin but their own free choice; so it is in the New Covenant.

Let's see if we can identify the exact point of Eve's transgression; *So when the woman saw that the tree was good for food, that it was pleasant to the eyes, and a tree desirable to make one wise, she took of its fruit and ate. She also gave to her husband with her, and he ate.* Gen 3:6 NKJV. The Hebrew word translated 'pleasant' here is usually translated as the much stronger word 'desire' and sometimes even by the English word 'lust'. We might say she admired, she lusted, she strongly desired, she took... The original prohibition had been that Adam was not to 'eat' of the fruit of this tree. The point in time of Eve's transgression was not when she looked, nor even when she lusted, or longed for wisdom, not even when she took it... she crossed the line and transgressed when she took her first bite.

God had given her inherent powers that were part of what it means to be human. She had the power to observe and to distinguish between one thing and another. She had the God-given authority to prefer one fruit to another. These inherent powers had not been distorted by sin at this time and were part of the way in which Eve was expected to function. She had a lust, a real appetite, for what she saw. Appetites are part of God's will for our race. To be without proper appetites is usually a sign of sickness or something out of order. She strongly desired what she saw. It was a God-given characteristic of humanity to be able to strongly desire something. Buddhism teaches that 'desire' is the cause of all suffering and that personal 'salvation' is possible only to those who have killed all desires. To eliminate all legitimate desire is to deform the human race and deface that part of God's likeness within it. She also longed to be wise; that too is part of our original constitution as human beings. The curiosity of our race is not an accident but part of the way in which we were made. All these attributes are present in Eve and she has not sinned.

Next she takes the forbidden fruit and even this was not specifically forbidden although it is folly to see how far we can go and still not sin. As we read the record we discover how subtle her enemy has been. He has drawn her attention to the single prohibition in the whole of Eden and invited her to 'test' the prohibition; *Then the serpent said to the woman, "You will not surely die. For God knows that in the day you eat of it your eyes will be opened, and you will be like God, knowing good and evil."* Gen 3:4-5 NKJV. Wasn't 'being like God' part of God's original plan for the human race? *Then God said, "Let us make man in Our image, according to Our likeness;* Gen 1:26 NKJV. If that is God's destination for the race why not take the short cut? If God has put all these legitimate desires in your heart why not satisfy them and become what you were destined to be?

Oswald Chambers observed that Adam's original sin was independence and that only later did it harden into rebellion. There is a truth there. Eve's short cut is a do-it-yourself solution in which she becomes what God intended her to be by her own effort and choice. Does the end justify the means? The presence of desires, of many kinds, that God has placed in each individual is not, in itself, the right to satisfy that desire. Man was not designed to be autonomous but to live in humble dependence upon God and to live within his schedules. Perhaps it was God's intention to give access to the tree of the knowledge of good and evil at some future time in Adam and Eve's lives. They 'snatched' at it and lost it all. Eve claimed her rights and lost her Eden and Adam followed her with his eyes wide open.

A route-map for the overcomer

We change the scene now, from an idyllic garden to a thirsty wasteland. Jesus of Nazareth has received the anointing of the Spirit who has identified him as the Son of

God. Now, under the leading of the Spirit, he is taken into the Judaean wilderness to be tempted. Will the Spirit ever lead us into areas where we are tempted? Certainly he will, but they are to be of his choosing not ours. His Sonship is immediately put to the test. He has neither eaten nor drunk for 40 days and he is hungry. Hunger is a legitimate response to a 40 day fast. There is nothing 'sinful' about being hungry. God has put many appetites within us and if they are not satisfied, and we are healthy, we will be hungry. This legitimate hunger becomes the setting for a temptation, and so will ours. The test now is to use his rights as the Son of God to satisfy his rights to relieve his hunger; *Now when the tempter came to Him, he said, "If You are the Son of God, command that these stones become bread."* Matt 4:3 NKJV. Why not? He has a God-given hunger and God-given powers, why not use the latter to satisfy the former? Because it would have been an autonomous act, an independent gesture which simply said 'My will be done'. Was this a real temptation or is it just theological theatre? Surely, this is a real temptation with real dangers.

His physical hunger is real but to satisfy it he must step outside the circle of God's revealed will for his life, and he will not do it. His answer is illuminating; *But He answered and said, "It is written, 'Man shall not live by bread alone, but by every word that proceeds from the mouth of God.'* Matt 4:4 NKJV. Tempted to behave as the Son *of God* he resolutely determines to live his life as a Son *of Man* in moment-by-moment dependence upon the will of God. He can satisfy his own legitimate longings or he can satisfy God's desires. He makes his choice. Next he is taken to the pinnacle of the Temple and invited to 'fulfil the Scripture'. He has made his stand on the word of God, and the second temptation starts from the same point. Why not move things on a little faster? Just imagine the audiences you will have when they have such solid proof that you are who you say you are. "Prove it", is a temptation based on an absence of faith not its presence. This is the temptation of the fanatic to settle all doubts by some spectacular event. Christ is, again, resolute; he will not put God to the test.

The final test of this series may be seen as a temptation to an even more radical short cut. He has come to win the nations for his father. He can have them; all he has to do is bow, briefly, to another's will and all the kingdoms will be his. He can then do with them as he likes. The great advantage to this fast-track is that it avoids the necessity of a cross. It is the great appeal of many of our short-cuts. It was rejected with the same conviction and as Matthew's account tells us... *Then the devil left Him, and behold, angels came and ministered to Him.* Matt 4:11 NKJV. In the older King James version Luke's account adds the comment; *And when the devil had ended all the temptation, he departed from him for a season.* Luke 4:13 KJV. This was not the last temptation to avoid the cross and one such later occasion brought out the strongest rebuke imaginable.

The trap

Peter had received a revelation. *Simon Peter answered and said, "You are the Christ, the Son of the living God." Jesus answered and said to him, "Blessed are you, Simon Bar-jonah, for flesh and blood has not revealed this to you, but My Father who is in heaven.* Matt 16:16–17 NKJV. The Father has revealed to Peter the true identity of Jesus of Nazareth. It was a particular blessing and Jesus said so. Peter had glimpsed something. Jesus was the Messiah, the coming King of Israel. The future was at hand. The enemies of Israel would be driven back and Israel would take its rightful place at the head of the nations. We then have a dramatic change of mood and Peter is not willing to follow it; *From that time Jesus began to show to His disciples that He must go to Jerusalem, and suffer many things from the elders and chief priests and scribes, and be killed, and be raised the third day. Then Peter took Him aside and began to rebuke Him, saying, "Far be it from You, Lord; this shall not happen to You!"* Matt 16:21-22 NKJV. Christ is beginning to speak about the cross and it draws from the volatile Peter an explosive protest. *"Far be it from You, Lord"* which can be more literally translated as "Be merciful to yourself".

No doubt it was said in all the kindness of Peter's affection for his master but it was a trap and Jesus spotted it; *But He turned and said to Peter, "Get behind Me, Satan! You are an offense to Me, for you are not mindful of the things of God, but the things of men."* Matt 16:23 NKJV. The word translated 'offence' or 'stumbling block' here was originally the wooden stick that triggered an animal trap. The temptation to 'be merciful to yourself' is the temptation to maintain 'my right to myself.' It is the temptation that God's will is not perfect and good and that I would do better if I took my life into my own hands. It was the temptation that undid Eve but not Christ. He rebukes the source behind the words and declares that this 'mind-set' is Satanic. This is the 'Not thy will, but my will be done' mind-set that originated in Satan himself and is the basis of all temptation to sin. It is the temptation that God does not have my best interests at heart and it will be better if I take the reins myself. To put the recognition of my rights before the revealed will of God, to satisfy my own hungers in my own way is a temptation that will beset even New Covenant saints, but there is a remedy.

Peter's suggestion is 'Pity yourself', Christ's counsel is 'Deny yourself'; *Then Jesus said to His disciples, "If anyone desires to come after Me, let him deny himself, and take up his cross, and follow Me. For whoever desires to save his life will lose it, but whoever loses his life for My sake will find it.* Matt 16:24-26 NKJV. This saying of Christ is repeated by Luke with a special focus; *Then He said to them all, "If anyone desires to come after Me, let him deny himself, and take up his cross daily, and follow Me.* Luke 9:23 NKJV. "Let him take up his cross daily'. The 'cross' in this sense is not tribulation and suffering but the free choice to give up my 'right to myself'; another Oswald Chambers' phrase. This is not a single crisis event but a daily process of choosing to live for another's pleasure and to do another's will.

Is it possible? Yes but only to the members of a New Covenant; *you shall be My people, and I will be your God.* Jer 31:33; Ezek 36:28. It is a wonderful freedom to find the place where I can be genuinely content for God to be God; he is so much better at it than I am!

But wait a moment... *And if any man sin...* does that undo it all? No. Even though... *His divine power has given to us all things that pertain to life and godliness, through the knowledge of Him who called us by glory and virtue,* 2 Pet 1:3 ...so that we can genuinely be the New Covenant people of God he has built in a contingency plan; *My little children, these things I write to you, so that you may not sin. And if anyone sins, we have an Advocate with the Father, Jesus Christ the righteous. And He Himself is the propitiation for our sins, and not for ours only but also for the whole world.* 1 John 2:1-2 NKJV. If we do transgress we shall need to be open and honest with God about it. We must acknowledge our sins to God and we shall receive forgiveness and cleansing. The continuing effectiveness of Christ's already provided propitiation is still in place. It will always be so. Our acceptance with him is not based on our progress in bearing our daily cross but upon him and his once and only cross.

In this chapter we examined and contrasted the experiences of Eve and Christ when faced with temptations to satisfy legitimate hungers. We examined the nature of temptation and sin in the experience of a member of the New Covenant community. We saw that the beachhead is often our legitimate desires that demand an illegitimate priority. We saw that the answer lies in constantly choosing to embrace my daily cross and to refuse 'my right to myself'.

26: Where do I go from here?

It depends, of course, on where you are when you ask the question. I was once given this topic to address a group of teenagers who had all made 'decisions' at a Billy Graham meeting. I conducted an experiment in which they followed a series of instructions that I issued step by step. Turn right, take 3 steps, turn left, take 2 steps etc. It was pretty chaotic but one person in the group actually arrived at the exit. It was no accident; he was the one I had in mind as I issued the instructions. It was all to illustrate the point that there is no single answer to the question "where do I go from here?' There are as many answers as there are people asking the question. So we should not expect a detailed prescription in this chapter but, hopefully, some practical pointers for anyone who wants to make progress in their Christian pilgrimage. The companion question to 'where do I go from here?' has to be 'where am I?'

It is absolutely necessary

Some of the heaviest burdens that new converts carry are in terms of labels. Among evangelicals one of the most misused labels is the phrase 'born again'. The phrase, taken from John Chapter 3, 'you must be born again' has been the title for thousands of sermons. We must, however, understand it rightly to avoid putting an unbearable burden on the shoulders of those who hear it. It is NOT a command, as is so often preached. It is the statement of a spiritual fact of life. Perhaps if we use the Old King James version it may be easier to make the point; *Marvel not that I said unto thee, Ye must be born again* John 3:7-8 KJV I have used this archaic English to illustrate the way in which Christ switched from the personal pronoun in the singular 'thee', to the personal pronoun plural in the word 'ye'. This is the equivalent of saying, "don't be amazed that I say to you, personally, Nicodemus, that everyone must be born again." Christ is addressing Nicodemus but the information he gives is not an instruction to Nicodemus but an explanation. If this were a command it would be in the Greek imperative; it isn't.

So the spiritual truth is expressed simply and follows very naturally from what preceded it; *That which is born of the flesh is flesh; and that which is born of the Spirit is spirit. Marvel not that I said unto thee, Ye must be born again.* John 3:6-7 KJV Christ is simply making the point that 'it is necessary that everyone is born again, from above.' This is a spiritual axiom; a statement that is self-evidently true. It is the starting point of the explanation not an instruction to be obeyed. I have actually heard the statement directed at a struggling believer; "you need to get yourself born again!" We can make as little contribution to our second birth as we did to our first. The matter is out of our hands. This is why in this famous passage Christ declares it to be the unique work of the Spirit, and his ways are untrack-able; *The wind blows where it wishes, and you hear the sound of it, but cannot tell where it comes from and where it goes. So is everyone who is born of the Spirit.* John 3:8 NKJV. The words 'wind' and 'spirit' are translations of the same Greek word in these two sentences.

This utter dependence upon someone else strikes hard at the root of our independence and there is an almost irrepressible determination in human beings to make some contribution to being 'born again'. But every conscious contribution we make only further disqualifies us. There are no percentages in true regeneration; either God provides 100% or the work remains undone. Every 'per cent' that I apply consciously, undermines God's unique gift. If I try to add faith, it will undermine God's work. If I try to add repentance, it will undermine God's work. 'Oh', I hear the cry, "that is so frustrating". Yes it is, and it is designed to be. By the way, did you know that the Hebrew language had no specific word for 'frustration' until the mid 20th century? That doesn't mean people didn't have the experience only that they were forced to describe it differently. They could call it anger, or disappointment, but not 'frustration'. What is 'frustration'? 'frustration' is really the way I feel when my 'will' is being thwarted... or frustrated. I want to be in control of this situation but I am not and I cannot bring my choices to bear. In short and at its most brutal, it is the way I feel when I am not getting my own way. Theologically, it is God not allowing me to be 'god', and my reaction to that realisation. Every human effort to produce regeneration will result in frustration. God has determined that the choicest gift of regeneration will be the consequence of his grace and because of that it can only be received by faith; *Therefore it is of faith that it might be according to grace,* Rom 4:16 NKJV. The Judaism of Christ's and Paul's day had reduced the Law to a ladder of achievement in which they thought that God received them because they had attained a particular standard. Against this notion Paul makes his most extreme objections. *God*, he writes in Romans 4:5, *justifies the ungodly.*

God, him say 'me OK'

We are accepted with God and declared to be 'right' with Him, not on the basis of our own right-eousness but because of what Christ has achieved at Calvary and our simple but absolute trust in him. Being 'justified', declared right with God, is never on the basis of a kept law, but on the basis of our reliance upon another. As Amy Carmichael was fond of quoting; *upon a life I did not live, upon a death I did not die, upon another's life, another's death, I stake my whole eternity.* That is Bible 'faith'; all my eggs are in one basket.

There is, however, a distinction between Justification and Regeneration. Justification is a change in legal standing; regeneration is a change in nature. Often the words 'justification' or 'conversion' or 'regeneration' are used as if they were synonyms but they are not. These are very distinct ways of describing different aspects of salvation. They may, at times, synchronise but that does not make them synonyms. And at times they do not synchronise and then the puzzles begin. David Pawson, in his book "The Normal Christian Birth" pointed out the confusion caused by failing to distinguish between conversion and regeneration. It is a simple fact of language that God is never the 'subject' of the verb 'convert' as it applies to human beings. There are lots of stories about people who were 'converted' by the evangelist but never by God and so are astray. From a Biblical perspective, however, God never converted anyone. People convert people, and sometimes people convert themselves but never God! God justifies and God regenerates; these are his work but conversion is man's work. It signifies the 'turning from one way to another'; this is man's work.

Justification, on the other hand, is God's work. There is a delightful Pigeon English definition of 'Justification' used, so I understand, by the people of Papua New Guinea. It is crude but wonderfully precise; "God, him say, me OK". Theologically it would be difficult to improve on that definition. Justification is not the way I feel or the way that someone else may feel about me, justification is the pronouncement, by the judge, that the charge against me, and its sentence of death, has not stood. I walk from the court a free man, not because I feel innocent but because the court has declared me to be 'just'. But justification is not an arbitrary comment from the judge, but the consequence of my only contribution, justification is always 'by grace' but always 'through faith'. Grace is the source, and faith is the channel. Faith does not create any virtue or deserving on my part but simply facilitates God's free grace; faith is response to revelation. In other words, the initiative always rests with God but the response rests with me. I cannot believe at my own whim but only because I have heard 'the voice of God' but when I have heard that voice I will be held responsible for my response.

Justification is part of the language of the law court that is one of the sources that God has used to communicate truth to us. It is the language of what Isaac Watts called God's 'condescending ways'. That is the Old English use of the word meaning 'to come down to another's level'. If Justification comes from the background of the law court then Regeneration comes from the vocabulary of life itself. It is not forensic but dynamic. Justification has to do with records and standing. Regeneration has to do with life and its impartation. Justification has many consequences and Paul quotes from a list of them that David included in a psalm; *just as David also describes the blessedness of the man to whom God imputes righteousness apart from works: "Blessed are those whose lawless deeds are forgiven, And whose sins are covered; Blessed is the man to whom the LORD shall not impute sin."* Rom 4:6-8 NKJV. It includes, according to this list, imputed righteousness, the remitting or putting away of trespasses, atonement in the covering of the stain and consequences of sin, and a refusal to keep a record of sin.

It is a wonderfully rich expression of what was no doubt David's own experience and blessing. The list comprises the blessings that are the consequence of justification. It appears in a chapter of Romans that Paul begins by asking the question; 'what was Abraham's experience?' The list is the answer, or part of it. The chapter concludes with the statement that the record of Abraham's and David's experience was not a mere archive; *Now it was not written for his sake alone that it was imputed to him, but also for us. It shall be imputed to us who believe in Him who raised up Jesus our Lord from the dead, who was delivered up because of our offenses, and was raised because of our justification.* Rom 4:23-25 NKJV. In other words this is not just for the blessing of Abraham and David but is the blessing of all *who believe in Him who raised up Jesus our Lord from the dead.* This is wonderful but there is more... much more. (Rom 5:9-10, 15, 17, 20; 11:12)

Much more

Romans Chapter 4 is the foundation for Chapter 5. It begins with the common experience of all those who are justified by faith, but it builds on that a brand new building. The theme of justification, now firmly established, settles into the background and Paul moves on to the issues of life and power; *Therefore, having been justified by faith, we have peace with God through our Lord Jesus Christ, through whom also we have access by faith into this grace in which we stand, and rejoice in hope of the glory of God.* Rom 5:1-2 NKJV. This justifying faith gives us 'access into this grace in which we stand' but the 'grace in which we stand' is the 'much more' grace of regeneration.

Paul's reference here to the 'glory of God' is all the more amazing if we contrast it with an earlier reference. When Paul was establishing the guilt of the whole of humanity he pointed out that there was no difference in the culpability of Jew or Gentile; *For there is no difference; for all have sinned and fall short of the glory of God*, Rom 3:22-23 NKJV. That is the law-court language; all fall short of the 'glory of God'. But now standing in 'this grace' we find Paul rejoicing in a restored hope of the 'glory of God'. That which was forfeited by the first man is now, potentially, restored through another man, Christ Jesus. And the hope that Paul has is not wishful thinking, the work has already begun; *Now hope does not disappoint, because the love of God has been poured out in our hearts by the Holy Spirit who was given to us.* Rom 5:5 NKJV. Literally, there is no reason to blush because the love of God has been poured out in our hearts... We have come again, in Paul's declaration, as in historical reality, to the era of the poured out Spirit. We are on familiar territory here. This is the language of Pentecostal effusions and of untrack-able winds. In Romans Chapter 5 we have moved into the consequences of the realised New Covenant.

Paul now recounts the reversal of Adam's sin. Adam, as the federal head of the race, sinned and that sin impacted all his race; all who are *in Adam*. Now the Second Man enters the scene and achieves something in his death that impacts his entire race. Adam, says Paul, was a pattern of Christ. We have moved from law courts into life and families. In Christ, the Old Man was decisively co-crucified with Christ. Our death he died, bringing to an end, for those *in Christ*, that whole Adamic racial solidarity. In Christ, we are finished with the Old Man and we put off his old ways; *Therefore, if anyone is in Christ, he is a new creation; old things have passed away; behold, all things have become new.* 2 Cor 5:17 NKJV.

How then do we get to be 'in Christ'? If we are assured of his acceptance and know that 'God, him say, me OK' how do we move from Justification to Regeneration? "If you are thirsty," said Jesus on one occasion, "come to me and drink." There is no technique available here but only personal engagement with Christ himself. *On the last day, that great day of the feast, Jesus stood and cried out, saying, "If anyone thirsts, let him come to Me and drink. He who believes in Me, as the Scripture has said, out of his heart will flow rivers of living water." But this He spoke concerning the Spirit, whom those believing in Him would receive; for the Holy Spirit was not yet given, because Jesus was not yet glorified.* John 7:37-39 NKJV. The Spirit is now 'given'. This promise is now 'live'; the day has come.

What do we mean by 'receiving the Spirit'? There are often consequences to receiving the Spirit, some of which may be seen or heard, but we must not confuse the consequences with the Spirit himself. Some have so specialised on these consequences that they describe them as 'proofs' of the Spirit having been received, but this is a damaging confusion which leaves some people believing they have received the Spirit simply because there have been consequences. There is an ancient description of receiving the Spirit that provides a valuable caution. It is in that famous chapter of Ezekiel where he describes the valley of dry bones. As he 'prophesies' there is activity; *So I prophesied as I was commanded; and as I prophesied, there was a noise, and suddenly a rattling; and the bones came together, bone to bone. Indeed, as I looked, the sinews and the flesh came upon them, and the skin covered them over; but there was no breath in them.* Ezek 37:7-8 NKJV. The word translated 'breath' here is the Hebrew word for 'spirit'. It is a sobering description. There is clear response to Ezekiel's prophetic ministry; things are happening, dramatic things, noisy things, rattlings and shakings. For many in our current era this would be sufficient proof but Ezekiel has more discernment; *but there was no Spirit in them.*

The 'son of man', as Ezekiel is called throughout this passage, then speaks to the Spirit; *So I prophesied as He commanded me, and breath/spirit came into them, and they lived, and stood upon their feet, an exceedingly great army.* Ezek 37:9-10 NKJV. There is an interesting parallel here with the ministry of the other 'son of man'. Christ brought the word of God and still does, there was much activity, dramatic things occurred and they still do. Bones were gathered together, sinews and flesh... but the body was still effectively a corpse until he ascended to the throne and 'spoke' to the Spirit. It is Christ's unique prerogative to 'give the Spirit'. If we are thirsty we must come to him and drink.

Why do we not see the power of the New Covenant more obviously in our day? In my view there are two particular reasons although in individual instances there are bound to be individual conditions. When Paul wrote his epistle to the Ephesians he twice refers to the way in which he was praying for them... and for any like them who might read the letter. We will conclude with a brief look at Paul's prayers for the saints; they cover revelation and realisation.

Revelation and realisation

Many live sub-standard New Covenant lives because they do not know any better. There is a clear link between faith and expectation and if expectations are low it is unlikely that faith will be any higher. It is challenging to see not only the way in which Paul prayed for the 'saints' but also to see what he desired for them. His first prayer in Ephesians is for 'revelation'; *that the God of our Lord Jesus Christ, the Father of glory, may give to you the spirit of wisdom and revelation in the knowledge of Him, the eyes of your understanding being enlightened;* Eph 1:17-18 NKJV. By revelation he means an inner insight into truth. In the epistle to the Colossians his prayer is for 'spiritual understanding'. He is praying that men and women will 'see' what God has had in mind. He subdivides this Ephesian 'prayer list' into three sections and asks that they may 'know'... the hope of Christ's calling, the riches of Christ's inheritance in the saints, and the exceeding greatness of his power toward us who believe. It is quite a list. The word 'know' implies to 'see with the eyes' or to 'perceive'. Perhaps they were already 'seeing' it but he is praying for the process to continue.

What is the hope of your calling? That you will go to heaven when you die? Oh, more, much more. Your calling is to be an image bearer of Christ himself. The hope is that the 'mystery/secret' would be expressed in the lives of God's people, that Christ would be 'in them' 'the hope of glory' as Paul describes it to the church at Colossae. This was Adam's original calling, to be in the likeness and image of God; to reveal the nature of God in flesh and blood. God has never given up on this project; it is why we were created. And the 'riches of the glory of his inheritance in the saints'? The language of 'inheritance' always echoes the land promised to a covenant community. The saints are Christ's inheritance in answer to the prayer 'ask me and I will give the nations for your inheritance'. The New Covenant community is his, Christ's. Certainly we have an inheritance of our own to look forward to but this is not that, this is Christ's inheritance; it is 'Christ's inheritance' in the saints. He wants them to see that the purpose of their calling is to be Christ's own people. It is the New Covenant fulfilment of an ancient promise. *Now therefore, if you will indeed obey My voice and keep My covenant, then you shall be a special treasure to Me above all people; for all the earth is Mine. And you shall be to Me a kingdom of priests and a holy nation.'* Ex 19:5-6 NKJV.

Then what of the third point on the list? He prays that they may see the nature of the power that is at work in them. He says it is nothing less than the power that was at work when Christ was raised from the dead and seated at God's right hand. What a journey that was! From the grave to the throne. This is the same power that is at work in God's people, not just to save them from hell but to give them a share in his death, his resurrection and his glory. If the power of God could raise Christ from a grave to a throne, what can it do in me? Is the

New Covenant too good to be true or can God deliver what he has promised?

Paul's second prayer list moves from the revelation to the reality, and its real-isation in the saints. It is vital that we see what God has done and is doing but the truth must become true in me too. *For this reason I bow my knees to the Father of our Lord Jesus Christ, from whom the whole family in heaven and earth is named, that He would grant you, according to the riches of His glory, to be strengthened with might through His Spirit in the inner man, that Christ may dwell in your hearts through faith; that you, being rooted and grounded in love, may be able to comprehend with all the saints what is the width and length and depth and height— to know the love of Christ which passes knowledge; that you may be filled with all the fullness of God. Now to Him who is able to do exceedingly abundantly above all that we ask or think, according to the power that works in us,* Eph 3:14–20 NKJV.

His prayer here focuses again on the work of the Spirit. It is through the power of the received Spirit that Christ is made real in the heart. When he walked on the earth and even when he was raised from the dead he was 'with' them, but his great promise had been that the one who had been 'with' them would soon be 'within' them. The indwelling Christ is the consequence of the indwelling Spirit. This as we have seen in our journey was one of the key elements in the New Covenant; a new heart and a new spirit and God's own Spirit indwelling, and the law written on the heart.

The word 'energy' is a union of two words; en and ergon, it is an inward working. The word is used often in the New Testament in its different forms. It is part of a sequence of truth that we also find in the word for power *'dunamis'*. *dunamis* is not external power but essential, inward or inherent power. That word is often translated 'ability' and appears twice in Paul's second prayer list. First he prays that *they may be strengthened with 'ability' through His Spirit in the inner man.* (Eph 3:16) He knows that only by the enabling power of the indwelling Spirit can Christ inhabit the heart in reality.

The 'able' God

Later, in the same prayer, he *refers to Him who is able to do exceedingly abundantly above all that we ask or think, according to the power that works in us,* Eph 3:20. It is because God has the ability/*dunamis* to 'do' that we can have the ability to 'be'. The transformed life of the New Covenant is not the result of greater effort but of greater grace. Paul, speaking by the Spirit, piles superlative on top of superlative here. He is not only able to do... above all that we ask or think, he is able to do 'abundantly' above all that we ask or think... and not only that but 'exceedingly, abundantly, above all that we can ask or think'. Language can take us no further. This is all the fulness of God's power available to fulfil all the promises of a New Covenant and to accomplish it 'according to the ability/*dunumis* that is working in' (*energeO*) the saint.

And to what purpose is all this provision of God given? That there might be *glory in the church by Christ Jesus to all generations, forever and ever.* Eph 3:21 NKJV. What we have examined may be breathtaking, but it is only the beginning. This New Covenant has made it possible for God's ancient longings to be fulfilled. Perhaps it is appropriate to let Paul have the final word...

To me, who am less than the least of all the saints, this grace was given, that I should preach among the Gentiles the unsearchable riches of Christ, and to make all see what is the fellowship of the mystery, which from the beginning of the ages has been hidden in God who created all things through Jesus Christ; to the intent that now the manifold wisdom of God might be made known by the church to the principalities and powers in the heavenly places, according to the eternal purpose which He accomplished in Christ Jesus our Lord, in whom we have boldness and access with confidence through faith in Him. Eph 3:8-12. NKJV.

In this final chapter we discovered that there is no formula that guarantees success but that the persistent appeal of the Bible is that we come to Christ when we are thirsty. We see that this speaks not of an evangelical formula but of personal encounter with a personal Saviour. No one can prescribe an infallible route but these promises stand, that those who seek shall find, and those who come will never be turned away. It is God's 'ability to do' that gives me the 'ability to be'.

Appendix 1: Receiving Christ

The phrase has become one of the most familiar in contemporary evangelical Christianity, but what does it mean? In most evangelical groups it has come to mean a personal response to the gospel. In evangelistic meetings or personal evangelism the enquirer is encouraged to make a response to a small subset of Bible doctrines often referred to as 'the gospel.' These are sometimes reduced to four steps, the concept being that agreement with these truths and the praying of a simple prayer of confession and commitment effects a transaction in which the enquirer 'receives Christ'. I came this way, as have many thousands of others. It was a starting place and not to be dishonoured. Every genuine response to God is of vital importance and not to be mocked.

It may come as a surprise to some reading this, however, that this concept of 'the gospel' and of 'receiving Christ' was the product of the evangelistic campaigns of the 20th Century. This pattern of evangelism has no roots in the history of the Church as we read in the Acts, nor is it in any other part of the New Testament. "But it can be a real help" says the objector. Yes, it may. The purpose of these thoughts is not to undermine or attack any. My anxieties lie in the fact that counselors or personal workers may 'go through the motions' and then declare that the seeker has 'received Christ'. This then becomes like a Catholic sacrament that is effectual as long as it is in accordance with a pattern.

As a point of reference let's think about pre-20th Century patterns. Some churches whose traditions go back to the turn of that century may still have what is called an 'after-meeting'. The idea was that people who had heard the truth and knew they must respond were able to withdraw from the main church service into a more private room where they could pray. Their praying was not the repetition of a 'sinner's prayer' but a confession of conscious sin and prayer for personal forgiveness. In some traditions 'helpers' would pray by the side of the 'seekers' until the seeker was assured that God had heard their cry and forgiven their sin. In the language of Paul in Galatians, they prayed 'until faith came'. It is interesting to read the histories of these times. Where a contemporary account would have "12 received Christ" those older records would say "12 found peace in believing" or "12 sought forgiveness in prayer" or "12 were comforted".

Sometimes the struggles of the 'seeker' could be alleviated by an occasional word of direction from a 'helper' pointing them to Christ Himself or to a word of promise. Later this spontaneous 'help' became more formalised in 'counseling techniques' which led the seeker through a prescribed list of Bible verses which brought them to the place of understanding and enabled them to pray the 'sinner's prayer'. It was much more efficient than spending hours in prayer, apparently.

The Bible verses used in this formalisation often included a few verses from the gospel according to John. *He came to His own, and His own did not receive Him. But as many as received Him, to them He gave the right to become children of God, to those who believe in His name: who were born, not of blood, nor of the will of the flesh, nor of the will of man, but of God.* John 1:11-13 NKJV. Seekers were then encouraged not to follow the pattern of the Jews of that time, but to follow the pattern of those who 'received Him'. The counseling format became the means of 'accepting Him' and the consequential blessings that followed. The reasoning was 'they received Christ' and became 'sons of God'; so you too may 'receive Christ' and 'become a son of God'. The pattern spread and became the norm for evangelical Christianity; to follow the counseling pattern was to 'receive Christ'.

It became such an integral part of contemporary Christianity that to just ask questions about this methodology was to risk being labeled 'non-evangelical'. Is that true? Not at all, but as John's gospel is so often used in this context I will try to unpack some of these key verses so that rather than importing our practice into Scripture we examine the Scripture itself to see how we should behave and what we might expect.

John's first chapter, as we have it now, is a wonderful introduction to his record and several themes begin here which can be traced through the remainder of the book. He introduces us to the person of the Word who was already present with God at the beginning of all things. He goes on to say that this Word *became flesh* i.e. human. As well as being an introduction it also contains a little summary of the impact of the Word, Jesus of Nazareth, upon the world that He entered, and of the response of that world to His presence. This response is detailed in the few sentences quoted earlier; *That was the true Light which gives light to every man coming into the world. He was in the world, and the world was made through Him, and the world did not know Him. He came to His own, and His own did not receive Him.* John 1:9-11 NKJV. John is actually describing three concentric circles; we will follow his account.

He came, says John, into the world as the True Light. In the earlier verses he had carefully made the point that John Baptist was not the True Light, but a witness to it. The ideas in this section have to do with God's witnesses. John was a witness, but the Word, Christ, was The Witness. He was the 'Real Light'. How did the world that He entered respond to that Light? The answer came a little earlier; *That light shines in the darkness, yet the darkness did not overcome it.* Joh 1:5 HCSB. There is a definite sense of conflict in this verse. The Light, which continues to shine, was not overcome by darkness. It hints at a concerted effort of the darkness to extinguish The Witness of the Light as it entered our world. (You can see how deep this idea goes in the Appendix 2: The Witness)

In the later verses this conflict is spelled out more precisely. *He was in the world, and the world was made by him, and the world knew him not.* The Greek word behind 'knew' is *ginoskO*; it is used in many different ways. It is often used in the sense of 'recognition'; *For every tree is known by its own fruit. For men do not gather figs from thorns, nor do they gather grapes from a bramble bush.* Luke 6:44 NKJV. and again... *And they told about the things that had happened on the road, and how He was known to them in the breaking of bread.* Luke 24:35 NKJV. It means much more than acquiring information. The world did not 'recognise' Him. Was this ignorance or defiance? We sometimes use the language of 'recognition' when we say that 'one state does not recognise another'. This is not ignorance but a settled determination to refuse specific status to another country.

There may be something of that feel here too. He who created the world was in the world but His creation refused to recognise his person and authority. The world refuses to recognise His status as the Light; the True Witness. That is the widest of our concentric circles, now we can focus more precisely.

The world would ultimately not only refuse to recognise the Light but would actually attempt to extinguish it. There was one place however that God had been specially preparing; His own land. *He came to His own, and those who were His own did not receive Him.* Joh 1:11 NASB The NASB here has tried to show the distinction in the original, literally 'He came to His own things, and His own people did not receive Him'. He came to His own things... Later He told a story with a terrible punch line; *But when the vinedressers saw the son, they said among themselves, "This is the heir. Come, let us kill him and seize his inheritance."* Matt 21:38 NKJV. This was the heir coming into His inheritance, the fulfilment of all the prophecies and rituals. This was His land, leased to His servants. This was true of the whole world but especially true of this place and time. Another version translates it; *He came to his own home, and his own people received him not.* Joh 1:11 RSVA Surely if all the world rejected Him there would be one place He could call home, where He would be welcomed?

This was the next of our concentric circles and now we come to the innermost core. *and his own people received him not.* Joh 1:11 RSVA They had been chosen for this; delivered from bondage in Egypt, joined in Covenant with God, entrusted with the oracles of God, served by judges and prophets and kings. All was lost in successive deportations that took the whole nation into exile. In the mercy of God a tiny remnant was restored to their land and given a new start; the prodigal nation. Super powers rose and fell. The Babylonian exile severed their dependence on the Temple and made them people of the Book. The Greek empire of Alexander and his successors gave them the tools for world evangelism and put the Book into the lingua franca of the day. The Roman Empire tamed the piracy of the Mediterranean, built thousands of miles of roads along which the gospel could speed, and guaranteed open access to their whole empire. *And when the fullness of the time was come, God sent forth His Son, made of a woman, made under the law, to redeem them that were under the law...* Gal 4 ...and his own people received him not.

As the word 'receive' is important to this topic we will pause to make it as clear as we can. In this first instance in John 1:11 the original word is *paralambanO*. It means 'to take to oneself, to associate with,' literally, the word means to 'take to one's side'. The negating of this then becomes ostracism. John uses the word twice, the second time will give us some idea of what kind of 'reception' the word has in mind; *And if I go and prepare a place for you, I will come again and <u>receive</u> you to Myself; that where I am, there you may be also.* John 14:3 NKJV. We see immediately that John does not have a passive reception in mind. Can you imagine the kind of welcome He has in store for us? That was the kind of 'reception' that might have been expected by His own people but His own people did not receive Him. The first time this particular word is used in the New Testament is also significant; *But while he thought about these things, behold, an angel of the Lord appeared to him in a dream, saying, "Joseph, son of David, do not be afraid to <u>take</u> to you Mary your wife, for that which is conceived in her is of the Holy Spirit.* Matt 1:20 NKJV. Joseph was to take her to his side and recognise her as his very own.

This is not passive acceptance, but a deep personal commitment that places the person by the side of the one who has welcomed him. In the main his people resolutely refused to do this. The three concentric circles had no room for Him, but John then introduces another group that is defined not by space or geography or culture but by their right response to the Light.

This group is defined by the phrase 'as many as received Him'. In his account of the gospel John will show how this group crosses every other barrier. It will include Jews and Samaritans, rich and poor, male and female. Its own defining criterion is that they 'received Him'. In what sense did they 'receive Him?' If we follow the line of John's thinking it will become plain. The preceding verses have had the Light in mind. John has carefully distinguished the Light from John who came to bear witness to the Light. Later Christ was to call John a 'lamp', not the endless source but a local reservoir of illumination. It is this True Light that the world refused to recognise, and the true Light that His own people refused to own. The gospel according to John is a life history of that Light. You may trace the story at your leisure; Joh 1:4-9; 3:19-21; Joh 5:35; Joh 8:12; Joh 9:5; Joh 11:9; Joh 11:10; Joh 12:35; Joh 12:36; Joh 12:46. It is a central point of John's writings and appears again in John's first letter; 1 Jo 1:5; 1 Jo 1:7-9; 1 Jo 2:10.

The second section... *And this is the condemnation, that the light has come into the world, and men loved darkness rather than light, because their deeds were evil. For everyone practicing evil hates the light and does not come to the light, lest his deeds should be exposed. But he who does the truth comes to the light, that his deeds may be clearly seen, that they have been done in God.* John 3:19–21 NKJV. is very significant. It follows on from the statement that the purpose of God's sending of His Son into the world was not in order to 'judge' but to 'save'. John goes on to say that the one 'believing' on Him is not judged: but the one 'not believing' on Him has already been judged as a result of his refusal to believe in the name of the only begotten Son of God. God's judgment then is based on the attitude of men and women to His Son. This must imply a meeting with Christ. It is not the idea or doctrine of Christ we are reading of here, but the person of Christ.

This is part of the most famous part of the Bible and the 'golden text'; *For God so loved the world that He gave His only begotten Son, that whoever believes in Him should not perish but have everlasting life.* John 3:16 NKJV. This is probably the best loved text in the Bible but even the best texts can become dangerous if detached from their context. For example, this single verse speaks of 'believing' but the kind of believing it has in mind can only be discovered by reading the preceding verses. 'Believing' here does not mean agreeing with facts as is usually the case in contemporary counselling patterns. The kind of 'believing' that John has in mind is the kind experienced by people in a unique situation; *And as Moses lifted up the serpent in the wilderness, even so must the*

Son of Man be lifted up, that whoever believes in Him should not perish but have eternal life. John 3:14-15 NKJV. In other words, the kind of believing that John has in mind is the kind found in Numbers 21.

The nation of Israel had sinned and the consequence of their sin was a plague of fiery venomous snakes. The context is so important that I will give the whole section here; *And Jehovah sent fiery serpents among the people, and they bit the people; and much people of Israel died. And the people came to Moses, and said, We have sinned, because we have spoken against Jehovah, and against thee; pray unto Jehovah, that he take away the serpents from us. And Moses prayed for the people. And Jehovah said unto Moses, Make thee a fiery serpent, and set it upon a standard: and it shall come to pass, that every one that is bitten, when he seeth it, shall live. And Moses made a serpent of brass, and set it upon the standard: and it came to pass, that if a serpent had bitten any man, when he looked unto the serpent of brass, he lived.* (Num 21:6-9 ASV.)

These people are not just sick or inconvenienced, they are dying and they know it. They also know why they are dying "we have sinned". Conviction of sin is a work of God's Spirit. They had not been persuaded of the facts of the case by an evangelist; they knew it. In fact, they took the initiative, they came to Moses. This is much more like New Testament evangelism where the appeal comes from the congregation rather than the preacher. They are desperate in their plea; this sounds much more like those old 'after meetings' too.

They are also narrowed down to a single solution; "pray unto Jehovah, that he take away the serpents from us." They know that there are not various options but only one possible solution; God must intervene. This is also much more like those old 'after meetings'. They are seeking a salvation that only God can provide. If God does not move on their behalf they are dead men. Currently their focus is upon the snakes, *take away the serpents from us*; that must change.

Moses does as they ask and God commands him to make a fiery snake of brass and to erect it on a standard/pole. There is only to be one brass snake and it must be 'lifted up' on a standard so that it was in sight of everyone who had been bitten. What a vivid picture this presents. I have a beautiful colour print by Harold Copping in an old Bible. I can't look at without weeping but let me see if I can describe it to you.

The tents of Israel spread out into the hazy distance. The scene is chaotic, people rushing out of their tents, some running, and some standing. As in any panic it is difficult to make out quite what is happening. Or it would be if it were not for a tent in the foreground that is much closer and has its own tragedy unfolding. In the doorway of the tent there is a young man; face down in the sand, a snake is wriggling over his arm and on its way to the next victim. There's an old man in the doorway, with white hair and beard, his attention is not on any of the chaos around him but is fixed on the horizon where a man holds a wooden stake with a single crosspiece; it has a brass snake coiled around it.

There are others in the doorway of the tent; a man and his wife are frantically trying to rouse a young man who looks to be the brother of the snake's earlier victim. The mother is cradling her teenage son in her arms, his eyes are closed; her face is pale with grief. The father is fear crazed; his eyes show white as he tries desperately to rouse his young son from his coma. His face strains to see any signs of life in his son, and his left hand points backwards to the horizon where the brass snake coils around the stake. There are no words, but I know what he is saying; "Look and live... look and live".

Young's Literal Translation does well to catch the sense of the verbs; *And Moses maketh a serpent of brass, and setteth it on the ensign, and it hath been, if the serpent hath bitten any man, and he hath looked expectingly unto the serpent of brass--he hath lived.* Num 21:9 YLT A paraphrase might say; any man looking away from everything else and putting his whole trust in the snake on the pole, lived. This is not just a wonderful story, this is a definition of 'believing' as used by John in John 3:16. God so loved the world that He gave His only Son so that any man, looking away from everything else and putting his whole trust in a Man upon a cross, should not perish but have everlasting life. This is John's desperate cry to all who have been bitten, and that is the whole race, "Look and live... look and live".

It is delivered to men and women who know that they have sinned and that there is no other remedy unless God takes away the snakes. I said earlier that men's focus must not remain upon their own condition or even its cause; not the bite and not the poison eating its way through their lives, but upon the one 'lifted up'. It is the truth often repeated by Amy Carmichael; *upon a life I have not lived, upon a death I did not die; upon another's life, another's death, I stake my whole eternity.* That's what the Bible means by 'believing'.

The man who hears and will not look is judged already. *This is the judgment,* says John, *that Light is come into the world and men loved darkness rather than Light, because their deeds were evil.* The judgment then is because of choices that have been made; not by Adam, but by those who do not come to the Light. Christ's life and words constantly bore witness to the nature of His Father and the nature of men. To those who will embrace the pain of the Light and will accept God's judgment on their deeds come to the Light and learn how to live there; *This then is the message which we have heard of him, and declare unto you, that God is light, and in him is no darkness at all. If we say that we have fellowship with him, and walk in darkness, we lie, and do not the truth: But if we walk in the light, as he is in the light, we have fellowship one with another, and the blood of Jesus Christ his Son cleanseth us from all sin.* 1 Jo 1:5-7 KJV The effectiveness of Christ's cleansing sacrifice is linked inseparably to 'walking in the light as He is in the light'.

Christ is Light, The Witness, and men's responses to His Witness determine their destiny. The contrast that John makes in the section under examination is important to note. *"For everyone practicing evil hates the light and does not come to the light, lest his deeds should be exposed. But he who does the truth comes to the light, that his deeds may be clearly seen, that they have been done in God."* John 3:20-21 NKJV. The contrast is not as we might have expected between 'doing evil' and 'doing good', but between 'doing evil' and 'doing truth'. John's focus is on honesty not personal merit. The

Light entered and its beams disturbed the dust of darkness. Men either scuttle back into the shadow or come to the Light.

It is Christ as the Light, God's Witness, that those earlier references in the gospel of John were addressing. Those who received His testimony/witness, received Him as the Light and the experience was open to 'as many as'. The ending of the third chapter gathers the themes together; *He who comes from above is above all; he who is of the earth is earthly and speaks of the earth. He who comes from heaven is above all. And what He has seen and heard, that He testifies; and no one receives His testimony. He who has received His testimony has certified that God is true.* John 3:31-33 NKJV. The older versions have 'he who has received His testimony/witness has set his seal to it that God is true.' To *set to his seal*, is to give personal recognition, approval and full-hearted consent to The Witness. Those who received the Witness added their signature in endorsement. It is the Amen of the whole of a man's life to God's revelation of Himself in Christ. We are not speaking of mental assent to doctrinal statement. Let me illustrate, for almost 70 years now I have believed that the Rolls Royce is the finest car in the world; I received this truth from my father who was an engineer, and I have never wavered in my faith. This belief, however, has never had the slightest impact upon my life. I have lived a life untouched by this truth I have believed. Biblical truth is different, and the Light which shines still in the person of Christ is not a matter of mental agreement but personal commitment; the putting of all the eggs into one basket. There are no Plan B's or contingencies; either He who was lifted high is my only Saviour, or I am lost. Either He is the Faithful and True Witness or I am lost. To those who received His Witness a door opened...

The words translated 'received' in John 1:11, and John 1:12 are different even though they have links. Let's dig a little deeper. Greek has two main words for 'receive'.

1. *dechomai*: means to receive, but in a passive sense. The imagery might be of the outstretched open hand. The gift must be placed into the open hand that 'receives' it. Perhaps a suitable English word would be 'accept'.

2. *lambanO*: means to receive, but in an active sense. Strong's Dictionary compares the words by saying it means to take (in very many applications, literally and figuratively [probably objective or active, to get hold of; whereas *dechomai* is rather subjective or passive, to have offered to one; while *lambanO* is more violent, to seize or remove.

3. *paralambanO*: is made up of para, by or to the side, and *lambanO*.

Thayer gives its meaning as

1) to take to, to take with one's self, to join to one's self

1a) an associate, a companion

1b) metaphorically, to accept or acknowledge one to be such as he professes to be. not to reject, not to withhold obedience

The essence is that the basic word lambanO means to take hold of, to grip. Let's try that in our key verse; *As many as took hold of Him to them He gave authority to become...* How different the sense is to the passive 'accepting Christ as Saviour'. One is passive condescension, the other is proactive ownership. There is another key feature of this verse that has been obscured by contemporary personal counselling. This verse may not say what you think it says.

The presumption in much contemporary evangelistic activity is that a response, followed by counselling and the 'sinner's prayer' guarantees new birth, and they say, this verse proves it. Even when we have redefined 'receive' to make it clear that this means much more than 'decision for Christ' there is more to examine. Perhaps the presumptions come partly from the King James Version pattern of translating two quite different Greek words by one English word; the one English word is 'power', and people love the sound of it. The word here translated 'power' is not *dunamis* meaning inherent power or ability, empowering, but the word *exousia* meaning 'to be lawful, or authorised'. A law-officer has *exousia*, and with it he can hold up the traffic. A weigh-lifter has *dunamis*, and with it he can hold up the law-officer. *But as many as received Him, to them He gave the right to become children of God, even to those who believe in His name,* Joh 1:12 NASB

283

The consequence of men and women receiving His testimony as the Light was that it qualified them for the next stage of their pilgrimage. Receiving His testimony was a necessary event which gave them 'the right' to become children of God. However, it takes more than *exousia*/permission to make a child of God; it would require the *dunamis*/inward power to accomplish that. At this stage John is really only referring to the 'right to become' rather than the dynamic which reconstitutes men and women as children of God.

We might paraphrase these verses... *John was not the Light, but was sent in order to bear witness about the Light. He was the Real Light, coming into the word and enlightening every man. He was in the world, and the world was made by Him, but the world would not recognise Him. He came to His own inheritance, but His own people rejected Him. But to as many as reached out and took hold of Him, to them he gave the right to become God's children; God's children who were not born from a bloodline, nor from natural origins, nor from man's determined purpose, but whose origin was God.*

The question is 'do men and women become children of God as a result of receiving the testimony of Christ?' Becoming a 'child of God' or as the next verses expresses it 'being born... of God' is not accomplished simply by agreeing with God's Witness. Such agreement is absolutely necessary but not sufficient, of itself, to effect regeneration. Regeneration is God's own work and He alone can testify to its accomplishment. This is part of the weakness of the modern evangelistic format that it puts the work of 'testifying/bearing witness' into the hands of a helper; God will not delegate this work.

The process of regeneration, if we dare call it a process, appears later in John's gospel with a warning disclaimer; *The wind blows where it wishes and you hear the sound of it, but do not know where it comes from and where it is going; so is everyone who is born of the Spirit.* Joh 3:8 NASB. That is to say man or woman, or counselling helper, who thinks they can pin this moment down is fooling himself. The wind, of course, can really only be described by its effects. It is a heavenly action with earthly consequences; Jesus replied, *"I tell you for certain that you must be born from above before you can see God's kingdom!"* Joh 3:3 CEV This is expanding the simple statement 'born... of God' used in John 1:13.

The miracle of regeneration was to be accomplished by 'Him who comes from above'. Nicodemus, the person on the other end of this conversation in John 3, was a recognised 'teacher of Israel'. I suggest you regard him as the best man in the Bible! He was not accused of hypocrisy, nor any sin. His coming to Jesus was an act of self-humbling; the older rabbi attending the younger. He has recognised the uniqueness of Christ's work and, unlike some of his fellow Pharisees, identifies it as God-given. I suspect we only have the bare bones of the conversation here, although enough to suit God's purpose in preserving the record. This is a man who from his earliest days has endeavoured to live as he should; I doubt that men come much better than Nicodemus. It was this 'best of men' to whom Jesus stated this spiritual axiom; *you must be born from above.*

This 'you must be born from above' must not be seen as a responsibility laid upon Nicodemus, as though the Lord had said 'you must get yourself born from above'. It was a statement of spiritual fact that applied to Nicodemus as much as to any man, even though he was the best. If this has been a burden to you, let me express it as plainly as I can. "You must be born from above" is not a command; it is a statement of fact. First the pronoun 'you' is plural in the original, so this was not addressed uniquely to Nicodemus the individual, secondly the pronoun is 'emphatic'. This gives the sense of 'it is necessary for all of you that you be born from above'. Not only Nicodemus, but 'all of you' is the range of the statement. The KJV's 'must' which makes it sound like a command is the Greek word *'dei'* which simply means it is absolutely necessary. Sometimes the street preacher quotes this verse as though it were the listener's responsibility, but you can no more make a man responsible for his heavenly birth than you can for his earthly birth.

We must not lay the burden of being 'born from above' upon the shoulders of the seeker or the person listening to the preaching; it is not man's responsibility but God's. What does

God require of me? that I achieve 'birth from above? Not at all. God requires that I believe His Witness, that I receive Christ in His office of Witness. This will open the door to God's work; to as many as received Him (the Witness) to them He gave the right to become children of God.

Well, you might say, how can a person be sure that they have been born from above? This truth is captured in the phrase 'the witness of the Spirit'. Notice we are back into the realms of a witness. Modern contemporary evangelistic counselling relies on a linking of Bible texts to convince the seeker of their regeneration. This is what A W Tozer inveighed against when he accused evangelicalism of 'substituting logical deductions drawn from proof texts' for the true Biblical doctrine of the Witness of the Spirit. Let's see how our 'expert witness' explains this.

This is a long passage which I will put in the words of the American Standard Version, as it avoids some technical difficulties with this passage, but mainly because it consistently uses the word 'witness' and shows the flow of ideas much more clearly as a result. *And it is the Spirit that beareth witness, because the Spirit is the truth. For there are three who bear witness, the Spirit, and the water, and the blood: and the three agree in one. If we receive the witness of men, the witness of God is greater: for the witness of God is this, that he hath borne witness concerning his Son. He that believeth on the Son of God hath the witness in him(self): he that believeth not God hath made him a liar; because he hath not believed in the witness that God hath borne concerning his Son. And the witness is this, that God gave unto us eternal life, and this life is in his Son. He that hath the Son hath the life; he that hath not the Son of God hath not the life. These things have I written unto you, that ye may know that ye have eternal life, even unto you that believe on the name of the Son of God.* 1 Jo 5:7-13 ASV. The repetition of the noun and verb 'witness' is very powerful. John opened his gospel by declaring that the Word was the True Light; God's revelation of Himself to His world. Now he says the Spirit is Truth. The mutual witness to the Persons within the godhead by the Persons of the godhead is an undergirding of the truth of Trinity.

It is the indwelling Holy Spirit alone who can bear witness to the believer. Others may give their opinions, and we may even have our own opinion, but the last word must belong to God Himself; *If we receive the witness of men, the witness of God is greater.* These verses are closely linked. God has borne witness to His Son. Those uniquely commissioned as eyewitnesses have borne witness to the Son; John is one of them. The Holy Spirit bears witness to the Son. The Holy Spirit bears witness to true faith in the heart of the believer. There are no human uncertainties here. The 'one believing into the Son of God' has the witness within him. This is how I may know... I will know. *The Spirit himself beareth witness with our spirit, that we are children of God:* Rom 8:16 ASV.

There is an interesting post-script to this in one of Paul's letters. To the Colossians, whom he had never met, he wrote; *As ye have therefore received Christ Jesus the Lord, so walk ye in him:* Col 2:6 KJV he uses the word *paralambanO* that we met in John 1:11 of His own people who refused to 'welcome' Him. How could Paul make this statement of people that he had never met? He had received information from a reliable source that certain things were 'true'; *...ye heard before in the word of the truth of the gospel; Which is come unto you, as it is in all the world; and bringeth forth fruit, as it doth also in you, since the day ye heard of it, and knew the grace of God in truth:* Col 1:5-6 KJV They had believed the witness of those who had preached the gospel to them, and had come to know the truth of God... for themselves... in truth. To these who have started well Paul says 'carry on'. The pattern does not change. We begin by acknowledging God's Word to us, we progress by continually receiving that same Word, and 'walking in Him'.

Appendix 2: The Witness

Tracing the words 'witness' and 'to witness' through John's writings is a surprising exercise. It is probably the greatest focus of his writing; in the gospel he uses the word or its associates 47 times; in the epistles 18 times, and in the Revelation 18 times. There is a case to be made for seeing John's focus on 'witness' as the great theme of all his writings. The power of the repetition is often obscured by the fact that translations use many words where he used one; witness, testimony, record, report are all translations of the one Greek word.

Christ is introduced in this gospel as the Word and the Light. Before Pilate we see His consciousness of His mission in his answers; *Pilate therefore said unto him, Art thou a king then? Jesus answered, Thou sayest that I am a king. To this end was I born, and for this cause came I into the world, that I should bear witness unto the truth. Every one that is of the truth heareth my voice.* Joh 18:37 KJV Christ came into the world... to bear witness to the truth. He has always been God's Witness to Himself; the 'spoken one', the divine communication, the Word. To a church which has ceased in its faithful witness the Risen Christ describes Himself; *And unto the angel of the church of the Laodiceans write; These things saith the Amen, the faithful and true witness, the beginning of the creation of God;* Rev 3:14 KJV)

He fulfilled in His own life that failed mission of Israel. *Ye are my witnesses, saith Jehovah, and my servant whom I have chosen.* Isa 43:10a ASV. As a people Israel were to have been the authentic 'Jehovah's Witnesses' but they failed in their mission. God's plan would be restored in Christ; *Behold, I have given him for a witness to the peoples, a leader and commander to the peoples.* Isa 55:4 ASV. The Word who was Light came into our word to bear witness to Jehovah; the Triune God.

As John develops his theme it is seen that he is focussing not only upon The Witness, but upon witnesses to The Witness. John's whole gospel is his own witness to The Witness; *This is the disciple that beareth witness of these things, and wrote these things: and we know that his witness is true. And there are also many other things which Jesus did, the which if they should be written every one, I suppose that even the world itself would not contain the books that should be written.* Joh 21:24-25 ASV. The community that completed the gospel with its last sentences certainly saw the links; they added their own witness to the apostolic witness to The Witness. They are setting their own seal to the authenticity of John's witness to The Witness.

This is where John Baptist comes into his story. John Baptist is the official witness to The Witness, and references to John Baptist's witness to The Witness fill the first chapter; Joh 1:7,8,15,19,32,34; John Baptist came in order to bear witness to The Witness. We ought not to forget that John the Gospel witness was a disciple of John Baptist before he followed Christ. John Baptist's authentic witness to the Witness was the means whereby John the Gospel writer became a witness.

John's promise of the Spirit includes the promise; *But when the Comforter is come, whom I will send unto you from the Father, even the Spirit of truth, which proceedeth from the Father, he shall bear witness of me: and ye also bear witness, because ye have been with me from the beginning.* Joh 15:26-27 ASV. We cannot pursue the theme more at his point, but it will make a fruitful study for any who will pursue it. The heart of it is found in one of John's mini-summaries; *What he hath seen and heard, of that he beareth witness; and no man receiveth his witness. He that hath received his witness hath set his seal to this, that God is true.* Joh 3:32-33 ASV. John is vitally concerned with the reaction of men and women to The Witness. Here he follows the pattern of the earlier verse in John 1:12. 'he that received His witness' is the equivalent of the phrase 'as many as received Him'.

Appendix 3: Bible Version References

Bible Versions quoted:

ASV: Philip Schaff, et al., *The Holy Bible, Containing the Old and New Testaments, Translated out of the Original Tongues, Being the Version Set Forth A.D. 1611, Compared with the Most Ancient Authorities and Revised A.D. 1881-1885, Newly Edited by the American Revision Committee A.D. 1901, Standard Edition.* New York: Thomas Nelson & Sons, 1901.

HCSB: Edwin Blum, ed., *Holy Bible: Holman Christian Standard Bible.* Nashville: Holman Bible Publishers, 2004. Revised in 2009.

KJV: This is the 1769 King James Version of the Holy Bible (also known as the Authorized Version).

NASB: NEW AMERICAN STANDARD BIBLE

(C) 1960,1962,1963,1968,1971,1972,1973,1975,1977,1995

NKJV: New King James Version. Arthur Farstad, ed., *Holy Bible: The New King James Version: Containing the Old and New Testaments.* Nashville: Thomas Nelson,

THE LOCKMAN FOUNDATION RSVA: revised standard version containing the Old and New Testaments,

2nd ed. of New Testament A.D. 1971.

YLT: Young's Literal Translation of the Holy Bible by J.N. Young, 1862, 1898 (Author of the Young's Analytical Concordance)